THE SPECTACLE MAKERS

(1629-1929)

The first 300 years in Minutes

By

Colin Eldridge

(Past Clerk and Director of Examinations)

Copyright © Colin Eldridge 2019
This book is sold subject to the condition that it shall not, by way of trade or otherwise, be lent, resold, hired out, or otherwise circulated without the publisher's prior consent in any form of binding or cover other than that in which it is published and without a similar condition including this condition being imposed on the subsequent publisher.
The moral right of Colin Eldridge has been asserted.
ISBN-13: 978-1-5272-4537-2

This book has not been created to be specific to any individual's or organizations' situation or needs. Every effort has been made to make this book as accurate as possible. This book should serve only as a general guide and not as the ultimate source of subject information. This book contains information that might be dated and is intended only to educate and entertain. The author shall have no liability or responsibility to any person or entity regarding any loss or damage incurred, or alleged to have incurred, directly or indirectly, by the information contained in this book.

CONTENTS

AUTHOR'S PREFACE i
INTRODUCTION 1
    I. THE CORPORATION OF LONDON AND COMMON HALL 2
    II. THE LIVERY COMPANIES 10
    III. THE MAKING OF SPECTACLES 16
IN THE BEGINNING 19
17th CENTURY 32
    PRELUDE 32
    JOTTINGS FROM THE MINUTE BOOKS 42
18th CENTURY 60
    PRELUDE 60
    JOTTINGS FROM THE MINUTE BOOKS 86
19th CENTURY 128
    PRELUDE 128
    JOTTINGS FROM THE MINUTE BOOKS 144
20th CENTURY 281
    PRELUDE 281
    JOTTINGS FROM THE MINUTE BOOKS 285
OBSERVATIONS 332
ENVOI 337
APPENDIX 344
    I. SPECTACLE MAKER LORD MAYORS 344
    II. SPECTACLE MAKER SHERIFFS 346
    III. VENUES FOR COURT MEETINGS 348
PICTURE ACKNOWLEDGEMENTS 350

AUTHOR'S PREFACE

The spectacle makers in the title are mostly members of the Worshipful Company of Spectacle Makers, a Livery Company of the City of London. The Company obtained its Charter, its founding, in 1629. The 300 years takes us to 1929 and the Minutes are the written records of the Company during that time.

Over the last twenty or so years, at work, as Clerk of the Company and during retirement, I have been reading and indexing the Minute books and indexing all Freemen, Liverymen, and Apprentices, etc. This seemingly boring task has been enlivened by various interesting incidents occurring from time to time in the records around which I have written a few articles some of which, in various forms, have appeared in *"From the Master and Wardens"*, the Company newsletter under its more formal title. In writing this book I have used these articles, and written more, and have tried to give the historical background in which spectacle makers found themselves at various times in their history and have elaborated on matters of, to me, more general historical interest that have cropped up. As background, I have given a brief history of the Corporation of London, Livery Companies and their governance, and the development of spectacles.

For me the first 300 hundred years of the Company's existence are the most interesting. Whilst the work and importance of the Company did not end in 1929 that story is more the remit for the Company history, due out to commemorate the 400th anniversary.

I am grateful to Neil Handley, David Brown, Past Master Frank Norville and Helen Perkins for their advice, criticism and encouragement. Not forgetting Hilary Dunne for her valuable proof-reading and my wife, Mary, for her gentle nagging about "this book you keep saying you are going to write". Many others have helped me along the way and I have acknowledged their assistance in the text. They have all done their best to correct my errors so any remaining are entirely my fault.

Colin Eldridge
(Clerk to the Worshipful Company of Spectacle Makers 1966 to 1998.)
Alderholt, 2019

INTRODUCTION

The Worshipful Company of Spectacle Makers is a Livery Company of the City of London, which obtained its Charter in 1629. It started as a "trade company" before admitting, a hundred or so years later, non-spectacle makers, obtaining Livery status in the early 19th century with its Liverymen producing 30 plus Lord Mayors and a similar number of Sheriffs before returning, in a way, to its old trade by introducing examinations for opticians at the end of that century.

Perhaps it would be as well to give a bit of background on the Corporation of London, the Livery Companies and spectacle making, before launching into the Minutes themselves.

I.

THE CORPORATION OF LONDON AND COMMON HALL

Whereas there may have been a settlement in the area before them it was the Romans who established London on its present site, building a bridge, turning it into a port and a commercial centre and eventually surrounding it with a wall. At its height, the population was around 50,000. London also adopted the law and practice of the Romans, including the status of a "citizen", later obtained by being admitted as a "Freeman". By the time the wall was built, London, and the Roman Empire, were in decline. The centre of trade and the population moved away from the walled part, which probably became uninhabited, to an area around what is now the Aldwych and Covent Garden. It was Alfred the Great who re-established London by tarting-up the ruins and building anew. The Saxons, as well as re-building London Bridge, which according to the children's rhyme was always "falling down", brought the focus of trade, and with it the population, back into the walled city.

William the Conqueror granted the citizens of London a Charter in 1067 confirming the rights and privileges the citizens had enjoyed since the time of Edward the Confessor, and in 1130 Henry I gave them a Sheriff. (The original role of the sheriff was to keep the peace in a shire or county on behalf of the king.) By 1141, the citizens were considered to be a single community and it was announced in 1191 as a "commune", which was the origin of the Corporation of London. The citizens, with the King's approval, could appoint a Mayor and by 1215, they could directly elect a Mayor. It would be some unspecified time years later that he, or we should now say or she, became Lord Mayor.

The "Folk-moot", called by the ringing of church bells, was a regular meeting of all citizens to consider and decide upon matters of general concern, with the Court of Hustings looking after the administrative and judicial processes. The non-legal part of the Court's activities evolved into the Court of Aldermen. Since medieval times the city was divided into "wards", a self-governing unit within the city, which were in place at least by 1127. Representatives of the citizens, who had to be Freemen, were elected at an annual "Wardmote" to serve the ward for a year and each ward had an elder man, who over time became an alderman, who was elected at the Wardmote. Also at the Wardmote the Alderman would appoint a Deputy, the organisation of the Wardmote being the responsibility of the Beadle, whose other functions were mainly ceremonial. The City is still divided into 25 wards.

Initially the City, also known as the "Square Mile", was run by the Court of Aldermen, but in time they sought more and more help from the commoners, which was eventually recognised with the commoners being represented by the Court of Common Council, a title recognised in 1376. Its formal title was "Mayor, Aldermen and Commons of the City of London in Common Council assembled" and is still the primary decision making body of the Corporation of London (now the City of London Corporation). In 1632, the King asked the Corporation to extend its privileges and institutions to the growing London outside the walls, but it refused. In 1637, came the "Great Refusal" when the Corporation instead of welcoming newcomers, still "foreigners" in City parlance, put pressure on unwanted "immigrants", and on an excess population, to transfer to the Ulster Plantation and the Corporation of Londonderry, which had been established for that purpose. Lord Glasman, in an article in the *"Financial Times"* in September, 2014, adds that *"the bowler hats and umbrellas of the Orange Orders derive from their sponsorship by the Corporation of London."*

One of the rights and privileges which the City retained over the centuries was "Common Hall" where liverymen took part in the governance of the city. Held twice a year this was a meeting of liverymen of the guilds, and subsequently the livery companies, for the purpose of electing a Mayor and various other city officials, including four "ale-conners". It is an interesting ceremony with liverymen entering Guildhall through the "Wicket gates", guarded by Company Beadles who traditionally had to "recognise" their liverymen, nowadays more often with a ticket of admission provided by the Clerk.

Two Aldermen who have served the office of Sheriff will be in contention for the office of Lord Mayor. Votes will be by acclaim, the Court of Aldermen, who have the final say, retire from the ceremony and on their return the order in which the contending two aldermen re-enter Guildhall will indicate who has been chosen. Whilst arguably the modern Lord Mayor is more of a ceremonial position, though he, or she, takes a large part in advertising and selling the City of London at home and abroad, this has not always been the case. The first named Mayor, Henry FitzAylwin, in 1215, was one of two guarantors charged with ensuring that the King kept his side of the bargain in Magna Carta. William Walford in 1381, during the Peasants' Revolt, allegedly killed Wat Tyler who appeared to be about to strike the King. The life and times of Richard Whittington, four times Lord Mayor, in fact and fiction, are a staple of the Christmas pantomime season. On the other side, the unfortunate Thomas Bloodworth has become a laughing stock as a result of his initial estimation of the significance of the fire in 1666, which eventually burnt down a large part of the City.

Common Hall is summoned twice a year, the first for the election of the Sheriffs. In 1130, Henry I granted a Sheriff to the people of London, along with control of the County of Middlesex, which also had a Sheriff, though control of the County has long gone the Sheriff has remained. The City thus has two Sheriffs, one an aldermanic candidate the other a lay candidate (unless the Aldermen have got their arithmetic wrong and are light on the ground). Usually if there are two lay candidates one politely withdraws, but there have been elections in recent years, held a couple of weeks after Common Hall. Common Hall is a ceremony all liverymen should attend at least once, particularly if a member of their Livery Company is standing for office.

There are a number of other ancient ceremonies which are still carried out in this day and age, not necessarily limited to liverymen. *"The Trial of the Pyx"*, at Goldsmiths' Hall, is the annual assay of the coinage of the realm carried out since 1282. Historically a coin was valued by its content, the weight of silver, etc. Entrepreneurs soon started shaving off bits of the coins thus altering their actual value, a habit a few of the kings also adopted, hence the need to "assay" the coinage to find out if its weight and content equalled its face value.

An even older ceremony is that of the *"Quit Rents"*, which has been carried out since 1211, and, with the exception of the Coronation, is the oldest legal ceremony. Here the Corporation is paying the rent for two pieces of land which cannot now be identified! The rent for one is two knives, one blunt one sharp and for the other, six large horseshoes and 61 nails.

"The Changing of the Quill" where the Lord Mayor, every three years, replaces the quill in the hand of the statue of John Stow in St. Andrew Undershaft. *"The Knollys' Rose Ceremony"* where a rose is taken from the garden in Seething Lane and taken in procession to the

Mansion House by the Master of the Worshipful Company of Watermen and Lightermen. The ceremony dates back to 1381, when Lady Knollys, in the absence of her husband, did some building work in Seething Lane for which she had no planning permission! As a penalty a rose has to be paid annually and in perpetuity, the decision of Sir William Walworth, whom we have come across before.

There are many more ceremonies but I will end with the *"Silent Ceremony"* where, on the Friday before the Lord Mayor's Show, the mayoral insignia, the seal, the purse, the sword and the mace are transferred to the incoming Lord Mayor. It gets its name from the fact that, apart from one short speech from the new Lord Mayor, the whole ceremony is carried out in silence. Usually that is, but Desmond Heap, the then Comptroller and City Solicitor, used to tell the story that on one occasion as he was handing over a large parchment he opened it quickly and with a satisfying loud bang, as parchment does. The audience, craning forward to see what was happening, or asleep in the silence, all jumped and then started conversations as crowds do when something unexpected happens, the silence was broken. He was politely asked not to do that again, I know as I was at the next occasion just to check up.

To bring things up to date, the Corporation of London was renamed, in 2006, the City of London Corporation. Treated as a London borough it can alter its own constitution by Act of Common Council. It owns and runs Smithfield and Leadenhall Markets, owns and part funds the Old Bailey, the Central Criminal Court for England and Wales and owns beyond the City, Epping Forest, Hampstead Heath, and Burnham Beeches. It built or owned and maintains, London, Tower, Blackfriars, Southwark and the Millennium Bridges. The Americans thought it was Tower Bridge they were buying when they acquired "London Bridge". Since 1996, a person of any nationality may be admitted as a Freeman if nominated or presented by a Livery Company.

THE SPECTACLE MAKERS

The City retains nearly all the ancient officers it has inherited: the Town Clerk, the Chamberlain, the City Remembrancer (who has the right to sit behind the Speaker of the House of Commons to ensure no acts of Parliament encroach the City's rights), the Comptroller and City Solicitor, the Recorder and the Common Serjeant (at the Old Bailey) and the Mansion House officers, the City Marshall, the Sword Bearer and the Common Cryer and Sergeant-at-Arms. It also has its own police force whose members were always taller than policemen from any other force! An Alderman, originally for life, has, since 1960, to offer him or herself for re-election every six years. As the resident population of the City has steadily declined, from 132,734 in 1851 to 7,568 in 1951 and with a daytime population of around 330,000, it became necessary to alter the qualification of the voters in Ward elections. Firms were allowed to nominate voters on the basis of the number of their employees on a sliding scale. As a result the business vote is around 24,000. Four of the more residential Wards elect 20 of the 100 Common Councilmen, the business dominated Wards electing the remainder.

In 2014, the Ward of Portsoken elected a member of the Labour Party, and in 2017 there were 5 Labour Party members. For what it is worth I don't believe that party politics should have a place in local government, we can blame Herbert Morrison for their introduction, for local politics usually bear no relation to national politics. The Corporation in my time in its service was an efficient, non-political local authority, whereas it has now become the PR department of the financial City, publicly acknowledging the amount of money it spends on this activity.

Visually the City changed in the mid 1960s when work started on the Barbican, a housing development once described, to the horror of the Chairman of the Barbican Committee, as "middle-class subsidised housing", which doubled the resident population of the City. It also exploded the old myth that London clay could not sustain high buildings, leading to the current plethora of seriously "high rise" buildings. A change from the times when Wren's churches, the tallest being St. Pauls, dominated the City skyline.

In passing it was considered, at least within the Town Clerk's office, that Barbican was the dream of Marmaduke Richards, one of the Committee Clerks and Housing Officer, and that he had manoeuvred over the years to keep the 55 acres, which was subsequently the Barbican Estate, intact. Richards was a Liveryman of the Spectacle Makers Company.

An organisation with such a long history and with considerable political and financial clout has not been without its critics. The Victorians had several formal reviews of the City and indeed of the Livery Companies. The general consensus on the City was that it was an anomaly but harmless and that the Livery Companies spent far more of their undoubted wealth on charity and education than they did on entertaining. In the 1950s and 60s the London Labour Party made a more sustained attack and at the time I left the Corporation to work for the Spectacle Makers, in 1965, I did not think the Corporation would have lasted through to my retirement.

Clement Attlee complained that *"over and over again we have seen that there is in this country another power than that which has its seat at Westminster".* Nicholas Shaxson in a book called *"Treasure Islands"* has pointed out that the Corporation exists outside many of the laws and democratic controls which govern the rest of the United Kingdom and is the only part of Britain over which parliament has no authority. George Monbiot, in an article in the *"Guardian"* of October, 2011, from which these quotes are taken, raises a very valid point. *"The City has exploited this remarkable position to establish itself as a kind of offshore state, a secret jurisdiction which controls the network of tax havens housed in the UK's crown dependencies and overseas territories. The autonomous state within our borders is in a position to launder the ill-gotten cash of oligarchs, kleptocrats, gangsters and drug barons…it deprives the United Kingdom and other nations of their rightful tax receipts".*

Brexit may well deprive the financial City of many of its current powers, "dirty money" may become non-negotiable, auditors may return to looking at and accurately reporting on the finances of the firms they audit, rather than concentrating on "tax avoidance schemes" but, though I am not a reliable prophet, I will be surprised if the alleged financial skills within the City do not return the City, in time, to most of its old glory. Indeed perhaps once again "my word is my bond" may return, lending money for long-term not short-term advantage may become the norm, and making profits for the advantage of all rather than for the very few become part of the capitalist ideal.

II.

THE LIVERY COMPANIES

The origin of the Livery Companies, through Guilds, Frith, Knighten and Adulterine, and the Greater and Lesser Misteries, is complex and foggy in early history to say the least. For these purposes I will simplify the issue, but for any reader wanting more detail then George Unwin in *"The Gilds and Companies of London"* is your man.

It should first be pointed out that guilds were not unique to London. All urban areas in Western Europe had some form of trade or guild control of trade and industry. By the latter part of the twelfth century commercial affairs were largely carried out within two types of guild – the guild merchant and the craft guild. The guild merchant consisted of tradesmen and owners of land, the great men of the area, royal officials, and officials of the area whose money came from their positions rather than as traders. The craft guilds on the other hand consisted of the artisans who made or processed goods by their own hand, offering them for sale in shops or at the local market. The craftsmen employed skilled and unskilled help and had one or two apprentices who gave their labour in exchange for learning the secrets of the trade. If the local organisation was sufficiently strong competitors from outside were excluded from trading in the area, as in Norwich and London. By the Charter of 1319 *"the crafts became the principal method of obtaining citizenship"* (Unwin) which, in London, also wrestled ascendancy away from the Alderman. In London during the fourteenth century the master craftsmen, producing luxury goods, became entrepreneurs, *"raising capital, hiring workmen, providing raw materials, and marketing the finished products. The craft guild eventually would reflect the division between the capitalists and the handicraft workers and become instruments by which capitalists would seek to create a monopoly over their trade and to discipline labor." (Unwin)*

Both guilds arose from social, religious, fraternal and trade association. Members of a trade tended to group together, socialising and worshipping at the same church and looking after the aged, poor and disabled of the area. Gradually the interest of the trade became of paramount concern, obtaining monopoly control to ensure that the trade was carried out to a certain standard, that the customer got fair service, that all members of the trade were equally treated and to provide training for future generations, became the aim. Hence modern Livery Companies have a patron saint, a company church and considerable charitable interests even though involvement in their eponymous trade may have completely disappeared.

During the fourteenth century a corporate structure was developed and by the reign of Henry V there were 111 guilds, though not all officially recognised, and the importance of obtaining a monopoly of the trade and maintaining standards had overtaken the social and religious aspects of the original guild. Royal acceptance of the guild monopoly was recognised by Henry VI by the granting of royal charters to the London Livery Companies, as the guilds had now become known, though the first charter is that of the Weavers' Company of 1155. The charter as well as confirming the monopoly control also gave the company perpetual corporate existence. Money could now be left to a company to pray for the soul of the donor in the knowledge that the prayers would be in perpetuity rather than, as before, in the hands of a human being who had the disadvantage of the same mortality as the donor.

The name "livery" derives from the feudal suits of livery. The original Livery *"meant the allowance in provisions and clothing made to the servants and officers of great households, whether of baron, prelate, monastery or college".* (Unwin) The term became restricted to the gift of clothing as a badge of service and of protection. When the early guilds started adopting "livery" for their members, to distinguish them from members of other guilds, they soon became known as "Livery Companies". For the companies the livery was in two parts, a gown and a hood, usually in two colours. Companies seem to have changed their colours quite frequently and the suits were given to members. Quite a costly business as the Brewers' Company in 1417, spent £185 on a new livery for all its members.

Entry to a Livery Company, the Freedom, was, and still is, obtained by one of four ways. By apprenticeship, or Servitude, starting at around the age of 14 and usually lasting for seven years. The terms were severe, being effectively a form of slavery, having to do exactly as he, usually he but not invariably, was instructed and to give up a private life, particularly as regards to sex, which was forbidden. (Probably why many of the frequent riots in the City's history involved apprentices). By Patrimony (and nowadays Matrimony) where a member's son or daughter, born after he or she become Free, was entitled to Freedom. By Redemption, by paying for it, the usual method nowadays and finally by Invitation, reserved for people of considerable distinction for the Company.

The next step up the ladder is that of a Liveryman. Usually proposed and seconded by existing Liverymen, the Freeman, if elected, is then summoned to a Court meeting, takes the oath and is "clothed as of the Livery". There was, and still is in some Companies, a further category of membership, namely the

Yeomanry. The definition of Yeomanry has changed frequently down the centuries. Initially they were "journeymen" and servants. Then they were the "bachelors", new to the Company. At a later stage they were Liverymen who were not householders. Later still Freemen awaiting their Livery. In many companies the Yeomanry had its own organisation and officers. In the Spectacle Makers Company the Yeomanry, whilst mentioned in the Ordinances, seems to play no part in the Company's affairs, the reason probably being that in its early years numbers were so small that there was no need of a different style of membership. Incidentally a Liveryman, as well as taking part in the ceremonial City and having the right to hold office, had the exclusive right, until 1832, of electing the four Members of Parliament representing the City.

Originally the Master and Wardens were chosen by the whole assembly of the Company, but over time the Master and Wardens, who had to choose their successors, took the advice of previous officers thus establishing an informal consultative body. In time, as trade disputes were settled by this body as well as the admission of Freemen and Liverymen and general Company matters, it came to be known, during the sixteenth century, as the Court of Assistants. Liverymen would be invited to join the Court as and when vacancies occurred.

Going up the seniority ladder come the Wardens, variously Upper, Middle, Lower, Renter (for a time the Spectacle Makers had a Rentor Warden, but that could of course be a spelling mistake). Traditionally the Renter Warden looked after the financial affairs. Top of the pile comes the Master, from master craftsman, sometimes called a Prime Warden or Upper Bailiff. These officers are elected by the Court of Assistants, now usually holding office for one year.

Until administrative affairs of the companies became more complicated, there was no need of Minute taking in the early days, and the Beadle was the sole permanent staff member, acting as the intermediary between the Court and members. As companies acquired halls, in which to carry out the growing work of the company, the work of a caretaker, clerk of works, and gardener were added to his role, whilst his wife washed the linen. By the fifteenth century the regular meetings of the Court required a regular record and the Clerk made his appearance, probably being one of the few who could read and write, even though in legal Latin. He eventually became the senior permanent officer, best described these days as a C.E.O. Remembering that the Master and Wardens are ephemeral beings it is the Clerk who is, or should be, the one able to keep his or her finger on all aspects of the company's activities. Of the 110 current Livery Companies, it is mostly those with halls, 39, who have full-time clerks.

The earliest known company halls were those of the Goldsmiths and the Merchant Taylors in the fourteenth century. The kitchen and crypt of Merchant Taylors' Hall survived both the Great Fire and the Blitz, the kitchen having been in more or less continuous use for 700 years. For the Spectacle Makers particular interest the oldest Livery Hall interior is that of the Society of Apothecaries, our landlords, though our offices are not in that part, even though in times of flood it can seem so! Part of the fabric of Apothecaries' Hall is also medieval coming from the original priory, part of which was adapted to form the original hall, and part of which was also adapted to form the Blackfriars Playhouse of which William Shakespeare was a partner. The crowds attending the theatre in their carriages formed the first "traffic jams" in the City to which the Court of Common Council took objection.

Nowadays to set up a Livery Company a group of people, usually more than 100, have to prove that they have been in existence for some time and are well established, that they have the necessary resources, that they are involved in a particular trade, craft or profession which must not clash with an existing Livery Company and that a large number of their members are involved in that trade, craft or profession. (Had these been the rules in 1629, the Spectacle Makers Company would not have been able to obtain a charter.) A charter having been obtained the incipient company still has to obtain the approval of the Court of Aldermen and have its Ordinances approved before it can announce itself as a City Livery Company. There was a long gap in the establishment of new Livery Companies between 1746 until 1932, but they are still being established, 110 at the time of writing and more in the pipe-line.

There is an order of precedence for the Livery Companies, originally established in 1515. Based roughly on wealth and power, the Great Twelve voted for themselves to establish 1 to 12 in the order, but not quite. The Merchant Taylors and the Skinners Companies had quarrelled over the years as to which should come first amongst them, so the Lord Mayor decided that they should alternate six and seven each year, hence "sixes and sevens". Subsequent companies came on at the date of their charter, the Spectacle Makers being number 60.

Whilst the historical relevance of the Livery Companies is easily appreciated, the continued interest in old, and new companies, with their concern for training, charity (more than 40 million pounds given each year), good fellowship, net-working opportunities, respect for their historical involvement with the Company and with the City of London in its ceremonial life, is a beacon of hope in a world which at the moment seems more concerned with self, keeping the others out, short-term profits, live for now and devil take the future, the very antithesis of the aims of the Livery Companies, both ancient and modern.

III.

THE MAKING OF SPECTACLES

This is just a brief look at the development of spectacles, a subject well beyond the scope of this book, only to indicate how they had developed up to the 17th century. Spectacles probably originated from Murano near Venice in the 13th century where the first white, or clear glass, had been produced. It was known that certain semi-precious stones could magnify when placed on manuscript. In time the stone was placed in a frame and used singly and held before the eye. The semi-precious stone came to be replaced with glass "lenses" which could be "ground" and then two were put in frames and connected, originally with rivets, and held before the eyes. The frames were made variously of iron, silver, bronze, tortoise-shell, leather, wood, bone or horn. (There is a reference in the *"Dictionary of Traded Goods and Commodities 1550-1820"* to horn discs in the making of mops *"these discs were waste products of the spectacle makers who sold the horn cut out of the frames for the glass to the mop makers at 6d. a hundred"*).(1) Much of the future development of spectacles was to come from Freemen of the Spectacle Makers Company, where a distinction was evolving between the pure maker of spectacles and the scientific instrument maker, who also made spectacles.

Spectacles came through the trade routes from Venice to Germany and to the Low Countries from whence they were imported and sold in this country by haberdashers and hawked around the streets, people trying them on to see which suited them best. In the *"Liber Albus"* of 1378, there is a description and valuation of wares in a haberdasher's shop, one Thomas Trewe, *"4 eyeglasses 2d."* In around 1430, comes the oft-quoted poem by John Lydgate, the *"London Lykpenye"*, which includes the lines, when he is describing a visit to Westminster Hall and being pestered by hawkers :

"Master, what will you copen or by?
Fine felt hattes or spectacles to reed
Lay down your silver and here may you speede"

and these are regarded as "fripperies" rather than essentials. There is a later written reference to spectacles in Newbery's book for children about a merchant who deals with:

"Al makers of glasses and workers with fyer…
Al spectacle makers for dim-sighted eyes..
I have spectacles made from of fine Burrall glasse,
And cases from Turkye, that never seen wasse"

The word "spectacles" has not always had its 21st century meaning, so bearing this in mind the *"Petty Customs Accounts"* of July, 1481, indicate that 44 dozen spectacles and 78 dozen spectacle cases (of these 3 Gross were noted as *"spectacle(brille) cases"*) were imported from the Low Countries. In the first two months of 1482, 278 dozen spectacles and 120 dozen spectacle cases were imported. Amidst Henry VIII's letters and papers of January, 1547, in a list of paid invoices appears *"For 10 pairs of spectacles at 4d. the pair"*. (Ibid)

The *"London Port Book"* of 1567/68 (2) shows William Hobson, haberdasher, importing 2 gross of spectacles amongst the paper, thread, combs, inkhorns, brushes and playing cards which he had on the "Pelican" out of Rouen in March, 1568. Richard Patrick, also a haberdasher, in April of that year imported 2 gross of spectacle cases. Hobson, realising that his spectacles needed cases, imported 2 gross of ungilt spectacle cases in May of the same year. Hobson is at it again in July, with 1 gross of spectacles and this time he has 20 gross of morris bells, as a loss leader? Patrick caught up in August with 6 gross of spectacles. The first known shop of a spectacle maker was that of Thomas Peale (subsequently a Freeman of the Company) next to St. Ethelberga's Church, which appears in the Church Warden's Accounts in 1623. The shop of John Marshall (who was a Freeman of the Turners Company not the Spectacle Makers - one that got away) at the sign of the Gun in Ludgate Street, is said to be the first shop set up for the sale of optical goods on a large scale and this was in 1688. Even when English spectacle makers started actually making spectacles rather than importing them they did not themselves sell direct to the public.

In passing, whilst John Marshall got away from the Company it put pressure on him to join for in January, 1687, it was ordered

"that none of this Society Shall for ye future Employ Jn. Cox Jn. Marshall or any other in grindeing of Convects or Concave glasses".

As Marshall was a scientific instrument maker, as were many currently on the Court, it may have been an attempt to ensure that all scientific instrument makers joined the Company. Didn't work with Marshall, but others were recruited. Edward Scarlett and James Mann, Jnr, who had been apprenticed to spectacle makers were "encouraged" to join by the threat of legal action in one case, and by arrest on the Court's orders in the other. This time it did work and both became Free of the Company. For many years later those who primarily produced scientific and mathematical instruments also sold spectacles in order to keep the wolf from the door.

IN THE BEGINNING

Whilst the Company obtained its Charter from Charles I in 1629, we should perhaps start a little before this. As has already been noted in the City of London in the 17th century it was necessary, in order to trade and take part in City governance, to be a citizen. This was achieved by firstly becoming a Freeman of a Livery Company, and then obtaining the Freedom of the City. This was not so difficult if you were a goldsmith or a fishmonger as the relevant Company was already in existence. But what if your trade was a new one, say making spectacles, and the number of spectacle makers was steadily increasing.

By 1628, there were at least 18 spectacle makers in London. They were in a number of different Livery Companies, principally the Grocers, Blacksmiths and the Brewers. The Brewers Company had the greatest number of spectacle maker Freemen, due almost entirely to one man, Richard Polson. They decided to establish a Fellowship or Society for spectacle makers, which process was set in motion by a petition to the King to obtain a charter. There seems there was no immediate desire or wish or perhaps ability, spectacle makers not being rich men, to become a Livery Company, though the By Laws of the Company clearly apply to "liverymen".

In the original petition to Charles I it is stated that there were 10 spectacle makers, though this may refer to the apprentices, as 18 is later stated as the number of those wishing to "translate", the technical phrase for the transfer from one Company to another, from the Brewer's Company. In fact there were 13 names of spectacle makers translated from the Brewers' Company on 11th November, 1634. The Charter of Incorporation was presented for enrolment on 21st May, 1633 and the Ordinances and By Laws, the working rules of the Company, were approved by the Court of Aldermen on 4th November, 1634, including the translations.

The Charter itself, duly granted by Charles I, is usually claimed as being dated the 16th May, 1629. However my immediate predecessor as Clerk, Roland Champness, pointed out in a letter to "The Optician" in November, 1957, that this date should be 23rd April. He wrote that *"the mistake has been perpetuated down the years because of an endorsement on the reverse side of the Charter indicating the enrolment of the Company by the Court of Aldermen of the City of London as being on May 16th. But the Monarch's seal dedicating the Charter bears the date April 23"*. For some reason his "correction" doesn't seem to have caught on for the 16th May is still the quoted date!

The original thirteen were the brothers Robert and John Alt, John Alt the Younger, son of Robert, the brothers Robert and Thomas Drumblebee, Thomas and William Peale, also brothers, John Bailey (Baylis), John Boote, Robert Clifford, Thomas Copeland, John Jenkinson and John Turlington. To these had been added in the Charter, Edward Gregorie, as Master, Thomas Fisher as a Warden, Robert Alt being the other Warden, and Francis Best.

Robert Alt John Alt	Father, John Alt, Farmer, SHEPSHED, Leics
John Alt, the Younger	Father, Robert Alt
Robert Drumblebee Thomas Drumblebee	Father, Thomas Drumblebee, Yeoman, SHEPSHED
Thomas Peale William Peale	Father, Richard Peale, Farmer, SHEPSHED

John Bailey (Baylis)	Father, Robert Bailey, Farmer, Houghton, Leics
John Boote	Apprenticed to John Turlington
Robert Clifford	Father, Rowland Clifford, Farmer, Diseworth, Leics
Thomas Copeland	Father, Ralph Copeland, Farmer, Wymeswold, Leics
John Jenkinson	Had been apprenticed to Thomas Ashe, whose father was a yeoman from SHEPSHED
John Turlington	Father, Henry Turlington, Farmer, SHEPSHED

Thus all the spectacle makers involved in the formation of the new Company had a connection, either with Shepshed or a village not too far away.

Some of them shared a further common ancestry in that they were connected to Richard Polson who is not known to us as a spectacle maker. His claim to spectacle maker reflected glory is as a master of apprentices. Robert Alt in 1602, John Thompson (his father was a farmer from Shepshed and John Thompson had been Thomas Peale's Master) in 1605, Robert Clifford in 1609, Thomas Ashe in 1609/10, John Turlington in 1610/11 and Thomas Copeland in 1617. These dates you will notice all precede the establishment of the Company in 1629, so they were all apprenticed to a Brewer. The Brewers' Company accepted as Freemen trades other than that of brewing. Though we know that Polson was a Freeman and Liveryman of the Brewers' Company the only claim he has to be a spectacle maker is that a number of his apprentices, as we have seen, became spectacle makers, but he provided the citizenry route that this new trade required. Strange to relate his father came from Shepshed.

St.Botolph's Church, Shepshed. Photo by Past Master Peter Mills of the 11th century church, where no doubt some of the original spectacle makers would have worshipped, the church has carved pew ends of the 15th century.

Whilst it can be understood that neighbours and friends, when it came to employment opportunities and particularly in London, would naturally congregate to people known to them, this does not explain why they became spectacle makers. Either they were spectacle makers when they left Shepshed, and if so what started spectacle making in Shepshed, or the first of the villagers, Robert Alt, took up spectacle making and it followed from there, in which case it may have been Richard Polson who encouraged Robert Alt. It is quite true that there were spectacle makers already at work in places other than Leicestershire, we know of half a dozen in London for instance. With the loss of the early minute books we don't know how many people joined the newly established Company, other than the initial 13, and therefore from whence they came.

Richard Polson is obviously the pivot in all this. What little we know about him comes from the researches of Jerome Farrell, the Archivist to the Brewers' Company and I am indebted to him for most of what follows. Richard Polson was born around 1573-74, the son of Thomas Poulsone of Shepshed. In 1598, he gave his parish of residence as Christ Church (Greyfriars). When he became a Freeman of the Brewers' Company, after an apprenticeship with a William Clever, his occupation was that of a "cheesemonger". (Leicestershire has a long tradition of cheesemaking and inns along the coaching route to London acted as key retail outlets for cheese selling). In around 1598, he married Marie Turlington. She was the daughter of Henry Turlington, a farmer from Shepshed. Her brother, John, was one of the first 13 Freemen of the Company in 1634.

I haven't been able to find much about the first 13 so far. Just the odd facts that John Turlington's father, Henry, married Marie Allte in Shepshed, but before getting excited about that it seems there were a lot of Allte's (or Alte or Alt) in Shepshed. However we do know from the Brewers' Company records that John Turlington, and 5 others, were appointed "whifflers" for the Lord Mayor's show in 1623. A whiffler, who is usually a young Freeman, marches at the head of his Company in the procession. Richard Polson was mentioned in several lists of those making a payment towards the Brewers' Company contribution to the Plantation in Londonderry and also included in the list of new Livery who gave a spoon to the Company in October, 1616. There is also a note beside a Minute of the Brewers which indicates that Robert Clifford, Thomas Drumblebee, and John Turlington were probably all at a meeting on the 6th November, 1627. Were they discussing trying for a Charter or, more likely, just about normal business? It is always unsafe to draw the conclusion you want from scant historical fact! I am indebted to the staff of the Brewers' Company for digging most of the above out of their records.

This leaves us with the first Master, Edward Gregory, Thomas

Fisher, a Warden, and Francis Boot. As these three came to us via the Charter it was assumed that they were perhaps royal appointments or of some other distinguished background. Searches were made amongst the courtiers of Charles I, Members of Parliament and citizens of London. Without success until Adrian Finch, who has been doing some work on the Clockmakers Company, emailed to say "do you know that your first Master, Edward Gregory, was a Freeman of the Goldsmiths Company?" No we didn't.

Having approached the Goldsmiths Company the position is as follows. An Edward Gregory, whose Master was James Duhamwell and whose father was Jerom Gregorie, Yeoman of Kineson(?), Oxfordshire, was admitted to the Freedom of the Goldsmiths' Company in 1606, after an 8 year apprenticeship, but there is no record of his occupation or location. Gregory took a number of apprentices, but the one who is of particular interest to us is Samuel Blaksley, for when his apprenticeship is recorded on the 25th September, 1611, Gregory is described as "spectaclemaker". None of his other apprentices are known to us as spectacle makers though one, Francis Perkins, 30th April, 1630, came from Shepshed.

Other connections, when Edward Merson, another of Gregory's apprentices, is made Free of the Goldsmiths, after Gregory's death in 1631, his service is testified by Gregory's widow, Martha. When Edward Gregory's son, Jeremy, comes to be admitted in 1647, the witnesses are "John Alte Spectaclemaker in Paules Chayne and Thomas Copeland Spectaclemaker Sermon Lane" both well known to us. Lastly when a William Bailey, the last of Gregory's apprentices, is admitted to the Freedom in 1650, his service "was testified by Martha Alte, late wife and executrix of Edward Gregory", she had moved onto another spectacle maker! (The information from the Goldsmiths' Company comes from the *"Mitchell Merry Goldsmiths' Database 2016".*) Whilst the foregoing is not absolutely definitive in itself there must be a strong possibility that Edward Gregory of the Goldsmiths' Company should be considered as our first Master, until some conclusive evidence can be produced to the contrary.

Whilst checking if any of Gregory's apprentices were spectacle makers for further confirmation, I was looking through the *"Middlesex Sessions of the Peace and Gaol Delivery for 1615"* (1), as one does, and in one entry amidst other names came the following: "... *for Thomas Fysher (Fisher) spectaclemaker and William Hudson, tailor, both of the same* (of St. Clement Danes) *for striking and wounding John Thomas of St. Giles in the Fields, drayman and of William Wase of St. Clement Danes, tailor, for the said John for abusing and reviling George Etheridge (Eldridge) and Thomas Johnson, two of the constables of the Liberty of the Duchy of Lancaster, in the execution of his Majesty's service"*. Fisher is a fairly common name, but I think it reasonable to assume that this is the Thomas Fisher referred to in our Charter. The fact that he was involved in some kind of fracas with one of my no doubt distinguished ancestors, and the brackets round the name are in the original report not mine, can be over-looked on this occasion. From the foregoing it would appear that Gregory and Fisher are spectacle makers and are probably named in the Charter for no better reason than because a Master and Wardens needed naming in such a document. It may also be because they were not in the Brewers' Company as were the other originals. That just leaves Francis Best to find and it seems likely that he will prove to be a spectacle maker as well.

I have so far unearthed, with the help of Gloria Clifton (3), 40 spectacle makers who became Free of the Company between 1629 and 1666. Unfortunately the facts about them are usually restricted to a bare name and an address at most. Of the 6 about whom there is some information, 2 come from London the other 4 from

Northamptonshire, Somerset, Wiltshire and Loughborough (also near Shepshed) but I don't know when they became Free of the Company. Gloria Clifton notes that the number of scientific instrument makers working in the British Isles (not necessarily the same as spectacle makers) whose names have been traced was, in 1601, 14 in the British Isles, at least 8 of whom worked in London, in 1651, 43 at least 30 of whom worked in London and in 1701, 151 at least 123 of whom worked in London. In the same book Clifton states that the number of optical instrument makers known to have been working in London between the early seventeenth century and 1720, was 53. Of those whose Company is known, 40, 20 were Free of the Spectacle Makers Company.

Incidentally the Shepshed connection continued for a number of years, 5 more Freemen of the Company coming from there between 1626 and 1701. We know a little about Shepshed. At the time of the Doomesday Survey it was *"a very considerable village, containing many more houses and inhabitants than any other village in the county".(4)* In 1564, there were 103 families and in 1630, one of the four freeholders was a Richard Peale, and there is a report of disputes between the Corporation of Derby and a *"Mr. Baylies concerning inclosures"* and that John Duport D.D. one of the translators of the Bible, was born there in 1655. None of this impacts on spectacle making and its whys and wherefores! Michael Wortley, the Honorary Archivist to St. Winifride's Catholic Church in Shepshed, wrote that he was unaware of any connection with spectacle making in the village, which in the 1600s was mainly pastoral (sheep) and agricultural. By the eighteenth century the village had turned to framework knitting. But bad times came after Waterloo, when many villagers starved to death, and it was only with the introduction of other trades, boot and shoe making being the major one, that conditions started to improve.

From the foregoing you will appreciate that I am not making the claim that Shepshed was the birthplace of spectacle making, but I think it puts forward a strong case for Shepshed being the birthplace of what later became the Worshipful Company of Spectacle Makers. If Shepshed was the birthplace, then Richard Polson has a strong case for being considered as the midwife.

To return to the Charter, after a long digression, it gave the right to hold Quarterly Courts *"to be kept at their Common Hall within the City of London called Spectaclemakers Hall"*. There is no further mention anywhere of such a building apart from in the By Laws. According to Mary Robischon (5) the incipient spectacle maker and clockmaker companies shared the same counsel, Thomas Copley, who drafted both petitions, and in due course became the Clerk to both Companies. I would suggest that he used the standard wording for such documents which included the reference to a hall.

Sir George White, the Keeper of the Clockmakers' Museum at the Science Museum, has confirmed that Thomas Copley was also their Clerk. I am indebted to Sir George for the additional information he has provided *"Thomas Copley was appointed Clerk for life under our Charter of August 22nd 1631....though the first Court meeting was on the 12th October, 1632. However I am absolutely certain that he was an attorney and that he guided the Company through its application for the Charter and also through the writing of the bye-laws. It rather looks as though Copley fell out with the Company c. 1635, or perhaps became ill? Certainly he was replaced on August 1st, 1636, by 'Thomas Shelton of ffurnivals Inn gent'. There may be a clue as to a possible problem that the Company had with Copley in the conditions that Shelton was ordered to work under 'that the said Clerk shall not at any tyme receive writings or Copies from henceforth in anywise touching the Company but shall from tyme to tyme bring in and redeliver the same from one Court day to another as occasion shall require'.*

Had Thomas Copley held back papers?

Sir George continues *"An odd reference appears in the Court Minutes, which one assumes refers to Thomas Copley, though it may not. It is dated 10th January, 1635, and is headed 'Mrs. Copley's demands'. It reads 'The same day Mrs. Copley came & demanded more money of the Company for hir husbands payment notwithstanding all we had done for him'. Sadly there are no other references which might shed light on his life and times in our archives"*. Unfortunately, as the Spectacle Makers have no extant Minutes of this period, I am unable to add anything further concerning Thomas Copley. But these references in the Clockmaker's Minutes give a little flesh to a character who, to the Spectacle Makers Company, is but a name in our Charter.

The By Laws, which were approved in 1630, had the usual impressive cast list of signatories *"Thomas Lord Coventry Lord Keeper of the Great Seal of England Sir Nicholas Hyde Knight Chief Justice for all Pleas before his Majesty to be holden and Sir Thomas Richardson Knight Chief Justice of his Highness Court of Common Pleas.* They lay down the running of a Livery Company, or at least give authority to *"make choose and have a livery"* and reference is constantly made to what Liverymen should do, which raises the issue of why the Company did not, relatively quickly, go the further step and approach the Court of Aldermen, etc. This would have cost even more money and, as we shall see, the Company for many years lived a hand to mouth existence and had few members, for there weren't that number of spectacle makers around at the time.

Having established the Quarterage as twelve pence per annum, a series of fines is set-out, mostly for things not done e.g. not coming to Court at the appointed hour or leaving without license, or not wearing gowns, or refusing to take office, or not paying Quarterage, which could indicate that not everyone in a trade was necessarily going to conform readily to the new arrangements.

The King ensured that they were duly obedient to him for if the Master and Wardens summoned the *"Livery or other of the said company"* for *"attendance upon the Kings Majesty his heirs or successors at his or their repair to or towards the City of London.....to any convenient Service or Attendance in Livery or otherwise by Horse or Foot and upon Warning thereof shall not attend, and sort provide and attire and furnish himself, and perform and do accordingly what he shall be so appointed he shall for every such Default or Neglect forfeit the sum of twenty Shillings".*

The By Laws continue to lay down other fines, including a fine for not paying *"any Taxations or Assessments",* misbehaving apprentices and various types of bad workmanship. Some By Laws covered the workings of the spectacle makers trade e.g. *"make any Spectacles working them only on one Side the other being wrought by Looking Glass Makers or otherwise after that forme".* Trades in general were worried about foreign competition and somebody gaining a commercial advantage. This was covered for spectacle makers by *"there is much Glass made for the Use of Spectacle-Makers as well within his Majesties Dominions as in parts Beyond the Seas and imported into this Kingdom which is not of any sufficient goodness to be employed for the use of Spectacle Makers, yet many evil disposed persons seeking rather their own Private Ends and benefit than the publick good in having it at a very cheap Rate, do convert it to that Use whereby many Inconveniences do happen, and is a very great Danger to the Sight of all such as do or shall use them and is a very great discredit to honest and good Workmen, for the better prevention whereof It is ordained that no Person or Persons which shall use the Trade or Mistery of Spectacle-Making shall at any Time hereafter buy any Glass either whole or broken in greater or lesser parcells from any person or persons whatsoever until such parcel be before the same shall be so bought as aforesaid brought to some Place appointed for that purpose where it may be converted to the use of the whole Society".*

Another By Law referring to the Stewards may interest their modern counterparts: *"shall yearly ...... nominate and publish two of the Livery or others of the said Company who shall the Place and be called Stewards for the Assistants Dinner for this Fellowship to be kept on the Feast Day of Saint Luke the Evangelist at the Costs and Charges of the said Stewards".* Not surprisingly there is a fine laid down for such as refused this obviously onerous task. The description of the Assistants Dinner which follows makes it seem, as no doubt intended, to be a very chummy affair *"at which Dinner for Maintenance of Brotherly love and familiarity the Master Wardens and Assistants and all or any of their Wives may be present as also the full Livery of the said Society".*

The By Laws continue with the various oaths to be taken on assuming office which are still in use. I will refer only to one more of the By Laws which may strike as odd to the modern reader. *"that if Request at any time shall be made to the Master and Wardens of the said Company to have the Livery of the said Company to accompany to the Grave within the Circuit of London Liberties and suburbs thereof or within three Miles compass the Dead Corps of any of the Livery deceased or of his wife at the Time of the Funeral Then the Master and Wardens if they shall think it fit shall cause a warning of the whole said Livery accordingly and every of the said Livery shall upon reasonable warning attend with his Livery at the Time and place appointed"* and if he didn't then of course a fine, in this instance ten shillings. This type of by law was, as already mentioned, a money earner for all the Livery Companies, for if a Liveryman wanted prayers said for his immortal soul, as was the fervent wish in that more religious and fearful time, it was no good asking his local vicar to carry out the job for he, too, was mortal. When the Livery companies were declared bodies corporate, i.e.

having eternal life, then a Liveryman could safely give payment to his company in his Will to carry out this purpose. It is no doubt an apocryphal story, but one Livery company had to draw the line on satisfying their deceased Liverymen's wishes when it found itself solemnly processing for this purpose three times a week.

17th CENTURY

PRELUDE

Map of London 1572

What could our spectacle maker expect of this City of London to which a few came in the first part of the seventeenth century? Whilst London was by the 17th century the principal city of the land, in 1500 it was three or four times the size of the largest provincial town at the time, Norwich, by 1700 it was fifteen times bigger (6), it wasn't very big by modern standards as can be seen from the map above of 1572. It was possible for our spectacle maker forebears to walk, on their Sundays off, to look at the Fleet River in deep countryside only a mile or so north. Peter Ackroyd states that *"there were healthful 'walks' in a number of carefully planned and plotted public areas. By the early seventeenth century Moorfields had been drained and laid out, creating 'upper walks' and 'lower walks', and a few years later Lincoln's Inn Fields were also designed for 'common walks and disports'*. Gray's Inn Walks *"were highly favoured and Hyde Park, although still a royal park, was open to the public for horse-racing and boxing"*. (7)

Over the century it became an even stronger magnet for the countryman, four fifths of the population were tilling the land in some form or another, to come to town to service the increasing population and their demands for more food, clothes and building. This century too saw the increase in overseas trade and emigration. Between 1636 and 1643, some 20,000 emigrants would leave for New England and 40,000 to Virginia and the other "colonies". (8) Bristol and Liverpool were also increasing in size and importance, but London had the lion's share of overseas trade, much of it being exported onwards. Though there was much industry in the City, including breweries and tanneries, and trades of all sorts serving the population, it was as a trading and a redistribution centre, together with the growing importance of finance, which really drove the City. The century also saw an expansion in the numbers and wealth of great merchants, many of whom would be Liverymen of the "Great Twelve", and involved with the East India Company, with its monopoly of trade in the Indian Ocean region. Though many of the imports were often re-exported, various goods were filtering down the "food chain" and becoming available, at a price, lower down the social scale. On a more mundane level the century saw the end of the English groat and the introduction of coins with a milled edge to prevent clipping. Now that gold was being imported a 20s gold coin was issued.

With the development of banking came the introduction of paper currency. For some time goldsmiths had been prepared to look after money and pay interest on the money deposited. A receipt was provided and in time this became negotiable. *"From 1667 paper orders or assignments of revenue were issued to those who lent money to the Crown or supplied goods. They could be exchanged and were paid in order as the revenues came in. They were issued in convenient amounts of £1, £2 and £5 and were effectively the government issue of paper money"*. (9) In 1672, financial pressure caused payment of these orders to be suspended for twelve months. It suddenly became apparent that if there was to be a "bank" it had to be independent of the Crown! This led to the establishment of the Bank of England in 1694, and the first issue of bank notes followed in the same year.

Whilst no doubt it was well known that the streets of London were paved with gold, other aspects of the City were not so welcoming. As Adrian Tiniswood writes *"it was noisy, filthy and smelly, and most Englishmen agreed that only Paris was worse. Charnel houses stood side by side with stately mansions; butchers' offal lay rotting in the narrow streets, and human waste blocked open drains. Commentators cursed the constant traffic jams and marvelled at the way in which the smoke from brew-houses hung like a great cloud over the houses and gardens of the nobility that lay between the City and the centre of government in Whitehall"*. (10) It might be worth noting as regards smell that, according to modern theory, living constantly with the smell the nose in fact no longer bothers to recognise it and it goes to the back of consciousness.

To a contemporary writer, John Evelyn, *"the buildings are as deformed as the minds and confusions of the people, for if a whole street be fired (an accident not unfrequent in this wooden City) the Magistrate has either no power, or no care to make them build with any uniformity, which renders it, though a large, yet, a very ugly Town, pestered with Hackney-coaches, and insolent Carre-men, Shops and Taverns, Noyse, and such a cloud of Sea-coal, as if there be a resemblance of hell upon Earth, it is in this Vulcano on a foggy day"*. *(11)* He doesn't here mention the plagues, of which there were a number over the years, the nearly last of which, 1665, was not long after the Company obtained its Charter.

But things were improving. Towards the end of the century piped water became available, at a cost, and street lighting introduced, though this was restricted to oil lamps on every tenth house. Window glass, though used since the time of Edward III, became available at a price even some of the poor could afford. The streets, there are no roads in the City, were full of people rushing hither and thither, the air full of the cries of the various sellers shouting their wares. To quote Peter Ackroyd (7) *"as long as the City has existed there have been entertainments... there were midnight dog-shows and duels of rats; there were street jugglers and street conjurors, complete with pipes and drums; there were performing bears and performing monkeys dragged through the streets of London upon long ropes... there have always been wonders and curiosities, John Stow recorded the minute skills of a blacksmith who exhibited a padlock, key and chain which could be fastened round the neck of a performing flea and John Evelyn reported seeing the 'Hairy Woman' whose eyebrows covered her forehead".* Fleet Street was the home of marvels *"In 1611 mandrakes were on show for a penny. A fourteen-year-old boy, only eighteen inches high, was to be seen at a grocer's shop called the Eagle and Child by Shoe Lane, a Lincolnshire ox, nineteen hands high and four yards long, could be viewed at the White House nearby. There was the usual diet of giants and dwarfs, anything out of its due size and proportion was welcome in 'disproportion'd London.* Also in Fleet Street was, at the beginning of the eighteenth century, a waxworks, Mrs. Salmon's, the forerunner of Madame Tussauds.

For entertainment our spectacle maker could go to Hockley in the Hole to "enjoy" bull and bear baiting, dog fights and prize-fighting with quarter staffs and swords, the object being a good clean cut, not a fight to the death and, as with wrestling, the result was fixed beforehand. There was also archery, jousting, bowls and football. Or he could stroll in Mulberry Gardens, where Buckingham Palace and its gardens now stand, or other tea gardens, to enjoy open air restaurants and entertainment, the forerunners of Vauxhall and Cremorne. To quote Peter Ackroyd again, referring specifically to New Spring Gardens *"small green refreshment huts sold wine and punch, snuff and tobacco, sliced ham and quartered chicken, while ladies of doubtful morals sauntered among the trees with gold watches dangling from their necks as token of their trade. The apprentices and their girls would visit Spa Fields in Clerkenwell or the Grotto Gardens in Rosoman Street where they were encouraged to consume tea or ices or alcohol, to the accompaniment of song, music and generally 'low' entertainment".*

Samuel Pepys was a frequent visitor *"it is very cheap going thither, for a man may go to spend what he will or nothing, all is one – but to hear nightingales and other birds, and here fiddles and there a harp, and here a jews trump, and here laughing, and there fine people walking is mightily divertising"* as he wrote in May, 1667. He also, as was his wont, noticed the *"ladies of doubtful morals". (12)*

Many spas were established on the sites of a chalybeate or sulphur well, whose medicinal cures were conveniently recommended by an obliging doctor. Or he could go swimming in "Parlous Pool", so named as many Elizabethan youths had drowned in its waters. (By the mid eighteenth century this had become "Peerless Pool", a large open air swimming pool some 60 yards by 30 yards in size). Or, should he want a drink *"There are endless inns, beer and wine shops for every imaginable growth, alicant, canary, muscatels, clarets, Spanish, Rhenish"* says Thomas Platter writing in the 1600s as quoted by Ackroyd.

Cockfighting, Henry VIII had the first cockpit built in England, was much in evidence, in time developing not just on bets on the winning bird or birds, but by charging gate money to attend, an early spectator sport. Should he be a gambling man then hazard, a game of pure chance, was available for large groups and whist for the more intimate card game.

Theatrical entertainment, though frowned on by the City Fathers, was available in inns and a few theatres. The first theatre in London was "the Theatre" opened by James Burbage in Southwark to be followed by the "Curtain". Later theatres were built around the Clink prison and Paris Garden all outside the City. Marlowe's plays were first staged at the "Rose", built in 1587. The "Swan" was built in 1596 and the "Globe", in which Shakespeare had a tenth share, in 1599. Performances took place in the afternoon, announced by a loud blast of trumpets and the waving of flags, recreated in the opening of Olivier's film of *"Henry V"*. Money was collected inside the door, 1d. for admission to the pit, 2d. to the gallery and 3d. for a seat, and placed in a box and then locked in the office, hence the modern "box office". (This last point is disputed as the money was also collected in cheap earthenware "money pots" which were broken up when full in order to get the money out. Quantities of these broken pots were found during excavations of the sites of the Rose and Curtain theatres by the Museum of London in 1988 and 2010 respectively).

As the Globe had no roof, except over the stage and the galleries, it was only used during the summer. In the winter the company would revert to the Blackfriars Playhouse, built in what was once the Blackfriars Monastery, which, after the dissolution had become a private house. Richard Farrant had purchased the house from Lord Cobham, the Farrant family lived on the ground floor and converted the upstairs as a theatre. By this means Farrant claimed that it was a private theatre thus avoiding the City's ban on public theatres. He further claimed that it was where the choirboys could practice *"for the better training to do her majestie service"*. The Playhouse went through various hands until James Burbage bought it in 1596, unfortunately he died the same year. Alterations had to be made to his plans for the theatre as the neighbours objected to a public playhouse. It eventually opened in 1597, with three galleries, and a capacity of 600 to 700, having been leased to the Master of the Children of the Chapel Royal. The boy actors proved very popular and rivalled the adult players hence the bitter comments in *"Hamlet"* about *"an eyrie of children, little eyasses, that cry out on the top of questions, and are most tyrannically clapped for't: these are now the fashion"*. The theatre was closed after the performance of a play which upset the French Ambassador in 1608, but Burbage and six fellow actors, including Shakespeare, then went into partnership to run the theatre, where no doubt some of Shakespeare's plays were performed. The Puritans closed the theatre in 1642 and it was demolished in 1655. The Society of Apothecaries would purchase what remained of the hall in 1632, and where the Spectacle Makers Company eventually established their first permanent office, as opposed to using the Clerk's or the Master's premises, in 1946.

Though Cromwell closed theatres, with the arrival of Charles II the theatre was revived, with patents being given to Davenant and Killigrew. Allegedly, after Charles had been kept waiting during a play *"for the Queen to finish shaving"*, the instruction went out that women were to play the female parts previously played by androgynous boys. The Pit in the theatre was very much a place to be seen and for social gathering and chit chat before, after and during the performance. There were also seats on the stage, the audience participating from time to time in the play itself. Oranges were sold in the interval where, allegedly, Charles duly "found" Nell Gwynne. Servants came and saved seats for their masters and subsequently took seats in the gallery, for free, until such time as their behaviour became unendurable, when their free seats were abolished, naturally causing another riot.

 *This is an enlargement from Wenceslas Hollar's "Long View of London of 1647". He mistakenly named it a "beere house", this has been omitted and "The Globe" substituted. Bit of a fiddle but it is a contemporary realisation. This is the second Globe Theatre, the first destroyed in a fire in 1613 started by a cannon misfiring and setting fire to the beams and thatch.*

Our spectacle maker would not necessarily watch the plays of Shakespeare at this time. The plays of Christopher Marlowe, Ben Jonson and Beaumont and Fletcher were revived more often than Shakespeare's. The Shakespeare cult was not to take off until Garrick ran the Shakespeare Jubilee at Stratford-on-Avon in 1769. He didn't quite make the 200th anniversary. No complete play of Shakespeare's was performed, it poured with rain and people who attended from far afield, anyone who was anyone in London attended, couldn't get away fast enough from this insignificant village in Warwickshire. But it started Stratford off as a tourist spot and continued the Shakespeare revival which Garrick had revolutionised by his "natural" style of acting, very different from the bombast which had gone before.

The first years of the Company's existence were also years of turmoil and upheaval. The King, who had granted the Company's Charter, was executed, not by some rival to the throne, but by the "Government of the People" as understood by the Roundheads. They in their turn were replaced by a returning monarch, but not without a considerable movement of power away from the Throne and towards Parliament, with the Common Law taking the place of the Royal Prerogative. This King too, was himself replaced in another minor revolution. How much of these political issues affected the average spectacle maker has to be a matter of doubt, though most of the original spectacle makers lived and worked in London, the hub of much of this national turbulence.

Cornhill in 1630.
A rather pretty picture of a main City thoroughfare at around the time of the Company's Charter. The street is a bit too clean, and the sky a bit too blue, but it gives an impression of London as lived in by our early spectacle makers.

17th CENTURY

JOTTINGS FROM THE MINUTE BOOKS

Though the Company obtained its Charter from Charles I in 1629, its records were destroyed in the Great Fire of London in 1666. Thus the first written record we have is of the Court meeting of the 3rd October, 1666, held in the Rayne Deare in Long Lane under the Mastership of John Turlington:

"This Court was principally called and appointed and kept for the Election of Master and Wardens of the Company for the year ensuing according to the Charter. But by reason it hath pleased the Lord this City is lately burnt down and thereby Members of this Company are dispersed into several remote parts as yet unknown whereby a full Court could not muster."

Fires were not infrequent in the City but that of 1666, well deserved the description of "The Great Fire of London". A survey, quoted by Adrian Tiniswood (10), found that 13,200 houses had been burned down or demolished, in 400 streets and courts. That meant that somewhere in the region of 70,000 to 80,000 people had lost their homes. Of the area within the walls, 373 acres had gone - well over 80 per cent - along with a further 63 acres in the extra-mural parishes to the north and west. 86 churches were either badly damaged or completely destroyed. Add to this the fact that Guildhall, the Exchange, St. Paul's, Custom House, the Excise Office, the General Letter Office and 44 Livery Company halls had also been destroyed. The Court minute could thus be considered as either a very concise appreciation or the result of shell shock. It was rough justice that the Lord Mayor, Sir Thomas Bludworth (he was the one who had said in the early days of the fire that "*a woman could piss it out*"), had also lost his official residence and had to make do with Carpenters' Hall.

**

There are some references in the records to matters prior to 1666. On the 20th October, 1644, John Throckmorton started his apprenticeship with John Jenkinson. However the note states that he left his apprenticeship to *"fight for the Restoration"*. He eventually took his Freedom some 25 years later on the 6th October, 1669. (This is not a record for Sir Frank Newson-Smith started his apprenticeship on the 6th October, 1894, but did not become a Freeman, by Servitude of course, until 6th January, 1944.)

**

The Charter of 1629 gave the usual rights of a Charter at that time for the oversight and rule of a trade. Establishing a Master with two Wardens, a Court of Assistants and inevitably a *"Learned Clerk"*. Included in the Charter was the essential right of search:

> *"...we do give and grant unto the said Master Wardens and Assistants of the Fellowshippe of Spectacle Makers of London and their Successors That the said Master Wardens and Assistants of the said Fellowshippe for the Time being for ever here after shall have the oversight Rule and search of all and singular Person and Persons whatsoever occupying exercising buying selling importing exporting trading or anyway using the said Art Trade or Mistry of Spectacle Making within our Realm of England."*

Much of the early minutes were taken up with "The Search", the first report of a search was in April, 1669, and the last in June,

1695. When the Guilds and Livery Companies, the one melded into the other over the centuries, were obtaining control over their respective trades, one important power ceded to them by the Crown was the Right of Search. This enabled the Master and Wardens to go into every shop within their purview carrying out their trade and seize any goods that they considered "not fit for purpose", though they probably used more direct language like *"badd wares"*, and take them to the Mayor's Court and, if their complaint was upheld, destroy the imperfect goods on London Stone. (In the 1960s with the increase in the importation of foreign frames it was suggested that the Court test out whether these powers were still operable. The idea was not proceeded with as there were on the Court at that time several spectacle manufacturers who did not want their frames to end up on London Stone, even though the Stone was behind a grill in Cannon Street and it would not have been easy to accomplish).

A typical example of the action taken is at the Court on the 3rd of August, 1671, when Widow Brignall, who was a Haberdasher, was found in possession of 20 dozen spectacles:

"Badd in glasse and frames and, after judgement in the Mayor's Court, in Canning Street on the remaining parts of London Stone where the same were with a hammer broken all in pieces."

London Stone in 1820 but likely very little changed in aspect from the time when Widow Brignall's 20 dozen spectacles were "broken all in pieces" 150 years before.

The reporting of these *"searches"* reads more like a genteel pub crawl. On the occasion of the search held on Tuesday, 9th April, 1695, and having *"searched"* some 52 shops the total haul was 78 pairs of white spectacles and 84 pairs of black spectacles mostly of looking glass *"wrought on one side only"*. These *"badd wares"* all came from 6 shops. 8 members of the Court took part in the search.

Each shop visited paid 4d. for the privilege unless, as 6 claimed, *"they had no money"*. Total income was therefore, reminding some readers and informing others, that at that time it was 12 pence to the shilling and 20 shillings to the pound, 15s.4d. Offset against this are the expenses:

"At the Horse Shoe	*2s.2d.*
At the Coffee House in Cateaton Street with the Constables	*7d.*
At the Feathers by Mr. Radford's	*1s.6d.*
At the Coffee House in Lincoln's Inn Fields	*2d.*
At the Constables in Thavies Inn Lane	*1s.0d.*
At dinner in the Feathers in Aldersgate Street	*7s.8d.*
At Lloyds Coffee House	*10d.*
At The Sun Tavern	*5s.3d.*
Total	*19s.3d."*

So they came out with a loss of 3s.11d., and taking action in the Mayor's Court as regards the *"badd wares"* and their destruction, knowing lawyers, will have cost the Company something.

The next search is that of the 18th June, 1695, in which 7 members of the Court took part. Some 35 shops were searched and this time, nobody claiming lack of money, the income was 11s. 8d. Expenditure on this occasion was:

"At the Coffee House	*6d.*
At the Bay Tree in Cannon Street	*1s.3d.*
At the Hoop Tavern in Fish Street	*4s.*
At the Cooks in Wapping	*9s.*
For Tobacco and Brandy	*1s.10d.*
At the Cock in Birchin Lane	*2s.*
Total	*18s. 7d."*

A loss of 6s.11d. This time the haul of *"badd wares"* was 67 pairs of black spectacles and 97 pairs of white spectacles, mostly of looking glass *"wrought on one side only"*. There were also 67 pairs of black spectacles with *"two slitts"* and 13 pairs of black spectacles with *"3 slitts"*. The report adds that:

"all the spectacles taken in this search as before were sealed upp at The Hoop Tavern at the Bridge foot and sent by the Beadle to Mr. Longlands house", William Longland being the Master.

**

The Company's finances at that time consisted of money coming in by fines, Quarterage, etc., against current expenditure. The money was held in the hands of the Upper Warden, he being responsible for the Company's finances, there being no bank account. If there was a deficit the money was "loaned" by the Master or one of the Wardens. In 1682, the Company owed Joseph Howe, a previous Master, some £42-3s-2d. :

"Mr. Joseph Howe shall receive all such moneys as shall be prove due or be paid or payable to or for the Companies use in any kind whatsoever from henceforth until he be paid his full debt".

**

The Company also took action outside the Search to defend the trade. Two actions in 1677 are typical. A fine of £40 for selling frames to a non-member and a fine of £37 for selling *"bade warres"* to one, Edward Bovery, a merchant.

**

In 1669, came the first bequest to the Company referred to in the Minutes, of £5, from John Turlington. There may have been other bequests to the Company before this and a search of the relevant wills might be appropriate. Turlington had other claims to fame, apart from his bequest. He was Master at the time of the Great Fire and until 1668, he was also Samuel Pepys' eye man. Pepys gave up writing his diary because he feared he was going blind. His first reference to this was in 1663 *"and so to bed, being weary, sleepy, and my eyes begin to fail me, looking so long by candlelight upon white paper"* From 1667, he complained more frequently. *"By then his eyes were suffering from his years of close work; increasingly they hurt if he read for too long, they reacted badly to bright light, and they felt sore and watered. None of the remedies he tried – spectacles, lotions, eye-drops, pills, purges, the use of a paper roll when reading – did much to help. Modern medical opinion is that he had long sight (hypermetropia), which made reading difficult, and some astigmatism. But he was not going blind and his eyes deteriorated no further. Whether they were helped by giving up the Diary or not, they served him adequately for the rest of his life".* (12.)

**

In January 1676/7, the old calendar, it was reported that John Hawes, who had come onto the Court at some time prior to 1666, was in the King's Bench prison. He was promptly removed from the Court of Assistants.

**

The Company became involved in legal actions from time to time as regards the Right of Search. One case in particular is recorded, namely Bolton and Throgmorton (who is Throckmorton in our records, Master in 1681). Bolton, (using the wording of the case report by Mr. Skinner, late of the Inner Temple, in cases adjudged in the Court of Kings Bench) *"declared in trespass, for taking and breaking so many dozen of spectacles, the defendant* (the Spectacle Makers Company) *pleads that the City of London is an antient city, that therein is and hath been an antient custom, that if any make and expose to sale ill and unserviceable goods, that the chief officers of the company* (Throckmorton in this case) *have and used to seise them, and carry them to the Guild-Hall, and empanel a jury; and if they find them ill and unserviceable, to break them"*. Pollexfen was for the prosecution and raised a number of points, one of which was that the custom was not good as *"'tis laid that the goods are to be carried to Guild-Hall, and a jury impanelled, &, but no notice given to the party; and that it is against reason to condemn the party's goods, and not give him notice, and hear him."* Saunders was for the defence and, having batted away the earlier points raised, said, *"Thirdly, that the custom was good enough, though the party had no notice, for 'twas but an enquest of office by which the party is not concluded, but may bring his action if his goods were merchandisable; upon the whole, the Court took the custom to be good, and reasonable; and the judgement was for the defendant, nisi"*. As you will see in the next century it was not long before the Courts ceased to uphold the *"antient custom"* of the City Livery Companies.

**

One event that took place from time to time and which our spectacle maker would have been able to attend was the Thames Frost Fair. (13) In all nine Frost Fairs are known to have been held. The first in 1564-65, the last in 1813. Perhaps the greatest of these fairs was that of 1683-84, which is reasonably well documented, particularly by John Evelyn. It was actually in two parts. Frost started forming on the Thames in mid-December and by the end of December booths and stalls were erected on the ice. By the 5th January the Thames was a solid sheet of ice. However by the 15th January, a thaw set in and everything was hastily cleared off the river. Three days later the frost returned and by the 19th January the ice was as thick as ever, the frost so severe that it was reckoned that it would last until March. Evelyn paid a visit on the 24th January: *"The frost continuing more and more severe, the Thames before London, was still planted with booths in formal streetes, all sorts of shops and trades furnish'd and full of commodities even to a printing press…Coaches plied from Westminster to the Temple, and from several other staires to and fro, as in the streetes; sleds, sliding with skeetes, a bull-baiting, horse and coach races, puppet-playes, and interludes, cookes, tipling and other lewd places, so that it seem'd to be a bacchanalian triumph, or carnival on the water."*

Evelyn added *"this humour* (of having one's name printed) *tooke so universally, that 'twas estimated the printer gain'd £5 a day, for printing a line onely, at sixpence a name, besides what he got by ballads, etc".*

According to a ballad of the time *"what cost 3d. ashore cost 4d. on the ice"* but for his money *"a visitor could buy a slice of roast beef, or plum-cake, and follow it with a tankard of either beer, ale, brandy or Spanish wine. If he happened to have a puritanical objection to strong drink, he could try a dish of famous new-made coffee or tea or chocolate…amusements offered were no less varied. The visitor could take part in a game of ninepins-recently imported into this country as ten-pins-or pidgeon. If he was feeling energetic, he could clap on skeetes and scim across the ice".* He could also get dizzy on Dutch whimsies *"Thee whimsies, which were probably the originals of the modern fair-ground round-abouts, appear to have been very popular".*

Our spectacle maker visitor could even take part in fox-hunting.

"This last spectacle, which tradition says Charles II saw, was where the fox is run on a leash across the ice pursued by large dogs also on leashes. At a given signal, when all the bets had been laid, fox and dogs were loosed and the chase began".

1683 - Frost Fair on the River Thmes near Temple Stairs by Thomas Wyke.

On the 2nd February *"a whole ox was roasted on the river near Whitehall"*. By the 5th February the thaw had set in. So ended the great Frost Fair of 1683-84. There were subsequent frost fairs but not of this magnitude. With the demolition of the old London

Bridge, with its 20 narrow arches, and the opening of the new bridge on the 1st August, 1831, the flow of the Thames was vastly improved. There have been no subsequent occasions when the Thames has frozen solid since. Of course with the arguable facts of climate change there is no saying that it will not freeze solid at some time in the future!

**

As already referred to, for many years the Company had problems with money. On the 9th January, 1672, meeting at the Rayne Deare, we find:

"This Court taking notice that they are already in debt for moneys laid out for the support and maintenance of this Company about £12-0-0 and now must of necessity lay out in and about the prosecution of unlawful workers the whole Master and Wardens and Assistants now present do promise to pay and lay down into the hands of Mr. Alt the Warden Twenty Shillings each man towards the charges aforesaid the same to be lent by them and they are to be repaid the same against this Company."

Admittedly, the Court did not have too many expenses, but they do seem to have had a meal after the meeting of the Court, hence in 1679, at a meeting held in the Cage in the Old Bailey:

"It is ordered this day by the Court that every of the Assistants that shall happen to be absent from any Quarter Court or other Court that shall be by summons appointed about the affairs and business of this Company shall from henceforth pay his and their proportionable charges of the expenses that the Master, Wardens and Assistants who shall be then present shall be at, at the time and times when such Courts are held.
It is also further ordered that if the Master, Wardens and

Assistants or any of them shall neglect to be at Court by the space of one hour after the time by the summons appointed that then every such person so transgressing shall pay to the use of the Company twelve pence."

Money was still proving a problem in 1686, for there was a bond due to John Burman, the Clerk, of £40, which the Assistants were instructed to cover. For the record at the next Court Burman resigned due to *"those misfortunes upon him that he could no longer officiate"*. A polite way, perhaps, of saying that he could no longer afford to sub the Company.

**

In January, 1679, the Assistants, together with the Clerk, were asked to pay the servants in lieu of the Company.

**

By the seventeenth century shops had replaced the market stall, a permanent structure rather than an itinerant stall put up and dismantled for the market or fair. A typical shop of the period was of the "One up, one down" type. On the ground floor would be a large unglazed window, glass didn't come in for shops until the next century. The window would have a horizontal shutter which could be closed at night. During the day the shutter was opened and the top part could be hooked up to provide a shelter, with the bottom half folded down to provide a counter. The shop keeper and his family would live "above the shop". The inventory of John Taylor, a member of the Company, gives some indication of how they lived and his total possessions at the time of his death:

THE SPECTACLE MAKERS

Roll Dated 9th June 1681.

Total value of goods £41. 1s. 6d.

Inventory dated 24th March, 1680
Sworn by Richard Neal, Goldsmith; John Rayshald, Founder; William Longlans, Spectacle Maker and John Lardye, Draper, before Sir Thomas Bludworth, Knight and Alderman.

In the Kitchen	8.	16.	3				
In the Garret	2.	2.	6				
In the Chamber up one pair of stairs	6.	13.	6				
In the Shop: 6 gross and a half of frames; 5 gross of rough frames; 18 dozen of glasses; 18 dozen of spectacles; 3 dozen of spectacle cases; a counter chair and stool; a cupboard; 2 nests of drawers; a flock bed and bolster; a blanket and lumber	6.	5.	0				
Apparel	5.	10.	0				
Linen	3.	15.	6				
Plate	7.	13.	9	40.	16.	6	
Ready money				20.	0.	0	
				£60.	16.	6	

Debts owing by the Testator at his decease:

To Mr. Page for rent	12.	10.	0			
To Mr. Underhill, brewer	3.	0.	0			
To the Scrivener that made his Will		5.	0			
To Mr. Skinner, apothecary	4.	0.	0	£19.	15.	0

Charges and other necessary expenses including charges of proving the Will and valuing the goods £4. 7. 0

Perhaps surprisingly for a newly fledged company, trade matters, apart from the Right of Search, occur but seldom in the Minutes. An exception was on the 14th April, 1692, at a meeting of the Court held at the Citty Armes, Milk Street Market:

"At this Court it being put to the vote whether a By-Law or Ordinance of this Company shall be made by this Court to prohibit the making selling or disposing of Leather Spectacle frames by any of the members of this Society the votes were as follows. The persons who voted for making such a By-Law (nine names). The person who voted against making such a By-Law, Mr. Christopher Cock (at that time the Upper Warden)-. Mr Thomas Sterrop would not now vote at all but desires further time to consider thereof."

Apart from being a splendid example of sitting on the fence by Mr. Thomas Sterrop, leather spectacles were part of the development of the modern spectacle frame.

**

Another example from the 16th December, 1692, again at the Citty Armes in Milk Street Market:

"Whereas at this Court notice hath been given that the Patentees for the Convex Lights are about to enlarge their time for the said Light and under pretence thereof endeavour to have it stated that none but the said Patentees set up or use any Convex Lights which will very much intrench upon and prejudice this Company in their right and property of using and selling Convex Glasses being a considerable branch of this Trade It is agreed and consented unto by all the said persons now being present that the name of the Master, Wardens and Assistants of this Company may be used in a Petition to the High Court of Parliament now assembled against the passing of such Act as aforesaid and in such Reasons as shall

be thought fit to be given in Parliament against the same."

A further example of a more widespread problem came at the Court on the 20th March, 1694, held at the sign of the White Beare at the corner of Barbican in Aldersgate Street, the Master being John Yarwell:

"Ordered that the Master Wardens and Mr. John Radford Mr. Joseph Howe and Mr. Samuel Thompson or any four of them do meet and consider of a method for making publication on behalf of this Company to vindicate their Art and Interest against Interlopers and their pretensions and that the same be managed at the Charge of the Company."

Plus ça change plus ça la même chose.

**

Going back a few years, oddities show up in the Minutes which may well have had a simple explanation at the time. For instance the Mastership of Gregory Tingay, 1685/86 shows a few anomalies. He was elected at the Court meeting on 30th September, 1685, with George Mason as the Upper Warden and James Throckmorton as Under Warden, as the office was then called.

I should at this point explain that then, as now, in the Court Minutes those present at a Court meeting were set out in their order of precedence, with the Master and the two Wardens at the top of the list. The next meeting was held on the 15th October, 1685, when John Yarwell's name appears at the top of the list and indicated as *"Master"* immediately followed by Gregory Tingay with George Mason and James Throckmorton duly indicated as Wardens. The next meeting was on the 7th January, still in 1685, as the new calendar was yet to be introduced. Yarwell appears at the top of the list followed by Gregory Tingay who is now shown as *"Master"* and George Mason as Under Warden, James Throckmorton was not present. However the Minutes go on to state:

"For Under Warden stood in competition James Throckmorton and William Longland and the election fell upon Mr. Throckmorton."
No reason is given in the Minutes for this "extra" election.

At the February meeting Yarwell is shown as *"Master"*, followed by George Mason with Gregory Tingay coming third with no indication of office. James Throckmorton was not present. At the April meeting Yarwell is again at the top of the list and shown as *"Master"*, with Tingay next, followed by George Mason as Under Warden, James Throckmorton is again absent. In July Yarwell *"Master"*, followed by Tingay and Mason, this time not shown as a Warden, and with James Throckmorton right down at the bottom as the penultimate name in order of precedent. The October Court was the Election Court, and William Longland becomes Master and George Mason and James Throckmorton Upper and Under Warden respectively. Tingay was not present. He had not however taken umbrage, as he appears at a meeting later in October, which is admittedly his last appearance. Thus whilst he was solemnly elected as Master he does not appear to have taken a Court meeting in this capacity.

It could be that Tingay was ill and Yarwell was standing in for him, but in previous instances in the Minutes if the Master was absent it had been stated that a Deputy was standing in. (Deputy in this instance meant someone specifically deputed by the Master to take the meeting as the By Laws demanded). It would be highly unlikely that someone would stand in for the Master if the man who was Master was actually at the meeting. Neither was he consistently late at a meeting with someone standing in until he arrived, for members of the Court, including the officers, were fined for late arrival at a scheduled meeting and no such fines are noted.

I suppose it could be argued that the Clerk made a mistake, but it would need to be a succession of mistakes and, as is well known, Clerks of Livery Companies do not make mistakes! The whole thing is of little import in the great state of things. Of course I might just have been reading these Minutes for too long!

This may be of no relevance to the above but in the *"Middlesex County Court Records, 1683"* the following appears: 26th February, 1683, the conviction of *"Gregory Tingly of St. Clement Danes, spectaclemaker, of having been present at an unlawful conventicle, held under colour of excercising religion, etc., at a meeting place in St. Margaret's, Westminster"* and was fined £10. (1) With the enforced change to the Church of England under Henry VIII, three *Conventicle Acts* had been passed to coerce people into attending the Church of England. (A conventicle is a small, unofficial and unofficiated religious meeting of lay people.) *The Conventicle Act, 1670,* had introduced fines for a first offence of 5s. and for a second offence 10s. Gregory Tingay was obviously a firm "non-believer" as this was at least his second offence. It is possible that his religious beliefs, whilst not stopping his fellow spectacle makers electing him as Master, precluded them from indicating him as such in his position in the Minute book, or perhaps they were covering for his absence at a *"conventicle"*?

**

Masters of the Company were no doubt eminent members of their trade but are remembered in history, if at all, only as Masters of the Company. John Yarwell, who was Master in 1684, and again in 1693, is the first Master to be known for his innovatory work, not in relation to spectacles, but as a maker of scientific instruments. It is known that he was visited by Robert Hooke, the wayward genius of the Royal Society, in the 1670s. He supplied lenses to Abraham Sharp who was Flamsteed's paid assistant at the

Royal Observatory. Yarwell and John Marshall were great rivals in the monocular and tripod microscope field, both as purveyors and as inventors, as their advertising at the time well indicates. Making spectacles required skill but the rewards were limited. Making scientific instruments required even more skill but, to judge by Yarwell, was a good deal more lucrative. By his will in 1713, he left £300 to the poor of the Parish of St. Paul, £100 each to Christ's Hospital and the Spectacle Makers Company and other bequests of £100 and £50 to his friends and family. He was hardly destitute. He also gained a Royal Appointment to William III. (14)

As an aside he couldn't always keep control of his children for in the report of the *"Middlesex Sessions of 1705"* (1) we find that Arabella Yarwell, daughter of John Yarwell, had dropped out of her apprenticeship to a sailmaker, for 13 years in 1694. *"The Court ordered the apprentice to return to her service."*

**

On the 30th March, 1699, Lucretia Clarke became, by Patrimony, the first female Freeman in her own right i.e. not a wife taking over her husband's business as was allowed by the Court.

**

It isn't often that one finds references to spectacle makers in other sources. To quote two, first in the *"Diary of Roger Whitley"*(Ibid) Tuesday, 28th January, 1690,*"The Sunne with the spectaclemakers, there were two Radfords, gave them a bottle of wine"*.

Secondly one John Norman (not in our records), who had a *"spectacle shop just outside Westminster Gate"*. The time is August, 1643, and feelings were running high about the apparently inevitable Civil War. He witnessed a large group of women, some say 5-6,000, attempting to hand in a *"Petition of Many Civilly Disposed Women"* to the Parliamentary leaders at Westminster, including John Pym. The women all had white ribbons in their hats as a symbol of peace. The scene became ugly, with the women blockading the entrance to

Parliament for two hours. Sir William Waller's horse regiment attempted to suppress the *"riot"*. There was *"much mischief done by the horse and foot soldiers"*. Two men were known to have been killed, and many more men and women injured. News spread that a women, one of the protestors, though some reports say she just happened to be crossing the Palace Yard, had been shot and killed in a nearby churchyard. Norman went off to see what had happened. Norman had been heard to say that *"he would rather see the streets run with blood than that we should now have peace"*. When he got nearer the scene he found that the *"pretty young wench"* who had been shot was his own daughter. (15)

**

References:

1. British History on Line Version 5 Institute of Historical research.

2. *"The Port and Trade of Early Elizabethan Documents"* edited by Brian Dietz London Record Society.

3. *"The Directory of British Scientific Instrument Makers 1551-1850"* Gloria Clifton Zwemmer in association with The National Maritime Museum 1995.

4. Nichol's *"History of Leicestershire"*.

5. *"Scientific Instrument makers in London during the Seventeenth and Eighteenth Centuries"* by Mary Robischon - a dissertation for a Ph.D. at the University of Michigan.

6. Roy Porter *"London a Social History"* 2000, Penguin Books.

7. Peter Ackroyd *"London the biography"* 2000, Chatto and Windus.

8. G.M. Trevelyan *"English Social History"* 1973, Book Club Associates.

9. The National Archive.

10. Adrian Tiniswood *"By Permission of Heaven the true story of the Great Fire of London"* 2004.

11. John Evelyn *"A Character of England"* 1659.

12. Claire Tomalin *"Samuel Pepys – the unequalled self"* 2002.

13. The following is based on *"The Great Frost Fair of 1683-4"* by Michael Srigley quoted in *"History Today"*, December, 1960.

14. College of Optometrists Museum et al.

15. Sara Read *"Maids, Wives, Widows: Exploring Early Modern Women's Lives"* quoted in *"History Today"*.

18th CENTURY

PRELUDE

After the turmoil of the previous century the 1701 Act of Union and the establishment of the "Kingdom of Great Britain", served to calm matters down. True there were revolutions, the Agricultural and Industrial, though perhaps not even recognised at the time and certainly not named, which were to have a profound effect, not least on the Livery Companies. The Agricultural Revolution involved changes in animal husbandry, the introduction of root crops, mechanisation and enclosures making bigger fields for sheep and the new machines, but forcing many people off the land and towards towns and cities, notably London.

There was also the little matter of the American Colonies fighting for, and gaining, their freedom. With Parliament and the "government" gaining the ascendancy over the monarch, bureaucracy expanded and central administration expanded exponentially. *"The political strategists of the 18th century were concerned not with thwarting parliament, but with how to make it work – in their interests. So, the art of political management was born in this period"* (Hannah Betts Guardian 2 January 2014). According to Roy Porter there were *"3,000 career officials working in Westminster"* by 1725. (1)

Communications improved, by 1765 London was linked to 180

towns by stage coaches, which as well as passengers, carried the mail, though it took 3 days to get to Manchester (by 1800 this was reduced to 18 hours) and the nationwide installation of the turnpike system. Coastal trade had existed for centuries and by the 18th century London had nineteen quays specialising in provincial traffic. Water transport was far cheaper than road, and the century saw improvement to rivers but, more significantly, the arrival of the "Canal Age", which increased navigable waterways, significantly reducing the cost of transportation and thereby the cost of the raw materials. The vast army of workers, "navvies", moving through the country caused a social and economic upheaval, which continued in the next century with the building of the railways which replaced, eventually almost completely, the canals. Communication was vastly improved in the latter part of the century by the introduction, by John Palmer of Bath, of the "mail coach" thus replacing post boys. It was said that letters sent on a Monday could expect a reply by Wednesday. I think for once I will avoid the comparison with the present day, except to say that the email of today is gradually eliminating the need for letters.

Crime was rife, though was gradually got under control by the establishment of the Bow Street Runners in the middle of the century. Much of the crime was of a minor nature, carried out not by hardened criminals, but by *"servants and seamstresses, and the labouring poor, down on their luck or out of work, starving, or just fatally tempted. Much crime arose out of the ambiguities of capitalism itself, involving mishandling of property"* (Ibid) but still resulting in execution, whipping or transportation.

Christopher Hibbert (2) considered that for most of the 18th century London *"was perhaps the most dangerous city in Europe"*. All roads leading to London were infested with highwaymen who had the cheek *"to post notices on the doors of the rich expressly forbidding persons to go out of town without ten guineas and a watch about them upon pain of death"*. The establishment of "Mr. Fielding's People", the forerunners of the Bow Street Runners, was opposed by the people of London, who regarded with horror *"any form of professional police force, regarding the police forces of Europe as a threat to individual liberty as well as an unjustified expense"*. This in spite of the fact that armed robbery and housebreaking were rife *"not only in the country, for robberies were frequent in Holborn, Fleet Street, St. James's Square, Park Lane, Piccadilly and Grosvenor Square"*. Much of the blame was put on the appalling street lighting which was said to be the worst in Europe.

In the City, St. Paul's was at last completed. It had taken 35 years, under one architect, Christopher Wren, and one master builder, Thomas Strong, in all that time. Wren, despite working on 50 other churches, found the time to visit St. Paul's every week to superintend progress. When the building was nearing completion he used to have himself hoisted up to the lantern in a basket, though he asked his son to perform the ceremony of laying the last and highest stone in the lantern. After returning from one of his frequent visits to his cathedral to his home at Hampton Court, Wren died, at the age of 91, and was one of the first to be buried in the Crypt, his tomb marked by a plain black slab, above it the inscription *"Lector, si monumentum requiris, circumspice"*, usually translated as *"Reader, if you seek a monument, look around you"*.

London in 1725.

In the middle of the eighteenth century as described by William Boulton (3) *"London, including Westminster, was bounded by Oxford Street and Holborn on the north, by the river on the south, by the outer boundary of the City on the east, and by Hyde Park, Arlington Street, and St. James' Street on the west. All the rest of modern London was suburban merely, or open and pleasant country interspersed with wild heaths, and dotted with ancient villages. The country stretched out fingers at Finsbury and the Tower. The fashionable dwellers in the Savoy and the lawyers in the Temple looked across the river to the hills of Surrey and Kent; and there is room for reflection in the fact that the Zoological Gardens which were not opened till 1828, had for years to be fenced against the hares and rabbits which nibbled the bark off their shrubs and dug up their bulbs"*. In his lyrical description he omits the "hovel development" to the east, and Southwark and its environs to the south of the river. Nor does he mention the "Winchester Geese", the name given to the prostitutes of Southwark who lived and worked in houses and hovels, many of which were owned by the Bishop of Winchester.

Bow Church and Cheapside, 1750.

Another City thoroughfare some 120 years later than Cornhill on Page 41. The street is noticeably more crowded with passenger coaches as well as goods traffic. More people in the streets under the big swinging shop signs. Cheapside was still a popular and expensive area so it would be unlikely that a spectacle maker would have his shop here but he, or she, might do a bit of shopping before the days of the big emporiums.

London grew throughout the century, particularly with the building of new bridges across the Thames at Westminster and Blackfriars. In 1700, the population was around 575,000 and by 1800, it was 900,000. It had become the largest city in the world where "*one in ten of all English and Welsh people was resident in London, whereas only one Frenchman in forty lived in Paris... Shadwell and Bethnal Green had dissolved into the sea of bricks, to the south, the Borough was spreading to Newington Butts, southwest, Tothill Fields in Westminster was edging into Chelsea and*

Knightsbridge; and Hammersmith, Chelsea, Paddington, Marylebone and St. Pancras were joining the metropolitan orbit. Chelsea rose from 350 houses in 1717 to 1,350 in 1795; Marylebone from 317 to 7,764". (1)

London became prosperous on commerce and those who served it. Overseas trade and empire were vital to this prosperity, and the Port of London the heart of the exchange. 80% of the country's imports, 69% of its exports and 86% of its re-exports came to London. Everything came to London *"tea, china, drugs, nankeens, muslins, calicoes, long cloths, cotton yarn, pepper and spices, salt-petre, indigo, raw and manufactured silks, sugars"* from the East Indies; *"sugar, rum, coffee, cocoa, pimento, ginger"* from the West Indies; *"fruit, wax, gums, elephant's teeth, palm oil, wine"* from Africa; *"tobacco, rice, indigo, cotton, corn oil, skins and naval stores"* from North America; *"hemp, linens, tallow, ashes, iron, masts, deals"* from the Baltic, according to Patrick Colquhoun as quoted by Roy Porter, and, of course, coals from Newcastle.

Industry flourished too in the City. Distillers: Booth's and Gordon's. Breweries: Red Lion, Truman's and Whitbread's. Cutlery, superior to Sheffield, clocks and watches, and silk weaving. Porcelain factories, a bell foundry, cabinet-making – Chippendale in Long Acre, Hepplewhite in Cripplegate and Sheraton, who was a designer of furniture rather than a maker. There were so many crafts that a trade directory of 1792, was able to name 492 in London. Retailing also came to the fore. Whereas historically goods were sold by hawkers and ***"them that jette about"***, *"high-grade retailing was becoming the province of stylish shops"*. Names known today were being founded in the 18th century: John Murray, publishing; Hawkes of Piccadilly; Fortnum met up with Mason; Hatchard's the bookseller; and James Christie (a Freeman of the Company) the auctioneer.

Banks developed, though here the names have changed,

absorbed by their subsequent larger brethren, Child's, Stone's, Martin's and Hoare's (several generations of whom were to become Liverymen of the Company). The Bank of England had been established in 1694, (along with the birth of the National debt), at first working from Mercer's Hall before transferring to Threadneedle Street in 1723.

Hoare's Old Banking House, 1838.

The currency at last settled down to a standard set of coins and values. The guinea or "gold crown" worth £1-1-0d. The shilling, pound sterling, and the crown, worth 5s., were coined in silver, the penny, half-penny and the farthing in bronze. Additional safety for paper money was introduced by the use of watermarked bank notes.

The increase in size of London and the change in the organisation of labour were having a dire effect on the Livery Companies. Labour was now organised by market forces and not by the old trade organisations. *"Law courts grew less inclined to uphold their* (the Livery Companies') *privileges, especially the crucial right of search, essential if companies were to maintain a closed shop. The mushrooming of the metropolis had long made such procedures difficult to enforce outside the walls; were they even legal? And, even within the City, companies grew reluctant to act for fear of prosecution for trespass. Many abandoned searches altogether, and concentrated instead on property management, charity and junketings".* (Ibid)

The last Spectacle Makers Company search was 1710. When the Company subsequently applied for a Warrant for a General Search from the Recorder of London, this in 1713, it *"could not be obtained"*.

What could our spectacle maker do for amusement in his or her spare time? London was more and more taking its enjoyment, al fresco. New Spring Gardens, to be renamed Vauxhall Gardens, was coming into its heyday. Patrons could get there by water, 6d. for a pair-oared wherry from Whitehall or 3d for sculls, and stroll the lawns, the dark walks and shady groves. When Jonathan Tyers took over the lease in 1728, New Spring Gardens took off. He employed sculptors to create colossal statues, including one of Handel by Roubiliac, and employed fine musicians in the Grove to play the works of Handel and Thomas Arne. *"Round and about the Grove were clustered the temples, the pavilions, the rotundas, the great rooms, the music rooms, the picture rooms, the covered colonnades for wet weather, above all the famous supper boxes built in straight rows or curving sweeps. In those famous supper boxes, where generations of Londoners ate the noted Vauxhall chicken and ham, were the paintings which gave a quaint interest to each, every picture displayed by its own little oil lamp"* so says William Boulton. (3) The chickens were renowned for their smallness, the ham for a *"thinness past belief"* nicknamed *"sliced cobwebs"*. The pictures were not mere wallpaper but by Hogarth and his pupils.

Wallpaper had started to replace tapestry as a wall covering in the time of Henry VIII. Not the least of the attractions were the lights, the sudden lighting of which, by the clever use of long fuses, and with a simultaneous crash of music from the orchestra, had a considerable effect.

Vauxhall Gardens 1751 by Samuel Wale.

Apart from a spectacle maker or two, Vauxhall was often visited by the Prince of Wales, together with the society of the day, to take part in the stately promenade with which the evening opened. To be followed by a concert with the best orchestra and voices of the day, with spectacles like watermills and cascades for those not so interested in the music. The dark walks also became famous for the romantically inclined. Johnson sums it up as *"that excellent place of amusement must ever be an estate to its proprietor, as it is particularly adapted to the taste of the English nation, there being a mixture of curious show, gay exhibition, music, vocal and instrumental, not too refined for the general ear, for all of which only*

THE SPECTACLE MAKERS

a shilling is paid, and though last, not least, good eating and drinking for those who choose to purchase that regale". Towards the end of the century it was considered that Vauxhall was in decline when the entertainments resorted to fireworks displays. Tyers, the inspiration behind Vauxhall Gardens, used an interesting form of public relations. He dressed up presentable people in the height of fashion and sent them off to mix with the crowds in the Mall at St. James and to remark loudly, that they would be meeting each other later *"at Vauxhall Gardens"*.

Staying al fresco, were the fairs. By the 18th century Bartholomew Fair, originally a cloth fair, had been in existence since the time of Henry I., founded by Rahere, Henry's Court Jester. The priory and hospice dedicated to St. Bartholomew were funded by the tolls of the fair granted to it by Royal Charter in 1133. Well before the 18th century it had gained sufficient standing to be opened by the Lord Mayor, who drank *"a cool tankard of wine, nutmeg and sugar"* at Newgate before the formal opening. The tradition continuing despite when, in 1688, the Lord Mayor, Sir John Shorter, flapped down the lid of his tankard so loudly that his horse shied and threw him and he died the following day. Ben Jonson's play, *"Bartholomew Fayre"* of 1614, rather gives the impression of a fair with which no Lord Mayor ought to be associated. Whilst there were tight-rope dancers, jugglers, puppet shows and the showing of monstrosities, there had developed theatre booths depicting portentous subjects such as *"The creation of the world"* and *"The siege of Troy"* and, by the 18th century, the cream of the great theatres came to perform.

In time the Fair *"became so great a nursery of dramatic talent that many actors afterwards famous obtained their first chance at Smithfield"*. Colley Cibber was a regular, as was Doggett, a name remembered now for an annual race on the Thames. These entertainments came to be called "drolls", perhaps forerunners of the variety theatre and the pantomime. The plots varied little from year to year. Not that that mattered as the handbills gave a full description of what was to follow. Henry Fielding produced *"The Beggar's Opera"* at the Fair, and these productions became so successful that the theatres closed during the Fair, and the whole cast re-located to Smithfield for the fortnight. There were many attempts to close the booths, not just by the Puritans, the City Marshall was killed in 1751, in one attempt. Other attractions at the Fair were the menageries of wild beasts, including tigers, lions, a *"Noble Cashaware"*, a leopard, rattlesnakes, a double cow, *"a little black hairy monster, bred in the deserts of Arabia"* and a *"young mermaid taken on the shores of Aguapulca"* and all for 6d. A broad enough mix to interest Sir Hans Sloane, who employed a draughtsman to make *"studies of such curiosities"*.

When Bartholomew Fair was reduced to three days, in 1750, the theatre side lost interest and the menageries took more prominence, but they had to be more daring, the keeper started putting his head in the lion's mouth, for the mere appearance of a lion was no longer a sufficient draw. Conjurors, vaulters, the tight-rope and slack wire, puppet-shows and ventriloquists, described as *"the wonderful man who talks in his belly and can fling his voice into any part of the room"* abounded. But Bartholomew Fair was on the wane. There were other fairs at St. Margaret's Hill, Southwark (which started in 1550), and Chapel Street and Hertford Street carnivals, remembered today in the name Mayfair, all following the Bartholomew's pattern, with theatre booths, gin stalls, gaming tables and gingerbread stalls. The fairs gradually degenerated and could more easily be suppressed, though Bartholomew Fair didn't end until 1850, the site to be used for Smithfield Market.

Another more aggressive outdoor pursuit for our spectacle maker to watch was that of the prize-ring. The earliest record of a public boxing match in England was in 1681. It included all the essential features of the sport, then and now. Whilst prize-fighting was much favoured by the "fancy" it was something which had a vogue amongst all classes of men through the ages. Prize-fighting probably started as a side show to the established sword, stick or quarter staff encounters referred to earlier in the 17th century. Prize-fighting was based on a sound commercial basis, and a Mr. Figg seems to have had, if not the first, then the most successful establishment, with a number of boxers around him, rather than indulging himself. Matches were arranged, usually as a result of a wager, the entrepreneur, in this case Mr. Figg, taking a large cut of the money paid by the spectators, which on occasion amounted to as much as £150.

George Taylor succeeded Mr. Figg at the Great Booth, Tottenham Court and amongst his team was a certain John Broughton, who was to change the face of prize-fighting. Broughton, having defeated Taylor, set up an opposition establishment in Hanway Street and was to retire after his only defeat, to die at the grand old age, for those days, of 84, with a fortune of £7,000. Broughton is said to have invented the defensive side of boxing, he certainly established rules which lasted some 100 years and attracted the all-important patronage that his enterprise required. His rules, whilst not establishing the size of the stage, introduced what we know of as rounds, a time limit between rounds, the appointment of umpires and referees, not hitting an opponent when he is down or hitting below the waist. His royal patrons included the Duke of Cumberland and Frederick, Prince of Wales. At Broughton's last fight in April, 1759, the wager was £200 a side and the gate money, estimated at £600 clear, was added to the stake. Broughton underestimated his opponent, failed to train, and was beaten by a *"prodigious blow between the eyes",* which effectively, though temporarily, blinded him. Consequently his patron, the Duke of Cumberland, lost his wager and £10,000, turned his back on prize-fighting and, without Royal support, the authorities were able to close down Broughton's establishment.

The fancy lost their appetite for the prize-ring and it effectively left London for the provinces. There was then a period of what were "fixed fights", with one or other of the fighters being paid to lose. But towards the end of the century a more "civilised" form of boxing returned with the introduction of "mufflers", which we would recognise as boxing gloves. The more scientific of the new fighters established boxing salons and gave lessons in the art to which the fancy, in this instance including Lord Byron, lame foot and all, took up as a new fashion so as to be able to defend themselves with their fists, swords now being more for decoration. Slowly the interest in prize-fighting returned and it became the fashion for a man of position to keep a tame prize-fighter of his own and to wager your man against another's. With such distinguished patronage, the "sport" returned to popularity. In the 19th century, with the improvement in training, fights lasted longer and longer, there was no limit except exhaustion or defeat. Ninety rounds were not unusual, and in 1856, a fight lasted 109 rounds, taking three hours and eight minutes. Let's leave this "amusement" with Boulton's words *"where two men with no quarrel between them, broke each other's jaws and beat each other blind and insensible, only to provide a spectacle and an occasion for gambling for a set of rowdies, who were careful to preserve their own skins from the same danger"*.

Still in the open air as Boulton (3) writes *"all classes had been quick to appreciate the value of a breezy open place, where fashion, jaded in the stuffy rooms and playhouses of the London of that day, could forgather in its chariots or on its horses, exchange repartees, and gaze over an open country right on to the hills of Surrey and Kent on the one hand, and to the northern heights of London on the other"*. He was particularly speaking of Hyde Park but it does emphasise the small size of London at that time *"lying purple in the distance in the hollow by the river between the Tower and the Savoy"*.

Hyde Park on a Sunday, 1804.

In the early part of the century "The Ring" in Hyde Park was the place where those wishing to be seen paraded in their coaches, or on horseback, going around in opposite circles, clockwise and anti-clockwise. Perhaps not for the basically poor spectacle maker, though he would have been able to observe the various military displays which started at the time of the Jacobite rising of 1715, and with various interruptions, continued over the years. Hyde Park was not the only London open space to be enjoyed, to some extent at any rate, by all and sundry. St. James's Park, once Charles II had had the Mall built, flourished. Strange contests developed: Dr. Garth and the Duke of Grafton running the *"short course of two hundred yards"*, races between servants, nude or not, hopping matches where a man had to hop a hundred yards in say fifty hops and much money was won when he did it in forty six, a fat cook running against a lean footman (the footman had a weight handicap), or an eighteen month old girl backed to walk three-quarters of a mile of the Mall in thirty minutes (the parents winning a large stake when she did it with seven minutes to spare).

There was much opportunity for *"promiscuous acquaintance"*, a lady of breeding exchanging words with a man she had never seen before(!), which was managed by the judicious use of wearing masks, leading to occasional extraordinary marriages. One quoted by Boulton in 1750, was of Sir Francis Delaval and the elderly Lady Isabella Paulet, who was of a bulky size and plain with it. Delaval had eased his task by bribing a fortune-teller, whom the lady frequently consulted, to tell her that she would meet a handsome stranger in the Mall. Sir Francis made sure it was he who was that *"handsome stranger"*, as she was worth £90,000 in funds and £150,000 in other property it was probably worth it. It was a little ungallant of him to proclaim afterwards that *"Look you, I bought Lady Delaval by weight, and paid nothing for fashion"*.

There were naturally disadvantages for, as the Park had immunity from arrest, the area had a crowd of *"unpromising individuals, who sunned themselves on the grass, filled the benches, begged alms or told fortunes, and picked pockets"*. However they themselves were subject to apprehension by the press-gang, who were not subject to the Park immunity, and who took as many as 150 away in one day. St. James's Park became more favourable to the spectacle maker when fashion left and went off to Green Park around 1786, when the well-bred suddenly adopted the fashion of taking their evening parade after dinner along the Queen's Walk, originally established by Queen Caroline. A modern phenomenon followed. With fashionable London displaying itself in the park, the houses on the west side of Arlington Street, with a view over Green Park, increased considerably in value.

There was also a revival of driving as a sport, the phaeton, the curricle, and the gig, drawn by four, three or two horses of the *"heavy breed"*. The high bred owners of these high bred horses began to dress like the coachmen and forsake fashion, and the ladies drove more ferociously and recklessly than their men folk. Added to this were, in various seasons, skating, prize-fighting and duelling with such a crowd assembling on the mere thought of seeing a duel that there was no room left for the duel to take place.

Lords Ground in 1837.

There was also cricket. In a primitive form it had been played since the 13th century but had been declared illegal, as it interfered with archery practice. A London club was formed in 1700, which played on the Artillery Ground at Finsbury, and this club moved to White Conduit Fields in 1780, and in due course the game became a national summer sport. One of the founders of the White Conduit Club was the Earl of Winchilsea, and it was for him and his friends that Thomas Lord superintended the ground. In 1767, the name was changed to the Marylebone Cricket Club, which settled in St. John's Wood in 1814. There was still no formal clothing or gloves and pads, and thousands of Londoners came to watch, not the exquisite cover drive or the late cut, but to bet on the result. There are many who feel today that the game has returned to its 18th century origins.

Before I am taken to task, I am not writing a history of cricket! The above history of cricket is limited to the City of London. Cricket in the Weald of Kent, initially, had been played for some time before this and competitive matches, and much gambling, had been going on for at least a century.

Lest it be thought that the 18th century had only place for outdoor amusement there were also the coffee-houses and the clubs. The club was to come to its heyday in the 19th century so it is perhaps more to the coffee-house that our spectacle maker might have made his leisured way. The coffee-house was a 17th century invention, first opened in Oxford in 1650, to be followed in the City by an establishment in St. Michael's Alley, Cornhill two years later, at the sign of the Pasqua Rosee. There is mention of coffee before this date. Sir Henry Blount, writing from Turkey, said that the natives had a *"drink called cauphe ...in taste a little bitterish..and that they entertained themselves two or three hours in cauphe-houses, which in Turkey, abound more than inns and alehouses with us"*. The ever watchful Evelyn had noted how a Greek came to Oxford in 1637 and *"was the first I ever saw drink coffee"*. (4)

It took time to become established, but by the beginning of the 18th century *"all London had arranged itself into groups of patrons for one or other of the different coffee-houses, and representative bodies of all ranks and conditions of Londoners had each a rendezvous in the house which best suited its taste"*. Garraway's for City merchants (and gambling). Jonathan's for stock-jobbers, Lloyd's for those with shipping interests, Batson's for surgeons and apothecaries, Child's or the Chapter, for the clergy of all ranks. Outside the City were coffee-houses, for the literary, the law, for the scholar and the wit. These were all for the *"professional men"*, who used them as their offices or places to meet and do business. Other social groupings were devoted to politics, the Whigs and the Tories.

The coffee-houses, and the Chocolate-houses, served coffee, chocolate, tea and wine and light meals, biscuits and sandwiches. Set meals were served at the taverns, whose main purpose was the sale of liquor. The coffee-houses were open, by our standards, at the unseemly hour of six in the morning and remained open for the next eighteen hours. Apart from the dedicated "professional" houses, they were places of gossip, news (copies of the day's newspapers were available to read) and good fellowship, where the "names" of the day could hold forth at length and at leisure, Dryden, Addison, Johnson and Steele, in a relaxed atmosphere after the insecurities of the previous century. From these social gatherings it was but a step to the more exotic clubs such as the Kit Kat Club, the Dilettante Society, the Literary Club, the Sublime Society of Beefsteaks and the Saturday Club frequented by the dining society of the age.

It is suggested that White's Chocolate Club, founded in 1693 by Francis White in St. James's Street, then a new part of the town, was the true precursor of the London club. It soon became popular *"by the fashion of its patrons and their generous views in the matter of gaming"*. Its patrons decided that they wished to have rooms of their own in which to meet, thus establishing White's Club sometime around 1736, the exact date being uncertain. Its origin was as an aristocratic *"lounging-place for the leisure of a lazy society"* and for a century its reputation lay in gaming. With a limited membership, and a tortuous election procedure, this led to a split in the Club before the final coming together in 1781.

Obviously all kinds of people attended the coffee-houses, for in the Master and Wardens Accounts for 1709, we find *"7s-6d. several times at the coffee house."*

Births, deaths and marriages were favourite subjects for wagers and suicides were a regular occurrence as a result of lost fortunes. Sir John Bland for one is said to have lost £32,000 at hazard at one sitting, and shot himself on the road between Calais and Paris. Lord Carlisle to have lost £10,000 at a cast of hazard. With the coming of the more uptight George III to the throne in 1760, with his strict views on morality, the tone at White's changed dramatically, with a move more into politics and subsequently party politics. The century also saw the establishment of other clubs, notably Boodle's and Brooks.

There remain to be mentioned the minor amusements of the century. Mr. Powell's marionettes, Mrs. Salmon's waxworks, just near Temple Bar, Mrs. Midnight's Oratory with its ox with six legs, its acrobats and fire-eaters, Mr. Bisset with his Cats' Opera and monkeys taking wine together, riding on horses and dancing minuets with dogs and a hare walking on its hind legs and beating a drum. The century also saw the introduction of the pantomime. Rich, at the Lincoln's Inn Theatre, produced in 1717, *"Harlequin Executed"*, which is accepted as the first pantomime in England and which Rich used to fight the ascendancy of the legitimate theatre of Colley Cibber at Drury Lane.

The equestrian entertainments of Mr. Astley were the precursor of the circus, though some claim that a certain Mr. Price, who rode on three horses at once galloping at speed, some 40 years before, was the true originator. Whatever the historical merits of the claim, Astley obviously had something for Horace Walpole, writing in 1783, said: *"I could find nothing to do at all, and so went to Astley's, which, indeed, was beyond my expectation. Astley can make a horse dance minuets and hornpipes."* He also added a pyramid of men, four at the bottom, with three on their shoulders, up to the single man at the top of *"The Hercules Pyramid"*.

The Vertue of the *COFFEE* Drink.

First publiquely made and sold in England, by *Pasqua Rosee*.

THE Grain or Berry called *Coffee*, groweth upon little Trees, only in the *Deserts of Arabia*.

It is brought from thence, and drunk generally throughout all the Grand Seigniors Dominions.

It is a simple innocent thing, composed into a Drink, by being dryed in an Oven, and ground to Powder, and boiled up with Spring water, and about half a pint of it to be drunk, fasting an hour before, and not Eating an hour after, and to be taken as hot as possibly can be endured; the which will never fetch the skin off the mouth, or raise any Blisters, by reson of that Heat.

The Turks drink at meals and other times, is usually *Water*, and their Dyet consists much of *Fruit*, the *Crudities* whereof are very much corrected by this Drink.

The quality of this Drink is cold and Dry; and though it be a Dryer; yet it neither heats, nor inflames more then hot *Posset*.

It forcloseth the Orifice of the Stomack, and fortifies the heat within it's very good to help digestion, and therefore of great use to be bout 3 or 4 a Clock afternoon, as well as in the morning.

uch quickens the *Spirits*, and makes the Heart *Lightsome*.

Is good against sore Eys, and the better if you hold your Head over it, and take in the Steem that way.

It suppresseth Fumes exceedingly, and therefore good against the *Head-ach*, and will very much stop any *Defluxion of Rheums*, that distil from the *Head* upon the *Stomack*, and so prevent and help *Consumptions*, and the *Cough of the Lungs*.

It is excellent to prevent and cure the *Dropsy*, *Gout*, and *Scurvy*.

It is known by experience to be better then any other Drying Drink for *People in years*, or *Children* that have any *running humors* upon them, as the *Kings Evil*. &c.

It is very good to prevent *Mis-carryings in Child-bearing Women*.

It is a most excellent Remedy against the *Spleen*, *Hypocondriack Winds*, or the like.

It will prevent *Drowsiness*, and make one fit for busines, if one have occasion to *Watch*; and therefore you are not to Drink of it *after Supper*, unless you intend to be *watchful*, for it will hinder sleep for 3 or 4 hours.

It is observed that in Turkey, where this is generally drunk, that they are not trobled with the Stone, Gout, Dropsie, or Scurvy, and that their Skins are exceeding cleer and white.

It is neither Laxative nor *Restringent*.

Made and Sold in St. *Michaels Alley in Cornhill*, by *Pasqua Rosee*, at the Signe of his own Head.

Pasqua Rosee 1652 advert on the virtues of coffee.

Should our spectacle maker be of a musical bent there was the music of Mr. Handel. Handel had come to London as the Kapellmeister to the German prince, George the Elector of Hanover, who, in 1714, became George I. Handel subsequently became a British subject in 1727. He set about writing operas, in the Italian style, and established over the years several opera companies, but it was an expensive business for it was up to the composer to do all the booking, and the paying, for the venue, the singers, the orchestra, etc. Added to which the competition for opera singers in London was fierce and though Handel and his backers managed reasonably well, by 1741, he had given up opera and concentrated upon oratorios.

Perhaps his best known oratorio, *"Messiah"*, had a mixed early reception. After the first performance in Dublin in 1742, Handel sought a sufficiently large venue in London and hired the Covent Garden Theatre. Unfortunately, the paying public considered that a theatre was not the right place for a sacred story. The future of *"Messiah"* was uncertain. In 1742, the foundation stone had been laid for the Foundling Hospital, for which Thomas Coram had been campaigning for some 17 years. George II had granted a Royal Charter to Coram, in 1739, to establish a new charity to care for abandoned babies. One of the hospitals founding governors was William Hogarth. He encouraged his fellow artists to donate paintings to be displayed at the hospital, which had the added advantage that, as there were no public art galleries at the time, this effectively turned the hospital into the first public gallery. London flocked to see the paintings and the charity became one of the most fashionable in London. Handel realised that the Chapel of the hospital would be an ideal venue for oratorio, far from the wrong associations of a theatre. Handel offered to organise a benefit concert in the Chapel, which was a great success both financially and musically.

One of the pieces he included in this first concert was his "Music for the Royal Fireworks". At its first performance on the river, it had to be played three times at the King's request, who could refuse such a request, and the rehearsal of which, in New Spring Gardens, had caused a three-hour traffic jam of carriages, such was Handel's popularity. For his next concert Handel included *"Messiah"*, it was grossly over-subscribed and it was repeated two weeks later. Handel was made a governor of the hospital, *"Messiah"* was performed every year in the Chapel of the Foundling Hospital until the 1770s. Handel himself conducted until his death in 1759. Not only was the future of *"Messiah"* assured, but £7,000 was raised from the concerts for the charity. Handel left his score to the Hospital which has benefitted ever since. We don't really know if any spectacle maker actually went to see the pictures or listened to the concerts or contributed to the charity, but it would be nice to think so. (5)

Handel was not the only "foreign" composer to appear in London. In 1764, the young Mozarts, brother and sister, were playing before George III. Their father, Leopold, got a cold and thought he was going to die, which stopped performances, and Mozart composed instead. He may have met J.C. Bach, also in London at this time, but certainly J.C. inspired him to write symphonies. He wrote his first symphony and several others in London. Between April and June, 1765, members of the public could go to the Mozarts' lodgings where, at a cost of 5s. they could hear him play his party pieces. If our spectacle maker was really hard-up he could still hear the young Mozarts at the Swan and Harp Tavern in Cornhill, for the princely sum of 2s.6d. This was in the June for by July 1765, the Mozart family had left London. It had not been as financially successful as Leopold had hoped.

Lastly there was Joseph Haydn. He came to London several times. The first in 1791, at the invitation of the impresario Johann Salomon. His music was already well known in London and audiences flocked to his concerts, making him financially secure for the first time in his life. He was to repay his debt by composing, among others, the London symphonies. He also had time for a trip down to Oxford to pick up an honorary doctorate and to perform his symphony No. 92, which, of course, became known as the "Oxford Symphony" though composed in 1789. Between his two visits to London Haydn had acquired a pupil, one Ludwig van Beethoven. This second visit in 1794 to 1795, was an even greater success as his music had grown in popularity in London. After two series of highly successful concerts, again under Salomon's auspices, including first performances of several of his own symphonies, the season ended with a final benefit concert for Haydn, which was a great success and perhaps the peak of his London career. (6)

One of the things which at least one of our spectacle makers must have done was to drink gin. The custom of drinking gin was brought from Holland by William III and as gin was free from tax it could be sold without license. The Government imposed a heavy duty on all imported spirits. By the early part of the century wildly excessive gin drinking had become almost a permanent orgy. The Westminster justices reported that it was *"the principal cause of the increase of the poor and of all the vices and debauchery among the inferior sort of people, as well as of the felonies and other disorders committed about this town"* as quoted by Christopher Hibbert. (2) By 1743, it was estimated that every eighth house sold spirits over the counter. *"It was sold in workhouses, prisons, factories, brothels and barbers shops: it was even sold privately in cellars and garrets as well as in the streets by hawkers. Eight million gallons were drunk each year, and this meant about two pints a week for each man, woman and child in London."* You could be *"drunk for a penny, dead drunk for twopence"*. Parliament passed several acts restricting the sale and imposing a tax but gin continued to be sold under a variety of pseudonyms "Ladies' Delight", "Cuckolds Comfort" and "King Theodore of Corsica". Control was eventually obtained over the gin craze by the Gin Act of 1751, which forced distillers to sell only to licensed retailers and brought gin shops under the jurisdiction of local magistrates.

Most of the above were organised amusements, though not the drinking of gin, but among the impromptu events were cudgel-playing, single stick and women fighting. The battle in Spa Fields between two women and two taylors for a guinea a head was won by the ladies who *"beat the taylors in a severe manner"*. There was also the "grinning match" which appears to be a contest between any number of people *"the frightfullest grinner to be the winner"*. The government was aware of these various delights, which gathered large crowds, as being fertile recruiting grounds and offered prizes and inducements to encourage attendance. There were also the "Garrat Elections" which were parodies of an election first held in 1750, in the hamlet of the same name. Doesn't sound of great interest except that the local publicans subscribed a purse for necessary expenses and large numbers gathered. There were election addresses and, as time went on, both Garrick and Wilkes assisted in the writing of the addresses. Candidates dressed in a caricature of the current fashions and came to the hustings in a carriage and six. Crowd estimates are notorious things but, for what it is worth, it was estimated that the average attendance was 100,000 which, even if well out, indicates a pretty good house.

Though difficult to imagine today swimming in the Thames was popular, including such eminent men as the Earl of Pembroke, Benjamin Franklin and Lord Byron, the well-known Hellespont man. There was also the race for young watermen, established by the comedian Mr. Doggett in 1728. As well as the Lord Mayor's Show on the Thames there was the Ranelagh regatta of 1775. The first of its kind in this country, it included a wherry race and a large number of private boats, each with four rowers dressed in one of the national colours, which assembled at Westminster Bridge. It was divided into three groups, red on the Middlesex side, blue on the Surrey side and white in the middle of the stream. The whole flotilla then moved up to Ranelagh with the Lord Mayor and the City Companies in state, with much music, saluting of cannon and an *"execrable supper provided by Mrs. Cornelys, the wine being very scarce"*. The reporters were eloquent upon the splendours of the festival *"the barges were on this occasion filled with above one hundred elegant ladies, and it is thought that the procession was seen by at least 200,000 people"*. A few years later it was suggested that prizes should be given for sailing-boat races, by the proprietors of Vauxhall, from which simple beginning has come the yacht racing and regattas of subsequent days.

The cruelty of many of the entertainments of the period has been noted but perhaps the biggest crowds, surely attracting some spectacle makers, were for the various executions. The better known or notorious the condemned the larger the crowd! The long trek from Newgate prison to Tyburn, or the shorter one to Tower Hill, was made that much more difficult by the vast crowds on the way. Oranges and gingerbread would be on sale, and for half a crown you got your seat reserved in the front row for a better view, and a chance to buy a small piece of the fatal rope, at a shilling an inch. Apprentices were allowed a "Tyburn Fair Holiday". On occasion the "deceased" had not died and efforts were made to revive him, and sometimes they took a long time a dying. If you were really lucky there might be a riot over possession of the body.

If you had had your fill of executions there were still such diversions on Sundays as the duck hunt where a tethered duck was "hunted" by a dog or dogs and could only escape by diving under the water of the duck pond. To add variety an owl was sometimes tied to the duck's back which, after a few duckings (sorry), would fly away. Then there was the cock shy or cock throwing where a cock or a hen, tied by the leg, had sticks thrown at it, at a distance of a chain, 22 yards, to knock it over. But that only took place once a year on Shrove Tuesday! Again as a variation the bird was put in an earthen pot, head and tail showing, and stones were thrown to break the pot, the successful thrower winning the bird. There was also the rat pit, but I expect by now you can imagine how that worked. All of these "diversions" have now disappeared, more due to the fact that building development filled in the duck ponds and rat pits, rather than a conscious effort to end such barbarous "entertainments".

Towards the end of the century came a completely different form of entertainment. Blanchard's first balloon ascent was in 1783 in Paris but the next year *"the secretary to the Neapolitan Embassy in London, accompanied by a cat and a dog and a pigeon, ascended from the Artillery Ground watched by the Prince of Wales. The following year two more men did the ascent from a field in Chelsea and balloon ascents from Green Park or Vauxhall Gardens appeared to have followed at monthly intervals".* (2)

18th CENTURY

JOTTINGS FROM THE MINUTE BOOKS

The Company was still small in scale and in influence, except within the narrow confines of its trade, and even that was diminishing rapidly. Since its establishment we only know of some 40 spectacle makers pre-1666 and only a further 80 odd were admitted up to 1700, and a further 120 or so to 1740, averaging something less than 3 a year, not enough to replace those dying off. The "pure" strain of a trade company would have to be compromised if the Company wished to continue. The decision was delayed until the middle of the century.

Every so often the Minutes take on a surreal modern line as on the 7th January, 1702, this time the meeting was held at the Kings Head in Aldersgate Street:

"For the avoiding any delay of business of the Company at their Quarter Courts and other inconveniences it is ordered that no Member of the Court of Assistants shall smoke tobacco in the Room appointed for keeping such Court, from the hour appointed for meeting of the Court on forfeiture for such time he shall do so of 1s. 6d."

"Smoking tobacco" was not new. Tobacco and various hallucinogenic drugs were smoked in the Americas since around

5,000 B.C., apparently used to achieve a trance-like state to try to contact the spirit world. The favourite implement for smoking in North America was the reed and smoking tubes. The Europeans arrived in the 15th century and, following down the various trade routes, it soon spread round the world. A Frenchman, Jean Nicot, who gave his name to nicotine, is reputed to have introduced it to France in 1556, and it soon spread to England, the first reported Englishman to smoke being a sailor in Bristol in 1556. Whoever first introduced smoking to England it was popularised by Walter Raleigh. It was mostly pipe smoking for the cigarette, in its modern form, did not come to England, via France, till the middle of the 19th century.

From an early stage there was opposition and James I wrote *"A counterblaste to tobacco"* in 1604, and attempted to enforce a 4000% increase in tax on tobacco. Didn't work though, for not much later in that century there were some 7,000 tobacco sellers in London. As reported later it was not until 1759, that the Company opened its membership to non-spectacle makers, so the first tobacconist to become a Freeman of the Company was John Slater on the 6th December, 1768, closely followed by Robert Kell on the 17th December. These were the tradesmen. The first tobacco broker did not become Free until Robert Anderson in February, 1830. There had been a Tobacco Pipe Makers and Tobacco Blenders Company originally from 1619 to 1642 and then again in 1663 to 1864 (their Livery was not granted until 1960 after the re-establishment.) It may be that its regulations were not to the liking of Slater and Kell and the other 2 who were admitted that century. In passing the word "smoking" doesn't seem to have come into use until towards the end of the 18th century. (7)

**

Money, and the raising of it, was always a problem for the Company as has been noted before. Various ways were tried as in the July, 1703, increase in fines:

"For the better management of the affairs and business of the Company and regulating the attending by the Members of the Court of Assistants not appearing at the Court of the Company. It is ordered that the Master and Wardens not appearing by the hour appointed for the meeting or within an hour after or not coming at all without lawful excuse or notice sent the Master shall pay 7s 6d., the Wardens 5s. and each Assistant not appearing within an hour after summons to pay 2s 6d."

On the other hand it may have been that they just had difficulty in getting members and officers to attend.

Another way with money is to cut down the expenditure in the first place, as they tried in January, 1704:

"At this Court consideration was had how to retrench the expenses and charges of the Company and how to raise money for defraying the necessary charges and disbursements thereof – Ordered: that until further notice the Younger Members or Yeomanry (not of the Court of Assistants) shall not be summoned to the Quarter Courts as formerly has been used."

One of the very few mentions of the Yeomanry in the Court Minutes, though it appears in the By Laws. I have already mentioned the Yeomanry on Page 13.

More scrimping and saving in January, 1706:

"Ordered that at the next Quarter Court, each Member of the Court of Assistants that shall appear at the next Quarter Court and dine with the Court of Assistants shall pay 1s. each towards the Eating (besides his Quarterage). Each member present having

paid one shilling to the Renter Warden for that purpose and Mr. Yarwell promised to allow a loaf of bread for next Quarter Court Dinner."

This 1706 decision was presumably brought in to cover the wanton and reckless increase in expenditure that had been agreed in October, 1705 when:

"till further Order at every Quarter Court where the Court is kept at the Tavern Every Person at Dinner shall be allowed a drink of Common draft Wine at Dinner on the Company's account and no more and what more they or any one shall call for they are to pay it themselves".

**

Perhaps because of their financial problems, the Company had in place a system whereby they had an audit each year. The accounts, such as they were, were the duty, initially, of the Upper Warden. The first recorded audit was in 1682, when Joseph Howe was required to *"produce the books"* though at the time he was not an office holder, becoming Master some 8 years later.

**

At the Audit meeting on the 9th February, 1709/10, it was noted that Joseph Cole, who was Upper Warden for 7 consecutive years, had received for the Company during that period £107-10-9 and had paid on behalf of the Company £111-0-9½.:

"he has paid more than he has received the sum of Three Pounds Ten shillings and one half penny which is due to him from the Company".

At the following Court it was agreed that this sum should be paid to Joseph Cole, and the Upper Warden was instructed to pay *"out of the Company's money when he has so much in his hands to do it"*. This is what is known as a "hand to mouth existence"!

**

Remembering the Company's financial position, and the fact that the Court regularly ate after the meeting, John Yarwell in June 1705, offered a *"loyne of beef"* for dinner. In October of the same year Yarwell was this time offering bread for the next Court meeting. At the same time Thomas Mayle joined in with John Yarwell and offered 5/- towards the next Quarter Court Dinner. This is the same Thomas Mayle who suffered the indignity of a double whammy at the Court in June, 1686, of being fined 1/- for arriving late and a further 1/- for *"departing without licence"*.

By 1712, the finances were looking up a bit for at the Audit Mathew Cooberrow, the Upper Warden, had received £14.4s.6d. and:

"that he had paid the sum of Thirteen Pounds, three shillings and Ninepence halfpenny, and that there resteth in his hands to Balance the account due to the Company the sum of One pound and Ninepence."

Even then the money was not put in the Company's name, not having a bank account, and was *"paid unto his successor Mr. Isaac Burbridge"*.

**

Though money was tight the Court could be generous. At the meeting in March, 1717, James Shelley, who owed Quarterage of 50s., which was a substantial sum at the time as Quarterage was 4s. a year, was allowed to dine with the Court at Quarterly meetings, provided he paid 5s. each time.

**

Court meetings at this time must have been somewhat livelier than I remember them in the 20th century for in July, 1721, Thomas Browne was fined 20/- for swearing *"opprobrious words"* at the Upper Warden, and he had to appear before the Lord Mayor as well.

**

The Master at this time, 1720 and 1721, was Edward Scarlett, Senior. His claim to optical fame is as the inventor of, or at the least the first to advertise, "Temple spectacles". Early spectacles had the problem of how to attach them to the head, or nose, so that the lenses would sit before the eyes. Scarlett introduced side arms for spectacles which had a hinge and spiral endings which pressed against the temple, as well as resting on the nose, greatly adding to the comfort of the wearer. Many of the Masters whose names have come down the centuries owe their fame to their development of scientific instruments rather than spectacles per se. Edward Scarlett was one of the exceptions. He is also quoted as the first to gauge and number spectacle lenses according to their focal length, he would then mark that number on the frame. He also succeeded his rival, John Marshall, on his death, as *"Optician to his Majesty King George II"*.

His son, also Edward, having been apprenticed to his father, initially worked with him before setting up shop at The Spectacles, 2nd house from Essex Street, nr. Temple Bar, before going to Macclesfield Street. Whilst carrying on his father's trade he also made advances in microscope design and development. (8)

He also appears in records completely outside optics. I am indebted to Mr. M. J. Bassett for this information. He had asked for information about the younger Scarlett and provided me with an extract from *"The Annals of Hampstead"* by a Mr. Barratt. This relates to Mr. Thomas Osborne, a bookseller, who having prospered, took a rather pretentious house in Hampstead. Wishing to "get in" with the Hampstead locals, his earlier efforts having failed, he asked Captain Pratten (later described in *"Hampstead Surveyed 1700 – 1762"* as Commander Pratten, Captain of the Suffolk, a 70 gun Man of War), an apparent leader of local society, how best this could be achieved. The gallant Captain advised *"that he should provide a public breakfast for the ladies and a duck hunt for the gentlemen. The proposal was supported by another Hampstead resident, Mr. Scarlett, a noted Macclesfield Street optician of the time, and inventor of a microscope for viewing opaque objects"*.

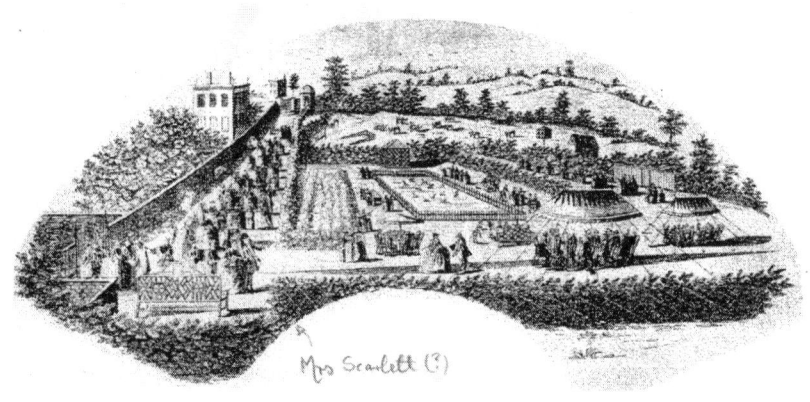

Mrs Scarlett (?)

The event went so well that, as the guests were still enjoying themselves, the resourceful Captain suggested that *"a cold collation"* be served. That proved even more popular and still the guests remained. It was suggested, again by the Captain, *"that as the day was so far advanced he had better send to one of the taverns for their dancing-tent and a band and so to make a good finish of so eventful a day... and the revels were kept up to a late hour"*. The Captain's last suggestion was to have a fan made with the scene of the happy, if lengthy, *"public breakfast"*, et al, engraved on either side and presented to each of the lady visitors. Above is one side of the pictorial fan-mount showing Captain Pratten entering the field with Mrs. Scarlett and her daughter, where Mr. Bassett has indicated, Edward Scarlett, for reasons unknown, is not accompanying his family. Perhaps the only known, or extant, picture of this particular mother and daughter, albeit a little distant and indistinct. The report in the *"Annals"* ends *"The omission of a portrait of Mr. Osborne is a matter for regret, but Captain Pratten was too intent upon his own glorification to think of so small a detail as that"*. One can only hope that Mr. Osborne won the approval of the neighbours which he so clearly, and expensively, sought.

**

The Master who followed Edward Scarlett, and was indeed Master for the next eleven years, was George Wildey also variously spelt Willdey, Welldy, Weldy and Weildy. Over his working life of some 24 years he had 15 apprentices of whom no less than 8 were girls. Only 3 of his apprentices are known to have to have traded subsequently as spectacle makers. This may be because his interests were varied, as indicated by his shop at the corner of Ludgate Street, near St. Paul's being "The Great Toy, Spectacle and Print Shop". Jeffrey R. Wigelsworth in *"Selling Science in the age of Newton"* quotes an advert of Wildey from the *"Post Man"* of 20th May, 1718, which includes *"cheap, useful, instructive ornaments for halls, rooms, stair gates, etc."* sheet maps of the World, *"a new and correct large sheet maps of the roads of England carefully laid down from Ogleby's actual Survey"* price 9d. *"though really worth 18d."*, globes, spectacles, reading glasses, telescopes, perspective glasses, etc., *"to so great perfection that he doth challenge and defy all the artists and pretenders to be so in the universe to make or show better than his are"*. Added to this were *"curious toys in Golds, Silver, and other metals, Agate, Amber Ivory and Fine Wood"*.

Later that year he was claiming the *"best Burning Glass in the World"* which *"in less than a minute melts iron, gold, silver, copper and brass"* which *"its greatest heat is in the air, in one it will serve for a hot bath, in another for a sun kitchen, where meat may be boil'd, bak'd, raosted (sic), stewed or broil'd".* He ends by claiming that *"whatever is done by other fire may be done by the Celestial Heat".* I can't help feeling that an 18th century General Optical Council would have had a whale of a time over professional advertising and even his contemporaries might have considered it a tad over the top.

**

Written on the very back page of the Court Minute Book for 1695-1738 is the following:

"At a Quarter Court held the 31st March, 1715 at the Fountain Tavern it was agreed between Mr. Joseph Cole, Master of the Spectaclemakers Company, Mr. Warden Scarlett and Mr Burbridge, as follows viz: If the said Mr. Cole shall be married before either of them, the said Scarlett or Burbridge, he will pay fifteen shillings as a Treat att the next Quarter Court after his marriage And if either of them, the said Scarlett or Burbridge, shall be marryed before the said Cole then such of them so first marrying shall pay Ten Shillings as a Treat for the Company at the next Quarter Court after."

Unfortunately there appears to be no further reference in the minutes, or written on any fly leaves, to this subject. Was it the result of a big argument, or a light hearted bet? It was signed by 7 Court members, but there were 11 at the meeting. Why did the other 4 not sign, were they anti-betting, or had they just left the meeting? What is even more annoying is that not only will we never know the answers to these questions, but we shan't know who won the bet either!

**

One can't expect the Minutes to be exciting or even surprising but there are exceptions, 1723 was one such. No doubt the local paper, the *"Daily Courant"* for example, might have had "Spectacle at the Sun Tavern" as a headline. Not being a sub editor perhaps I should leave the story to the "official account".

In the Court Minutes for the meeting of the 9th January, 1723, (this is the old calendar so effectively 1724) appears the following:

"As the Company was at Dinner a Serjeant of the Wood Street Comptor (one of the Sheriff's prisons CE) *came into the rooms and arrested John Williams at the suite of George Stone the Company's late Clerk in an Action upon the case for 9s and 9d. And they being of the opinion that it was a vexatious Suite Mr. George Wilbey, Master and Mr. Thomas Sterrop, Upper Warden, went the same day to the Comptor and became Bails to the same Action. And it was then ordered that this Company Should indemnify the said John Williams from all costs and Damages touching the said Suite."*

The story behind this vexatious action starts a little earlier, at a meeting of the Court in the Sun Tavern on 3rd December, 1722 when:

"This Court thought fit to declare that Mr. Stone their Clerk (after hearing the allegations on both sides) has been guilty of something of a breach of Trust But did Further declare that he should hold the office of Clerk of this Company until he should be guilty of committing a Misdemeanour."

Possibly the language had a little different meaning then, but one is left with the impression that they were saying "we will get you next time when you do something worse".

If this is so, then at the meeting on the 3rd October, 1723, they got their chance for:

"On complaint made that George Stone the Companys Clerk had for some time past taken exorbitant fees on Several accounts relating to the Company but more particularly Ten Shillings and Sixpence on the Admittance of every Assistant whereas his Due according to the old Accustomed fees was no more than five shillings and being desired to answer for himself he affirmed there was an Order of the Court made in the Clerk's favour to entitle him to the Ten Shillings and Sixpence and being required to produce the same Mr. Stone desired time till the next Court Day which he was accordingly granted."

As there were at the time only two Minute Books in existence, which would have taken little time to look through, it seems very reasonable of the Court to give Stone this opportunity. He was to make good use of it. The next Court was a Private Court i.e. a special Court *"held at 5 in the afternoon at the Sun Tavern, St. Paull's Churchyard London"* on the 18th October. The first issue was:

"Complaint being made that Mr. Stone the Companys Clerk had been guilty of a Contempt by not proceeding at Law against Mr. Rogers for his Quarterage pursuant to Severall Orders made. It was therefore Ordered by this Court that Mr. Stone should not proceed at Law against the said Mr. Rogers."

On the evidence this would seem a strange reluctance on the part of the Clerk not to have proceeded with the action as he was under suspicion elsewhere, perhaps there are still waters running deep – we shall never know about that. The next minute comes to the nub of the issue:

"Mr. Stone being desired to produce the Order of Court made in the Clerk's favour to entitle him to the fee of Ten Shillings and Sixpence for making an Assistant he produced an Order of the Court made in the year 1674 which is near fifty years ago."

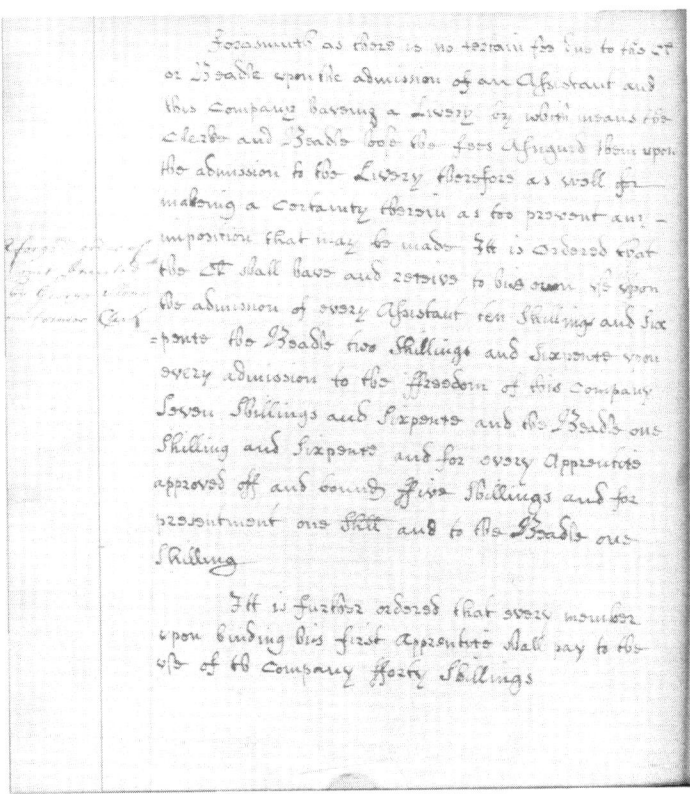

The page in the Minutes of the 26th March, 1674, which Mr. Stone produced appears above.

So far so good. But Mr. Stone, who should have been diligently searching for the Order referred to, had been seeking an empty page in the Minute Book long enough ago to be beyond the memory of any of the current Assistants, and had then concocted an appropriate minute. On the next page is a sample of the handwriting in the Minute Book of the earlier part of the meeting of the 26th March, 1674.

On the next page is a sample of the handwriting of the following meeting of the 2nd July, 1674.

It is hardly surprising, on the written evidence, that the Court should be suspicious. The Court minute continues:

"which Order being perused by every Member present they were of opinion (Nemine Contradicente) that it was Spurious; Of the hand writing of the said Mr. Stone and entered by him without Authority."

It is difficult to differ from this conclusion. The Minute goes on to report:

> *"The said Mr. Stone being Ordered to withdraw withdrew accordingly and after some debate the Court was of opinion (Nemine Contradicente) that for the forging the Order and other ill practices he ought to be expelled and being called in was accordingly expelled from being Clerk of the Company."*

No rules on "unfair dismissal" needed to trouble the Court. At the next meeting John Williams was asked to officiate as Clerk *"till the said Company thinks fitt to proceed to an Election"* which it duly did on the 27th January, 1723 (actually 1724), when John Williams was duly elected.

The Account for the Quarter in which all this took place is not neatly divided but the Upper Warden, for it was he who at the time looked after the Company's money, paid out £10-17-8p for: *"All charges of this Court including the Clerk's Bill of Law charges and half a yeares sallary for the Clerk and Beadle."* The Court had stuck by their new Clerk as they had promised.

You will have noticed the inset in the Minutes of the 26th March, 1674, in the left hand column which is in a different hand, and reads: *"A forged order of the Court Inserted by George Stone our former Clerk"* and this was presumably written at the Court on the 18th October when the issue was resolved. Incidentally the Clerk was still pursuing Stone for money owed some two years later.

The Court Minutes of this period have for a number of years been limited to the admission of Freemen and the indebtedness of the Company. George Stone's escapades provide unexpected light relief.

**

The Proceedings of the Old Bailey, as reported on the Web site oldbaileyonline, at about this time make surprising reading, not so much for the theft or shop-lifting of spectacles, as prevalent in the 21st century as in the 18th no doubt, but the punishments. In May, 1721, for pickpocketing *"2 pocket-books and a case of spectacles"* the punishment was death. In the same year the theft of a *"linen handkerchief to the value of 4d."* the sentence was transportation. In 1724, having bought 6 pairs of spectacles, but pocketing others, the punishment was again transportation.

**

Not all spectacle makers and their apprentices were law-abiding folk. The Court in October, 1737, freed John Porter from his apprenticeship for leading a debauched life and: in *"the lock of St. Bartholomew's Hospital"*. He had at one time been apprenticed to John Cuff.

**

Cuff was another innovative Master. He had been apprenticed to James Mann, Junior, Master of the Company in 1735 and 1736, who was an optical instrument maker, the provision of spectacles not being his primary concern. Cuff, according to the *"Oxford Dictionary of National Biography"*, *"made and sold, both retail and wholesale, optical instruments, barometers, thermometers and mathematical instruments."* As well as making standard microscopes he had several innovative designs. He perfected the *"microscope for viewing opake object and the solar or camera obscura microscope.... but Cuff's solar microscopes, with their ability to project a magnified image onto a screen, proved popular."* He was closely associated with Henry Baker, F.R.S., who encouraged Cuff's microscope innovations. It was for Baker that Cuff developed his double reflecting microscope, made entirely of brass, with a side pillar and having a fine-threaded focus, in 1743. This was widely copied at home and abroad and strongly influenced future design. He also made an aquatic microscope for studying properties of specimens in water.

Whilst his premises were next door but three to the Royal Society, where he was a frequent visitor, he was never elected as a member. Though he was very well respected as an optical workman, and never lacked for work, he was not good with money and was declared bankrupt in 1750. By the sale of his household effects he raised enough money to continue, but when Benjamin Martin set up shop between Cuff and the Royal Society, the competition proved too fierce and he moved to a rather catchy address, the Double Microscope, three Pair of Golden Spectacles and Hadley's Quadrant, opposite Salisbury Court in Fleet Street. (A pretty good reason for the introduction, albeit a few years later, of post codes.) He didn't stay there long, within a year he was forced to sell his stock-in-trade at auction and give up his retail shop, though he still had apprentices. In 1770, he asked for and obtained his discharge from the Court of the Spectacle Makers Company and he died in 1772. (For historical accuracy, it should be noted that Martin himself was declared bankrupt in 1782). (9)

There is still at least one mystery concerning Cuff. In the Royal Collection is a painting by Zoffany, which according to the Royal Collection, was commissioned by George III to depict Mr. Cuff, a Fleet Street optician, from whom he obtained microscopes. Despite this Royal identification there is still argument as to whom is portrayed. *"The portrait was been called variously An Optician with his Attendant, in a rough draft of the inventory of Kew it appears as Mr. Cuff, but in the published inventory as A Mathematician, when lent to the Royal Institution in 1827 it was hung as Two Old Men, subsequently it has been known as The Lapidaries. In 1859 a pencil note was visible on the stretcher reading Dollond the Optician in the Strand, London".* I do hope the final verdict turns in favour of John Cuff, it would be nice to have a cheerful picture of one of our famous "old boys". Research, which at the time of printing is about to be published, by Julian Holland, may well settle this issue in favour of Cuff.

**

After the expulsion of the Clerk, George Stone, in 1723, for overstating the fees to be paid to the Clerk and the Beadle for certain duties, it was decided to regularise these payments. The charges were thus agreed as: for admission to the Court of Assistants £5-0-0 and a bottle of wine to the Company, to the Clerk 5s and to the Beadle 2s. For the admission of Freemen 13s. 4p plus a bottle of wine to the Company, 4s. to the Clerk and 18p. to the Beadle. You didn't buy any old bottle of wine for the amount was stated as 4s!

For the Binding of an Apprentice 2s 6p. to the Company, 2s 6p. to the Chamberlain of London for the Orphan's Tax, 8s 6p. to the Clerk and 18p. to the Beadle. The relatively high payment to the Clerk is probably due to the fact that at this time the Clerk was expected to accompany the Apprentice to the Chamberlain's Court to witness the signing of the Indentures. Added to these figures is a charge of 1s. for the Poor's Box. As this is not included in the total to be charged one can only assume it was a "voluntary contribution".

However this was regulated at the Court meeting held at the Sun Tavern, St. Paulls' (sic) Churchyard on Thursday, 13th January, 1725 (remember that the calendar had not been "adjusted" so in modern parlance this would be the January of 1726*)*:

"Ordered that Every person that shall hereafter be made a free Member of this Company and every Apprentice that shall be Bound to any Member thereof shall pay to the Poors' Box one Shilling at least and as much over and above as they please."

The Clerk's low salary, £5 per annum increased to £10 in the early Eighteenth Century, is accounted for by the fact that he was paid on a "piece work" basis, for it was not his full-time job. (I believe when I was appointed Clerk in June, 1966, I was the first full-time holder of the office.) In addition to the fees and fines as above, every Court he attended he received 6s. 8d., for the writing of letters, 6 letters a £1, for the annual account, 6s. 8d, for making a fair copy of the list of Freemen, 10s., and for meetings with the Master etc., etc., he was given a further fee. It is known that the first Clerk, Thomas Copley, was a lawyer, and in the light of the charges above, his successors were either lawyers themselves or had learnt the legal way to charge.

The Clerk did get the odd bonus, in 1767, he was given a present of a pair of spectacles value stated as £4-14-6 and in 1797, a different Clerk: *"a pair finely ornamented spectacles pebbles silver mounted with silver case"* value £5-15-6. At least one of his successors does not remember the Company giving him a pair of spectacles as a present, despite Assistants grumbling at the state of the spectacles he occasionally wore, and the suspicion that they may have been "foreign made".

P.S. I was given a pair of 19th century reading spectacles by the Norville Optical Company, as a bit of a joke, after that Company had provided spectacles of the appropriate period for the Blists Hill Open Air Museum. These spectacles, called "Ironbridge", appeared in Norville's catalogue for general sale. I don't know how many were subsequently sold. I certainly got no commission.

**

In September, 1747, the Court started meeting at the Queen's Arms Tavern in St. Paul's Churchyard, amongst all the booksellers. They might have encountered David Garrick there from time to time as this was where a club met, not the Garrick Club that came a century later, formed by a few intimate friends of the actor so that they could enjoy his society. According to Boswell, and somewhat later, in 1781, Dr. Johnson, who had taught Garrick in Lichfield where they had become friends, started going to the Queens' Arms.

"he carried me to dine at a club which, at his desire, had been lately formed at the Queen's Arms in St. Paul's Churchyard. He told Mr. Hoole that he wished to have a City Club, and asked him to collect one; but said he 'Don't let them be patriots' The Company were today very sensible well-behaved men". (4) The Spectacle Makers continued to meet there until April, 1784, when it *"ceased to be a Tavern"*. Thus they had every chance of meeting not just Garrick and his fan club but also Johnson and Boswell.

**

In 1750, and again in 1752, John Phipps, who had joined the Court of Assistants in 1728, when he was 26, declining to take office as the Under Warden in 1739, was excused attendance at Court meetings *"by reason of residing in the country"* and in 1757, was again excused attendance and all fines as he was 55. Perhaps he had become disillusioned with his work for of the two apprentices he had one, William Stoaks, *"ran away"* in 1741.

**

When Past Master Frank Norville was browsing in an antique shop in Norfolk in 2002, he came across a large box which, on closer inspection, had the old arms of the Company painted on the front, and the Past Master, having bought the chest, donated it to the Company. After a bit of research, and with the help of the Master Furniture Maker, it was dated around 1760. With this in mind it is most likely be the chest "presented" to the Company by Thomas Ribright for which he was repaid £2-12-6, the cost of the chest, at the Court on 6th October, 1763. There is no mention of it being a plate chest in any case, according to the Minutes, the Company did not yet own any silver or plate to put in it!

The "Norville Chest".

On the 27th June, 1771 a Mr. Kittle was paid the sum of £5-12-6 for painting the Arms of the Company and from the Master and Wardens Account books he was paid a further 10s 6d. for alterations to the Arms. Were these the Arms painted on the side of the aforementioned chest? Perhaps, but on 3rd October, 1771, a *"sash case for Arms"* was purchased for the munificent sum of £12.

The College of Arms has confirmed that the Company had no official Arms until the grant in 1950. Yet first there is the reference to a case for Arms and on 1st January, 1778, there is a payment, £2-12-6, for the Seal of the Company Arms.

From this it can be assumed that the Company adopted the Arms which appear on the side of the plate chest at some time before 1739. This is the date given in Bromley and Childs *"The Armorial Bearings of the Guilds of London"* as the first reference to the Company Arms which was in W. Maitland's *"History of London"* of 1739. The Arms adopted in 1810 are very different from the 1739 version. Incidentally the 1810 Arms were adopted because:

> *"the stock could not be properly bought in as ordered at the last especial Court, by reason of his not having the seal of the Company".*

Is this Mr. Kittle's Handiwork?

Perhaps this was the very reason for the original Arms, the 1739 version, being adopted for the Seal to be made for the envisaged purchase of stock. Oh life would be so much easier if my predecessors had written accurate and full Minutes as all Clerks do today!

**

Along with other of the Livery Companies, recruitment had become more and more difficult. As manufacturing moved away from the City so it became more difficult to "control the trade".

This was a problem not limited to the new "trade companies". Ian Archer in his *"History of the Haberdashers Company"*, a very much larger company, states: *"Whereas an average of 119.5 freemen were being admitted each year between 1605 and 1614, by the first decade of the 18th century the figure was 87.6, and during the decade 1737-1747 50.4 per annum"*. (10) The number of Freemen admitted each year had been in single figures since 1667. The ten years to 1759, saw the admission of only 26 Freemen. Something needed to be done. The Livery Companies, when they originated, accepted only Freemen who were tradesmen of that trade i.e. a goldsmith joined the Goldsmiths' Company. The older companies tended to have members who were employers rather than artisans, and it was only a century or so after their establishment that even these employers started to drift away from their original trades and branch out as merchants. The newer companies, such as the Spectacle Makers and Clockmakers, stuck strictly to their trade and, as we shall see later, fought hard to keep it so. But when times are hard the old prejudices weaken, and Freemen came to be admitted who were not spectacle makers, or necessarily of any trade whatsoever. The Court, at the meeting on the 27th December 1759, agreed that:

> *"taking into consideration the Company's affairs Agreed that it would be for the benefit of the Company to augment the number of their Members as much as possible, and it was therefore Ordered that for the future the Clerk be at liberty to Swear-in and admit Members by Redemption out of Court, any Order or Ordinance to the Contrary not with standing Each person paying on his admission the sum of one pound eleven shillings the said sum to be distributed as follows:*

To the person who brings the Member	£1-1-0
To the use of the Company	3-0
Stamps	2-0
Clerk	4-0
Beadle	2-0."

(Note that I am quoting from the Minutes verbatim and can't account for the mathematics).

If the new Member was not a Spectacle Maker he, or she, was exempt from taking office in the Company and could take as many apprentices as they wished, on paying the usual fee of Nineteen shillings.

The effect on the number of Members was immediate. At the above Court 11 new Freemen were admitted – a mixed bunch, 2 Exchange Brokers, an Ironmonger, a Grocer, a Victualler, a Ticket Porter, a Painter, a Tea Merchant, a Serjeant at Arms, a Taylor and a Pawn-Broker.

In the first full year after this new policy was introduced, the number of new non-Spectacle Maker Members was 40. In 1762, the number was 45 and in 1766, 56. As the total annual income of the Company in 1757, amounted to £35-17-8, in 1766, to £57-14-5 and in 1778, to £101-15-10, the fines and Quarterage of the non-Spectacle Makers were worth having. Perhaps even worth considering the opening of a bank account, instead of using the pocket of the current Upper Warden as the piggy bank! But this is the first major change in the Company's fortunes since its Charter had been accomplished.

You will have noticed in the 1759 admissions there was mention of a victualler. Now I don't want to malign my 18th century predecessors, for the Clerk and the Beadle were no doubt assiduous in seeking out potential members as it helped their pocket money. But presumably they, the Clerk and the Beadle, would approach people in the places they normally visited in their off moments to recruit new members. Could this account for the fact that of the 471 new Freemen recruited between 1760 and 1775, 439 were non-Spectacle Makers and of these no less than 115 were victuallers. From the Artichoke in Fleet Market to the Swan and Sugar Loaf in Fetter Lane and onto the Rose and French Horn in Wood Street, by way of the Bowl and Pin in Peters Hill, to the Faulcon and Magpye, Gough's Square, thence to the West Country Barge in Queenhythe, followed by the Fleece and Sun, Threadneedle Street, through to the Ship and Raven, Leadenhall Street, coming to the Blue Coat Boy, Newgate Street and back to the Devil Tavern in Fleet Street via the Green Dragon in St. Andrew's Hill, did this pair drink on behalf of the company. The victuallers of these worthy establishments were duly recruited.

The Clerk and the Beadle also managed to add 1 Vintner (for their enjoyment of the higher life), 7 Apothecaries and 1 Surgeon (to look after their health), 5 Shoemakers (necessary for all that walking), 1 Lottery Officer (well it might have been them), 2 Hairdressers (to keep them tidy), 10 Booksellers (for their erudition), a Staymaker (for their no doubt fuller figures with all those Court dinners), 3 Musical Instrument Makers (for their entertainment), a Gingerbread maker (for the sweet tooth) and a Bed Joiner (no don't ask). They also signed on 4 "opticians", the new word first used in the Company records about John Berge, an apprentice of Peter Dollond.

The following picture, as well as showing The Devil Tavern, shows what a restriction Temple Bar was becoming. A bar is first mentioned in 1293, but was probably only a bar or chain between a row of posts. By 1351, a wooden archway had been built with a small prison above. Though not damaged in the Great Fire, Christopher Wren designed the fine arch in Portland stone. This lasted until 1878 when the then Corporation of London had it dismantled and rebuilt in Theobalds Park in Hertfordshire.

Temple Bar and the Devil Tavern.

A Temple Bar Memorial now stands in its place. The old arch mouldered away until brought back into the City in 2004 to form an entrance to the new Paternoster Square redevelopment

On prestige visits to the City the reigning Monarch still has to wait at the bar for permission to enter the City whilst the Lord Mayor presents the Sword of State as a mark of loyalty.

**

Prior to the decision to admit non-spectacle makers the Court had decided in June, 1759, to tell Freemen about the By-Laws and Ordinances. As you will appreciate from reading it they were shutting the stable door long after the horse had bolted as they had not activated these powers for some time, and were about to admit as Freemen those to whom spectacle making was foreign.

On the next page is the original printed notice, hence the "f" for "s" or "ff" for "ss"as the case maybe.

At a General Court of the Master, Wardens *and* Assistants *of the Company of* Spectacle-Makers *of* London, *holden for the said Company the* 28*th Day of* June, 1759.

IT was resolved and ordered, That a Committee of the said Company do examine the By-Laws and Ordinances of the said Company, and make Extracts of such of them, as they shall judge necessary, in order that the same may be printed and delivered to the several Members of the said Company, together with the Freeman's Oath, to the End that no Members of the said Company may pretend Ignorance thereof for the future, and are as follow, *viz.*

That a General Quarter Court will be holden for the said Company on the first *Thursday* next after *Lady-Day, Midsummer-Day, Michaelmas-Day* and *Christmas-Day,* yearly, and every Year.

That all Members of the said Company, and all and every Person and Persons that shall trade in buying Spectacles to sell the same again, within the said City and Liberties, or within three Miles thereof, shall then and there satisfy and pay for Quarterage Twelve-pence in Money, every Quarter, to the Master, or one of the Wardens of the said Company for the Time being, for the Use of the said Company, upon Pain of every Time denying or offending in that kind, to forfeit the Sum of Ten Shillings.

That no Person or Persons whatsoever, shall take to himself any Apprentice or Apprentices, without Leave or Licence first had at a Court of Assistants, and then to have but one, until he shall bear Office in the said Company, and then not to exceed the Number of two at any one Time, upon Pain of Five Pounds.

That no Person whatsoever, either foreign or free, of what Trade or Condition soever, shall intermeddle or practice to make any Spectacles, or any Part thereof, or any thing else belonging to the same Trade or Mystery of Spectacle-making, unless he or they have first served seven Years as an Apprentice to some professed Workman of the same Trade, upon Pain of Forty Pounds for every Offence.

That if any Person whatsoever shall hawk, or jett about, and put to sale, any Spectacles, at any Time whatsoever, every Party so offending shall forfeit Five Pounds.

That no Person, Member of this Company, shall take or entertain to be his Apprentice, any Person above fourteen Days by way of Trial, next after the receiving of him, and then shall present him for his Apprentice at the next Court of Assistants, to have him bound, and in case of Failure he shall forfeit for every Month wherein he shall have so kept him in his Trade and Service, the Sum of Five Pounds.

	l.	*s.*	*d.*
Fees to be paid on Admission	0	19	0
Ditto on being made free	1	5	10
Ditto on being turned over to a new Master	0	19	2
Ditto on Admission of a foreign Brother	1	15	10
Ditto for every Master binding first Apprentice	2	0	0

The Freeman's OATH is as followeth, *viz.*

YOU shall swear to be true to our Sovereign Lord the King's Majesty, his Heirs and Successors, and at all Times obedient to the Master and Wardens of this Fellowship and Society, and their Successors after them, in all honest and lawful Things touching the Affairs and Business of this Fellowship. You shall be ready at all manner of Summons, and bear Scot and Lot in all manner of reasonable Contributions of and to this Fellowship and Company of *Spectacle-Makers,* of the City of *London.* You shall to the best of your Skill, Power and Ability, uphold and maintain the Weal of this Company. You shall not know or suspect any manner of Meetings, Conspiracies, Plot or Devices against the King's Majesty, his Heirs or Successors, or the Government of this Fellowship, but you shall the same to the utmost of your Power let and hinder, and speedily disclose to the Master, or one of the Wardens of this Society. And this City of *London,* and Fellowship of *Spectacle Makers,* you shall keep harmless, as much as in you lies. Also you shall be ready at all Times to be at the Quarter Days, and every other Assembly, Matter or Cause that you shall be warned or called unto for the Affairs of this Fellowship, unless you shall have lawful and reasonable Excuse in that Behalf. And all the *Ordinances* of this Fellowship or Society, ratified according to the Laws of this Realm, or otherwise lawful for this Fellowship or Society to make and ordain, you shall to the uttermost of your Power well and truly submit yourself unto and keep. So help you GOD.

On the 1st April, 1779, authority was given to purchase: *"£50 of Old South Sea Annuities"*. This is a reminder, some 60 years before, of the "South Sea Bubble" where the South Sea Company had obtained a monopoly of trade with South America, then underwrote the National Debt, which stood at £30 million, on a promise of 5% annual interest from the Government. Shares immediately rose to up to 10 times their value. This encouraged speculation in all sorts of weird and wonderful companies e.g. for trading in hair, for insuring of horses, for improving gardens and, best of all *"for carrying on an undertaking of great advantage, but nobody to know what it is"*.

Fortunes were made overnight as the value of these stocks rose like rockets. Only, as rockets do, to fall when it became known that the South Sea Company was not making a profit. (One of that company's activities was buying and selling slaves, which did show a slight profit.) Trust was lost and the market crashed spectacularly, recent fortunes turning to debts, for the people who had borrowed money to buy shares now had no money left to pay the interest on the money they had borrowed in the first place. There had been a lot of skulduggery in high places. Many heads rolled, some by dismissal, some by suicide. 462 members of the House of Commons and 112 Peers were involved in the crash, not to mention two mistresses of George I. (11)

This was all in the 1720s, so perhaps the Company had learnt, for instructions were given to sell South Sea Company stock and by the 18th May, 1810, I am pleased to say that the Clerk was able to report that £250 of stock had been sold, making a profit of £173-8-9d.

**

At the Court meeting on 30th June, 1774, William Eastland, asked for a guinea (£1-1-0d) to clear his debt and release him from the Poultry Compter, which was agreed.

A compter was a small prison, run by the Sheriff, for minor offenders, including debtors, and religious dissenters as well as criminals. It is not surprising that Eastland wanted out as a contemporary description of the conditions said it was a place where *"riot, drunkenness, blasphemy and debauchery, echo from the walls, sickness and misery are confined within them"* and another *"the mixture of scents that arose from mundungus, tobacco, foul feet, dirty shirts, stinking breaths, and uncleanly carcases, poisoned our nostrils far worse than a Southwark ditch, a tanner's yard, or a tallow-chandler's melting-room"* as quoted by William Smith in 1776 in the *"State of Gaols in London, Westminster and the Borough of Southwark.*

N.B. "mundungus" described offal or refuse and later to a foul smelling cheap tobacco.

**

Edward Nairne was the Master from 1769 to 1773, and again in 1795-96, had had early promotion to the Court, having been admitted to the Freedom on the 5th October, 1749 and then joined the Court on 28th December the same year, being excused the fee as *"so early called to office"*. He was then Under Warden from 1760 to 1762 and Upper Warden from 1764 to 1768. When he retired from the Court in June, 1800, he had been a regular attender at its meetings for some 50 years, which is all the more surprising considering the busy life he had led.

Having been apprenticed to Matthew Loft he then set up shop at 20, Cornhill and employed, amongst others, Jesse Ramsden. He became one of the most famous English instrument makers. He collaborated with Benjamin Franklin, Joseph Priestley and Henry Cavendish. He was elected a Fellow of the Royal Society in 1776. He made a range of optical instruments for the Royal Observatory and Harvard University. He was involved in trials of electrometers, devised wooden telescope tubes, mercury thermometers for extreme cold, frictionless magnetic dipping needles, a marine barometer, an equatorial telescope, portable wind gauge, a new form of compound microscope and a range of air pumps and improved their calibration for John Smeaton. He also did considerable work on the design and improvement of electrical machines. He worked on lightning strikes with Franklin and invented a new medical electrical portable machine which, for the first time, allowed the generation of both negative and positive electricity, used for the treatment of nervous disorders, toothache, deafness and lockjaw which was used well into the next century. He died on the 1st September, 1806 at the age of 80. (12)

**

There is little in the Minutes about day to day proceedings. We know that there was an annual election for the various officers, but don't know if they held up their hands for the man they wanted, or was it a secret ballot? The Election Court of Wednesday, 2nd October, 1782, made matters a little clearer. In the election for Master the minutes state:

> *"there appearing an equal Number of Scratches for Mr. Peter Dollond and Mr. Shuttleworth a Doubt arose with Regard to the Decision whether the Master, whose situation was delicate as being interested in the Event, could with Propriety give his casting Vote. WHEREUPON the Clerk was directed to apply for Advice and the Election was postponed until the General Court to be held on the day following."*

I realise that you must be on the edge of your seats as to the result so I will not linger. At the Quarterly Court on the Thursday the same members attended as the previous day. To quote again:

"The Clerk acquainted the Court that he had consulted several Clerks of Companies and other Gentlemen skilled in Election Matters, and particularly with the Nature of the present Question, who were clearly of Opinion that the Decision rested with the Master WHEREUPON Mr. Dollond the Master gave his casting Vote in Favour of Mr. Shuttleworth, and he was declared to be duly elected."

Being used to the 20th century procedure, where the "election" was pre-arranged in order of precedent and the Clerk would advise the senior Past Master present who to propose, I had not appreciated that there was real voting, presumably by some form of ballot paper hence the *"scratches"*. Traditionally a modern Chairman with an equality of votes would cast his vote for the status quo. As Peter Dollond had been Master for eight years he presumably took the feeling of the Court to be that a change was necessary! The Clerk, incidentally, had only a few hours to make his enquiries – with no telephone, internet, Twitter, etc., he would had to have made the rounds on foot, or on horse back.

**

The Dollond family were to have a profound effect on the Company. The family were Huguenot silk weavers, Jean and Susanne had fled from France and settled in Spitalfields, as did many other Huguenot weavers. John, who was their eldest son, trained as a silk weaver, but his main interest was mathematics, to which he added a particular interest in astronomy and optics. These interests he passed onto his son, Peter, who in 1750, though also trained as a weaver but encouraged by his father, set up shop as a spectacle maker. The enterprise was successful and in 1752, John gave up weaving and entered into partnership with Peter. By 1759, they opened a shop near the Exeter Exchange in the Strand trading as "J. Dollond and Son" at the sign of "Golden Spectacles and Sea Quadrant".

John Dollond had begun work on improving refracting telescopes, one of the problems being the chromatic aberration causing distortions. Eventually, with the aid of others research, unacknowledged by Dollond, he was able to produce a compound lens for refracting telescopes which was free of both chromatic and spherical aberration. Prompted by his son, he obtained a patent for his new lens, which he duly reported to the Royal Society. John failed to mention the work of others which may have preceded his "invention". In particular Chester Moor Hall, a barrister and an amateur dabbler in optics, had, it was claimed by Jesse Ramsden, (who was married to John Dollond's daughter, Sarah), in a paper to The Royal Society, developed an achromatic object-glass made from a combination of two lenses of different types with different refractive powers in 1730.

He had asked Edward Scarlett (Master 1720-21) and the elder James Mann (Master 1716), to make a lens each, one convex of crown glass the other concave of dense lead crystal. Both spectacle makers asked George Bass (Master 1747, and 1754 – 1757) to produce the lenses. Bass realised that he had been asked to make two lenses which fitted together perfectly and gave a colourless image, soon finding out that the work was for Hall. Subsequently Bass passed this information onto John Dollond, who appreciated the potential and was then able to produce good quality achromatic lenses in commercial quantities. The Royal Society made him a Fellow and in 1760, he was appointed optician to the King, George III.

John Dollond had financed the cost of the patent with a

partnership agreement with Francis Watkins (Master 1763), Watkins sharing in the profits. On John's death in 1761, Peter inherited his father's share of the profits and, in 1763, acquired the whole rights, claiming that Watkins had broken the articles of partnership. In 1755 Peter Dollond became a Freeman of the Spectacle Makers Company, which his father had never been. As has been mentioned before, the first use of the term "optician" in the Company's records appears as applied to John Berge, who was Peter Dollond's first apprentice.

Peter was a better businessman than his father and exploited his patent to the full. In 1763, he took proceedings against Watkins for infringing the patent and in 1764, extracted a bond of £500 from Martha Ayscough, widow of James Ayscough (Master 1752), that she would not make achromatic refracting telescopes. This caused problems with the London spectacle makers. 35 of them signed a petition to the Privy Council calling for the patent to be revoked. This was supported by the Court of the Spectacle Makers Company who resolved on the 28th June 1764 *"£20 to Mr. Grubb, Attorney at Law, to vacate the John Dollond Patent"*, the Master at the time was Francis Watkins, Dollond's old partner. Didn't do any good though for the Privy Council refused to hear the Petition.

Following further cases between 1764 and 1768, Dollond established his right to enjoy the privileges of the Patent. This created a precedent in the case law on Patents. In a later case, Dollond v. James Champneys (a spectacle maker but not a member of the Company, he was a Stationer) Lord Mansfield decided in favour of the patentee on the grounds that it was *"not the person who locked up his invention in his scrutoire that ought to profit by such an invention, but he who brought it forth for the benefit of the public".* (This is the same Lord Mansfield who is reputed to have completely revised the law on wills and intestacy in his time and whose will, on his death, took seven years to sort out. To be fair he is also remembered, by laymen as well as lawyers, as the Judge in Somersett's Case of 1772, which ruled that slavery had no basis in Common Law nor established by legislation. Slavery was therefore illegal in England and Wales. 15,000 slaves were immediately freed in England).

The reason for the excitement and opposition to the Patent was that with Peter Dollond's successful defence of his Patent, his consequent reputation *"provided the company with the de facto right of refusal on the best optical flint glass. This privilege permitted Dollond to maintain an edge in quality over competitors' telescopes and optical instruments for many years"*. Suddenly the level playing field was no longer quite so level.

In 1766, Peter Dollond went into partnership with his younger brother John, and moved shop to St. Paul's Churchyard. They continued to make optical innovations and supplied a wide range of mathematical, philosophical and optical instruments. Supplying instruments for Captain James Cook, further improvements to the achromatic telescope objective, introducing mahogany telescope tubes, and supplying instruments with plated brass draw tubes. Towards the end of the century, their workshops provided all the new refracting lenses and eyepieces for the Greenwich Observatory and the refractors were in demand overseas. Despite the younger Dollonds assiduously reporting their inventions and improvements to the Royal Society, neither of them was elected as a Fellow.

In 1805, a year after his brother's death, Peter Dollond took into partnership his nephew, George Huggins, who promptly changed his name to Dollond. George had been apprenticed in the Grocers Company and subsequently became Free of the Spectacle Makers in 1807. George also proved to be an innovator with Patents to match. The firm continued to supply observatories around the world, providing instruments for the Arctic expedition of 1821, and for surveys of Australasia. George carried on the firm alone after Peter died in 1820.

George was elected a Fellow of the Royal Society, was a founder member of both the Astronomical Society and the Royal Geographical Society and was appointed optician to Queen Victoria on her accession. At the Great Exhibition of 1851, he was awarded a medal for his invention of a type of weather station. He died, unmarried, in 1852 bequeathing his property to his nephews. Amongst his nephews, and one of his apprentices, was another George Huggins who, on succeeding to the business, followed family tradition and formally took the name of Dollond. On his death in 1866, he was succeeded by his son William. William became too ill to continue with the business in 1871, and sold to L.R. Chant, a former employee. Though no member of the Dollond family remained with the firm the name was retained and, in 1927, the firm was acquired by James Aithchison to become Dollond and Aitchison. By the time I came into optics in the middle 1960s the name apparently struck fear into independent opticians, and was despised by many university lecturers, though many of their students were happy to work their pre-registration year with the firm. Graduates working for D. and A. also found that if they firmly expressed their professional views the allegedly more commercial approach of the firm was not insisted upon.

As to the Dollonds and the Spectacle Makers Company, the angst which must have been caused by the action over the Petition seems to have abated, because Peter joins the Court on the 30th March, 1769, and is Master on three occasions, the first for 8 years, then again in 1797 to 1798, and lastly in 1801 and 1802. Thus serving 12 years altogether, which makes him the Master serving the greatest number of years, though George Wildey did his 11 years in one go. Peter lived long enough to become one of the seven first Liverymen of the Company on 27th November, 1809. George was Master for two years, 1811 and 1812. Lastly another

George served as Master in 1862, an optician amidst a plethora of no doubt worthy City dignitaries. The family may have caused the Company problems in the early years, but more than made up for it in loyal service for more than 100 years, for William, the last in line, became a Freeman on 14th February, 1867 dying in 1893. (13)

Whilst the name Dollond was known in optical circles it is difficult to know whether it was a "household name" at any time. Writing about a spa called Bermondsey Spa and its creator, the artist Thomas Keyse, Henry C. Shelley (4) reports a conversation between J.T Smith and the artist about several paintings by Keyse which adorned the walls. They were obviously very lifelike for when the artist asked for an opinion of a painting named *"The Bull's Eye"* the answer came *"Why it would be a most excellent one for Adams or Dollond to lecture upon"*. This is in the latter part of the 18th century.

**

Mention of Francis Watkins leads into an enquiry the Company received from James Rothwell, Senior Curator and Adviser on Silver to the National Trust, which gives an indication of the methods of prescribing spectacles at that time. He quotes from the National Archives, State Papers Turin, wherein the Earl of Rochford, who was the Envoy in Turin, orders spectacles on the 17th November, 1761. *"My Lord Rochford desires you would buy him at Watkins a Pair of Spectacles mounted in silver and in the neatest manner possible. They are for a Lady between Thirty and Forty, and are not to magnify and Help the Sight, but meerely to preserve it. If you shew this letter to Mr. Watkins, he will understand the Order at once. But to avoid mistakes the Glass must not be Green, nor the Form of the Barnacle kind, but the plain fashion of Our Forefathers, to plant upon the Nose. Need I repeat that he cannot make them, nor the Case to hold them, too neat for the Person for whom my Lord intends this present"*. The order was satisfactorily carried out for the reply came *"My Lord's Spectacles came in the same packet with my letter dated 9th December and he is obliged to you for having that Commission executed so handsomely, and Mr. Watkins Workmanship is much admired. His Lordship desires you will send him in the first Packet after the Receipt of this, a Pair of the neatest Spectacles from the same hand, but not mounted in Silver. They are for the Nose of a Lady that has smelt Sixty Winters and more, and who has no other defect in her Eyes than what is owing to the Wear and Tear of Time. Mr. Watkins knows what will suit her age. And put them up in the same form as the former pair in a plain neat Shagreen Case."* Obviously fascinating and interesting things move around in the diplomatic bags of the time.

**

With the opening of the Freedom of the Company to, effectively, all and sundry, a few names known in other walks of life begin to appear. The name Spode is not one that one would normally associate either with London, or spectacle making, but Josiah Spode II, son of the founder of the Spode pottery, became a Freeman of the Spectacle Makers Company and had a showroom in London.

Josiah Spode I (known thus as his father's name was also Josiah) was born in a village in what is now Stoke-on-Trent in 1733. His father died a pauper, but it is believed that the family became impoverished, in part because they had paid for Josiah's education, as he was an accomplished violinist before his success as a potter. Whilst it is stated that he was an apprentice of Josiah Wedgwood, records appear to show that from the age of 16 he worked with Thomas Wheildon, one of the best potters in the area. As he stayed with Wheildon until he was 21, which sounds like an apprenticeship, perhaps he worked the first two years of his apprenticeship with Wedgwood and was then "turned over" to Wheildon. He then seems to have worked for a time in partnership with other potters as there was a pottery on the Spode site before that company was founded. Spode established a business in Stoke-on-Trent in 1767, founded his pottery works in 1770, becoming the outright owner in 1776.

In 1780, *"he perfected the non-fading, blue transfer printed underglazed china that became the hallmark of Staffordshire potters in the 1780s. The next breakthrough at the Spode works came in 1794 when Josiah Spode II (our Spode) mixed calcified ox bone with ordinary china clay and stone, creating a bone china which approached porcelain in quality yet could be produced inexpensively on a large scale".* Josiah Spode I also kept an eye on market trends and by contributing land for the canal, which came to be built alongside his factory, he added to the success of his business, for until then transport had been very difficult. Water transport meant that both raw materials and finished wares could be moved more easily, and with less fear of breakages. Thus making the whole industry, and Spode with it, more efficient and distribution more effective.

The Spodes became associated with William Copeland, a London broker and tea merchant, and *"in many cases Spode lifted design concepts directly from the elaborately decorated papers used to wrap the tea leaves Copeland imported from China. Trade with Asia was booming in the early 1800s, and as Europeans became entranced by Oriental design, Spode patterns became wildly popular".* It was time to open a London showroom.

It was Josiah Spode II who was sent to London and, together with William Copeland, opened the London showroom and shop in Cripplegate. Spode II, the eldest of Spode's eight children, was born in 1755. He had married Elizabeth Barker whose father had been apprenticed to the aforementioned Wheildon, keeping the trade secrets nicely in the "family". As it appears in the Spode Museum Trust story *"To become a tradesman in London it was necessary to become a Freeman of the City. Josiah became a Freeman by joining one of the livery companies. It didn't seem to matter whether it was relevant to the business as he joined the Spectacle Makers Company in 1778",* on the 11th March, with his address as 29, Fore Street. (He may also have known William Clowes, who was another potter, and who had come south from Longport in Staffordshire with his shop at 119, Minories, who became a Freeman of the Company the same year as Spode II, but in the June). The showroom *"exposed Spode China to the burgeoning British merchant class and to sea traders who soon carried it around the world. Spode's success at selling inexpensive bone china with an Oriental flavour brought importation of Chinese pottery almost to a halt".* Such was the success of the London marketing that bigger and bigger premises had to be taken, finally moving to Portugal Place in 1794, buying the freehold in 1802.

On his father's death in 1797 Josiah Spode II, our Josiah, went back to Stoke to take over the running of the business. On his death in 1827, he was buried next to his father in the graveyard of St. Peter's Church in Stoke. The Spode Company rededicated the family tombs in a special service in 2000.

During his life he had built The Mount, the biggest mansion ever built in Stoke, and not on the factory site as other potters did. He had become a rich man. At his death in 1827, his whole estate was valued at £225,271.13s.8d less debts of £87,135.13s.8d. He had probably out-performed, from a purely financial view, all the other Freemen and Liverymen of his casually adopted Livery Company. (14)

**

It was in 1773, just before Josiah Spode came to the City, that the first "Stock Exchange" was established in premises at the corner of Sweetings Alley and Threadneedle Street. Joint-stock form *"we may regard with some degree of over simplification, as being at the outset a development of the older merchant venture in which now others, besides the venturers themselves, could participate".* (15) By the beginning of the century *"the whole commercial scene was changing rapidly...and the joint stock form was increasingly attractive. It appealed to the merchants who wanted to spread the burden of what we would now call capital-formation, and to individuals who had spare money that they could put out to profit".* (Ibid) The problem was how to introduce these two classes to one another. At the same time the Government was considering how to borrow money from individuals who, for the first time, had some money to "invest", the joint-stock Company was a convenient vehicle through which the individual could lend his money to the Government.

"It was natural that, as the idea took hold, the exchange of investments should also almost imperceptibly become a separate, expert and specialised business. The borrowers in this new type of business, whether they were traders or the Government, wanted medium and long-term loans. The lenders, especially the smaller lenders, wanted to be able to get their money back as nearly as possible on demand. It would obviously provide a satisfactory compromise of these conflicting aims if the lender who wanted his money were able to find someone else ready to take over his loan". *(*Ibid*)* There had been dealers in securities working inside the Royal Exchange regulated by the City authorities. They moved out to Change Alley, to carry on business in and around Garraway's and Jonathan's Coffee houses. In due time brokers and stock jobbers became separate activities *"the broker deals with the public, acting as buying or selling agent; the jobber holds stocks and shares as principal, and deals only with the brokers".* (Ibid) It was this group of brokers and stock jobbers who moved into the new premises with the name, for the first time, of the Stock Exchange. The South Sea Bubble, which burst in 1720, did not enhance the reputation of the

Stock Exchange, though that organisation was not solely responsible for that blot on capital appreciation. It was many years before the Stock Exchange regained its reputation as an "honest and trustworthy exchange".

**

On the 21st, August, 1778, Samuel Wilkinson started his apprenticeship with Rees Beynon. His father was Master of the Shoreditch Workhouse, shades of Dickens yet to come.

**

Very occasionally ethnicity raises its head. March 1798, Joseph Bear obtains his Freedom of the Company and there is a note that *"he was rejected by the Court of Aldermen as a Jew"*. The Jews have been persecuted throughout history and their treatment in the City of London was no different. Though the Jewish community had contributed considerably to the Crown it did not stop Edward I expelling them from the City, and indeed England, in 1290, thus being able to cancel all the debts and take over their property. The Edict of Expulsion was not formally overturned until 350 years later by Cromwell. Jews did not return to City government until David Salomons was elected Sheriff in 1835. He was unable to take up the post immediately because of the Christian nature of the oath required, but did so later in that year when *The Sheriffs Declaration Act* was passed. In due course he became an Alderman and in 1855, Lord Mayor.

References:
1. Roy Porter *"London a Social History"* 2000, Penguin Books.
2. Christopher Hibbert *"London the biography of a City"* Allen Lane 1977.
3. William B. Boulton *"Amusements of Old London"* 1901.
4. Quoted by Henry C. Shelley in *"Inns and Taverns of Old London"*.
5. Extracts from Caro Howell's article in the *"Guardian"* 13th March, 2014.
6. Incorporates text from David Wyn Jones' article in the *"Oxford Dictionary of National Biography"*.

7. "History of Smoking" – Wikipedia.

8. *"The on-line museum and encyclopedia of Vision Aids".*

9. Incorporates text from Giles Hudson's article in the *"Oxford Dictionary of National Biography".*

10. *"The History of the Haberdashers Company"* by Ian W. Archer. Philimore 1991.

11. *"The South Sea Bubble"* – History UK.

12. Incorporates text from Simon Schaffer's article in the *"Oxford Dictionary of National Biography".*

13. The greater part of the foregoing on the Dollonds is taken from the article by Gloria Clifton in the *"Oxford Dictionary of National Biography".*

14. Extracts from the Spode Museum Web site.

15. *"The years before the Stock Exchange"* by Nicholas Lan from *"History Today"*, November, 1957.

19th CENTURY

PRELUDE

The 19th century was to be a time of great change for the Company. From a small, hard-up group of like-minded tradesmen, albeit plus a few "foreigners" introduced in the previous century, it became, firstly, a full-blown Livery Company which would produce more than 30 Lord Mayors and 30 Sheriffs. Secondly, at the end of the century, a return to its trade by becoming an examining body for opticians, and subsequently dispensing opticians.

As to the wider world, to quote from the National Archives *"the period from the late 18th century to the mid-Victorian years witnessed a major shake-up and changes in both the economy and society. This was seen in the organisation and finance of industry and commerce, the skills and work practices of production and technology, massive population growth and the development and disciplining of labour... at least for a few decades, mass manufactured items were produced more efficiently and competitively in Britain and the country had the commercial, financial and political power to edge out rivals... in some industries, most notably textiles, massive changes took place in technology and in the organisation of production causing dramatic productivity growth. This in turn brought a steep decline in prices...an unprecedented range and variety of products thus came within the grasp of a new mass market both within Britain and overseas…more people were buying a greater variety of textiles, clothing, shoes, household and domestic items – on their list was china, cutlery, mirrors, books, clocks, furniture, curtains and bedding, as well as a variety of small wares, such as buckles, ribbons, buttons, snuff boxes and other fancy goods. More beer, butter, bread, milk, meat, vegetables, fruit, fish and all other food stuffs were now being bought rather than made or grown at home."*

As to London in this century, it too was to see great changes. It became the world's largest city, the capital of the British Empire and a global, political, financial and trading capital. In 1800, London's *"built-up area was some five miles across east to west and home to 960,000 people, by the century's end had swollen to the greatest city the world had ever seen. Now seventeen miles across. Now 6.58 million people, nearly seven times greater. This huge bulk would far exceed – in terms of the aggregation of humanity at least – anything that the next century would add to London".* (1)

As to the financial City, the increase in discounting, effectively giving short-term credit, and stock-dealing, together with the growth of insurance in all its forms, and the joint stock banks, vastly increased City activity and employment. This gave the City a financial lead and international superiority which was not to be seriously questioned perhaps until Brexit and its effects after 2016. There were 570 stock and share brokers in London in 1861, as opposed to 5,000 in 1901. 86 bankers were listed in 1861 but 224 in 1901.

London spread into Islington, Paddington, Belgravia, Holborn, Finsbury, Shoreditch, Southwark and Lambeth. In Pimlico Thomas Cubitt, the brother of our Liveryman, had started acquiring land in the 1820s, but the area, known as "Cubittopolis" to some, was not completed until after his death in 1855. Known as South Belgravia to its residents, but Pimlico to the rest of London, was said to be *"the largest single area of London developed by one man"*. (Ibid)

Writing at a time when migrants are a contentious issue, it is noteworthy that the century saw immigrants from Ireland, Germany, France, Russia, Poland and Jews from all parts of Europe. There were also Italians, one of whom is credited with the introduction of ice cream, sold by street sellers who were most likely Italian, in 1850. Add to these immigrants from China, India and Africa it is hardly surprising that by 1900, 33% of the population of London came from those born elsewhere.

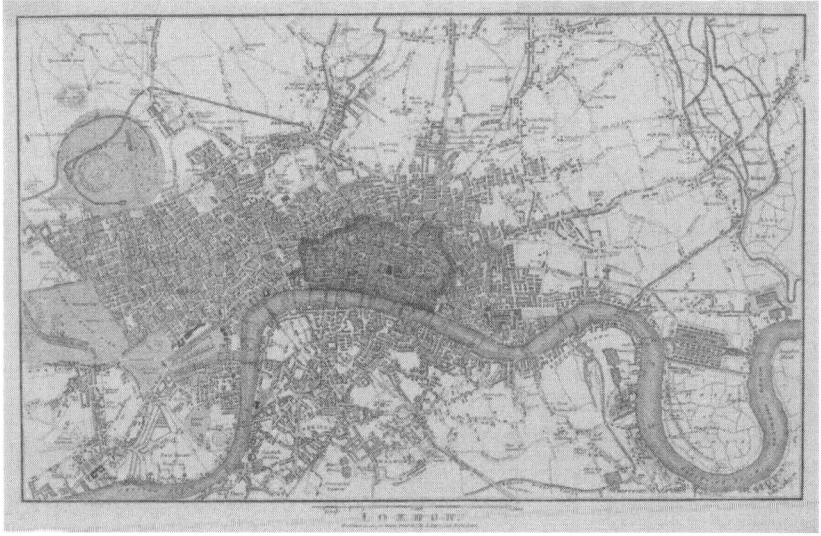

Map of London 1815.

By the 1840s gas was being used for street lights, electric light was first used in Holborn in 1883. Public transport at the beginning of the century was mainly stage coach, hackney carriages and ferry-boats. In 1829, George Shillibeer, having first tried it out in Paris, introduced a twenty-two seater coach, initially horse drawn, with fares as low as sixpence, which he called "an omnibus". By 1850, there were 1300 buses on the streets, all run by a multiplicity of companies. In time the London General Omnibus Company took over the competing companies and by 1875, boasted that it had 50 million passengers a year. By the end of the century the motor car had appeared, but no one was quite sure of its purpose.

The railways, too, developed quickly around the country, transforming London, though they stopped short of the City of London, an ugly terminus could not sully the environs of the City. There would be many applications to Parliament for railways to enter London. Very few were to be agreed, and particularly not into the richer areas of central London. The first City terminus was Fenchurch Street with Blackfriars, Ludgate Hill, Cannon Street and Broad Street to follow. By putting a Parliamentary stop on above ground development around the City and Westminster this encouraged an unexpected development, the "underground" railway system.

Trial trip on the "Underground", 1863.

First thought about in 1839, the Metropolitan line was eventually opened in 1863, the first in the world, though worked by "steam" engines, with deep level electric tube trains in the 1890s. Trams came along in the 1870s.

The railways had another major effect on the City of London. *"Railway mania was a formative factor in the City's reinvention in the nineteenth century as a specialist financial and commercial district with no room for a resident population……growth in banking was mirrored in the multiplication of insurance companies, the equation between speed and risk representing a minor Victorian neurosis. Share dealing flourished at almost unprecedented levels during the 1845-47 mania, facilitated by the development of the electric telegraph around the same time. It produced an unprecedented volume of work not just for brokers and jobbers but for printers, engravers, trade and other newspapers, all substantial City enterprises."* (Ibid) All these enterprises needed grand headquarters buildings in the City, each naturally more impressive than the next, which pushed buildings upwards into third and fourth storeys, as well as being more expansive on their first two floors.

You had to be able to afford the fares, but those that could, steadily moved out to "suburbia". The workers had to await the introduction of "workmen's fares" by the *Cheap Trains Act* of 1883, until they too could move to "suburbia", not the same suburbia as that for the better-off of course. Casual workers in markets and docks had to stay close to their work, no green, leafy suburbs for them. They mostly lived in the East End, an area variously described as *"a modern Babylon", "an inferno",* a *"city of dreadful night", "outcast London",* not that anyone who considered themselves anybody ever went there to find out if these descriptions were actually true. People now "knew their place", and lived in neighbourhoods full of people like themselves. The class system was catching up with a vengeance. *"By 1900, detached and semi-detached villas with their own private gardens typified middle-class suburbs; the better off working classes lived in suburban terraced housing; in inner London an increasing proportion of both rich and poor lived in purpose-built flats – the latter in philanthropic dwellings and, after 1890, in blocks of council flats, the former in luxury apartments that first appeared near Victoria Street in the 1850s and around the Albert Hall in the 1870s"*. (2)

Even in death class counted. *"Private cemetery companies divided their cemeteries into separate consecrated and unconsecrated areas for different denominations and graded the size and cost of grave plots"*. (Ibid) Even in the pub there were different compartments; lounge, saloon and public bar.

The City, though asked several times, first by Charles II, refused to take any responsibility for any area outside the old City. It was said because the Aldermen feared that they would lose control, and therefore their power, if a wider area was considered. Consequently the local government system for the rest of London grew piecemeal through the vestries and parishes until, in 1855, the Metropolitan Board of Works was created, which was London's first metropolitan government body. It had some success, but as it was not a directly elected body, which did not endear it to Londoners, it was replaced by the London County Council in 1888.

London in the 19th century was a decidedly unhealthy place, with frequent outbreaks of cholera. No real attempt was made to improve the situation, mainly because the cause was not appreciated. The fact that raw sewage was pumped straight into the River Thames, as it had been for centuries, which polluted the drinking water, which of course came from the Thames, was not sufficiently appreciated until the "Great Stink" of 1858. The first modern public lavatory, with flushing toilets, opened in London in 1852. On the other hand the "green lung" was increased with

Regents Park opened to the public in 1838, Victoria Park in 1845, and Battersea Park in 1858. The mind was also catered for with the opening in 1852, of the Victoria and Albert Museum, the Science Museum in 1857, and the Natural History Museum in 1881.

London continued as a great port with the building of 9 massive new docks down-river of Tower Bridge. The "casual labour" policy in the docks was to lead to the Great Dock Strike of 1889, *"the most sensational metropolitan labour dispute of the nineteenth century"*. (1) Within a week the whole port was completely paralysed and the Lord Mayor, amongst others, helped to broker a resolution. The dockers "won", getting their minimum of four hours work when taken on at the gate, and pay went up to 6d. an hour, at the same time accelerating the growth of trade unionism.

Despite the general view of the Industrial Revolution happening "up North", London remained a manufacturing centre with flourmills, sauce factories, sugar refineries, and breweries. The first tinned foods were produced in Bermondsey. The leather industry still flourished, with hat making, together with boot and shoe making. Chemicals were made in Silvertown and clocks, watches and jewellery in Clerkenwell. At the beginning of the century *"London was a City of small workshops, in 1851 86% of industrial employers in London had less than ten workers and only 17 establishments employed more than 250 persons. By the early 20th century new and larger-scale industries in suburban London - Greenwich, Woolwich, West Ham, Enfield – were increasing in importance. In 1907 there was an average of 20 employees per factory or workshop in Greater London; but the figure in Woolwich was 69"*. (2) Some of these "larger-scale industries" are still recognisable today: Clarnico's sweets, Bryant and May matches, Tate, the sugar refiner, Keiller's jam, Siemens' cable works, De La Rue and Waterlow and Sons, for stationery and Crosse and Blackwell's pickles. Mass production and lower quality goods for sale to the proletariat, had taken over from hand-produced goods for the wealthy. Together with a general increase in wages and greater security of employment, this led to what some have called *"the consumer revolution"*.

David Waller, in an article in "History Today" in November, 2015, argues that *"in the late 18th and 19th centuries, London was the Silicon Valley of its age, home to a largely forgotten concentration of technological expertise"*. One example he gives is steam power, though the dominant manufacturer was Boulton and Watt in Birmingham. By 1804, there were 112 steam engines at work in London, compared to 32 in Manchester, and by 1825, there were about 290 steam engines in London, compared with 240 in Manchester, 130 in Leeds and 80 to 90 in Glasgow. *"Even in 1851, more than 370,000 Londoners worked in manufacturing, making the capital the largest manufacturing centre in the U.K."*.

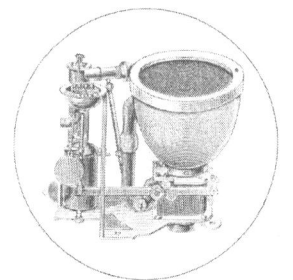

As to innovation, Waller quotes the flushing lavatory of Joseph Bramah (holder of 18 patents) from his factory in Covent Garden, where he also produced the beer pump and the hydraulic press. Precision engineering, much of that due to the work of Henry Maudsley. He worked with Bramah before being talent spotted by Marc Brunel, father of Isambard Kingdom. *"Together they built 49 machines for the Portsmouth Block-Making factory, the first steam-powered, metal machine tools that literally shaped the modern industrial world....it largely dispensed with human workers and constitutes the world's first assembly line... Maudsley opened a factory on Westminster Bridge Road where he invented the slide-rest, a form of automatic lathe that transcended the limitations of human skill and introduced new standards of accuracy. He built a machine capable of making*

measurements down to $1/1000^{th}$ of an inch". Many engineers of future note were attracted to Maudsley's factories, including Isambard Kingdom Brunel; James Whitworth, who *"introduced standard measures for nuts, bolts and screws – an overlooked contribution to the Industrial Revolution";* James Nasmyth who invented the steam hammer; Bryan Donkin who, apart from inventing tinned food referred to above, also *"pioneered sophisticated paper making and printing machinery".*

Another invention quoted by Waller is the computer *"the brainchild of Charles Babbage the eccentric, brilliant and very rich resident of Marylebone, who spent his life and much of his fortune trying to build what he called the "Difference Engine". He was a great statistician, writer and inventor".* Another of Maudsley's engineers, Joseph Clement, made the thousands of delicate components for the machine, which was never finished in Babbage's life-time. *"In 1981 a team from the London Science Museum succeeded in building the Difference Engine to Babbage's original design, showing that it was only lack of money that stopped the machine being constructed in the 1830s".* For good measure Waller adds the first commercial electric telegraph; Charles Bessemer's invention, in his St. Pancras workshop, of the first process for the mass production of steel; and William Perkin's invention of synthetic dyes in his Cable Street workshop. All of which are probably sufficient arguments to back up the original claim that the Industrial Revolution was not limited to the Midlands and the North alone.

What hadn't changed was the amount of poverty in London. It has been estimated that by the end of the century, 20% of the population were living at subsistence level and a further 10% living below. The conditions of the "middling sort" however, improved over the century. Railways and steam ships made it possible to import cheap grain, so bread became cheaper. Refrigeration made possible cheap imports of meat from Argentina and Australia. The consumption of sugar also increased, though perhaps a modern eye would not consider that a long-term improvement.

In the 21st century the rest of the country rightly bemoans the fact that everything is centred on London, and it was the nineteenth century that established London's predominance. As all roads, and subsequently canals and railways, led to London, all communications came from London. Particularly with the insulated telegraph wires which followed the railways out of London, so too the telegraph cable. By 1866, London was connected to Paris, Constantinople, Bombay and Washington, which had caused Reuter to move his news agency to London in 1851 *"his office at 5, Lothbury dominated the world supply of telegraphic intelligence for the rest of the century. The communications revolution cemented London at the centre of the nation's news"* (1)

Despite the various restrictions put on the printed word by various governments, London's annual production of stamped newspapers was 16.3 million in 1820, and by 1826, there were 179 newspapers and magazines listed in the London guide. (Ibid) With the reduction in stamp duty in 1836, the flood-gates opened. By 1850 the sales of the principal London papers increased to 31.4 million. There were 79 newspapers, 60 weekly periodicals and 227 monthlies. When the paper duty was repealed in 1861, there was another dramatic increase. *"In 1883 a guide listed the principal newspapers published in London. There were fifteen morning and nine evening papers, some of them specialist commercial prints. The Weeklies, etc., list ran to 383 titles. Of these fifty were local newspapers meeting the needs of expanding London and its suburbs. The total number of registered newspapers published in London in 1881 was 549; in 1895 823".* (Ibid) Much, but not all of this, came out of Fleet Street.

Leisure time, almost unknown at the beginning of the century, was greatly improved by its end. The 1871, *Bank Holiday Act*, gave workers a few paid holidays a year. By the 1870s, some skilled workers and clerks began to have a week's paid annual holiday. Most workers had had Sunday off since the beginning of the century, so by the 1890s, when they also got Saturday afternoon off, the "weekend" had arrived.

I had assumed, up to the beginning of the 19th century at least, that the average spectacle maker, unless he was also a scientific instrument maker, was at the poorer end of the wage scale. In this century things changed as most new Freemen and Liverymen were not in the trade and came from more affluent society. Their leisure activities were not therefore prescribed by the need to be free or cheap. I mention this because Vauxhall Gardens was still going strong, *"the most celebrated public gardens in Europe"*. There was dancing, music, eating, drinking, a theatre, lamplit walks, fireworks, balloon ascents and Italian jugglers. As well as all this was the Heptaplasiesoptron, an exhibition including mirrors, water, palm trees, serpents, revolving pillars and lights. It was considered very much a middle-class pleasure-ground requiring, even in the 1850s, full evening dress, and admission cost 3s.6d., which went up to 4s. in 1826. But it was being overtaken by Cremorne Gardens and by July, 1859 the coloured lights were showing *"Farewell for Ever"*. (Ibid) The gardens slowly died away to be replaced by tea gardens, often attached to pubs. Leicester Square was another area of entertainment, where could be found, museums, galleries, exhibitions and panoramas displaying vast landscapes and cityscapes. The Great Exhibition of 1851 was the major attraction moving, in due course, from Hyde Park to Sydenham.

The theatre was developing as another London attraction, particularly if you wanted a riot. The re-opening of Covent Garden Theatre Royal caused one because the price of admission was increased. The audience raised such a noise that nothing much was heard from the stage, and this continued for months until Charles Kemble, the actor manager, went back to the old prices. Vaudeville was gaining in popularity, catered for by many of the pubs, which developed into the "music hall", which then went back into theatres. Perhaps surprisingly, Shakespeare was particularly popular, especially at Sadler's Wells, where it was said that if an actor forgot his words there was always someone in the audience who could prompt. The theatre was considered as a place where all classes of society could mingle, divided up into their correct "class" by virtue of the price of seats. *"The reckless enthusiasm of the London theatre audiences, their out-spoken criticisms rudely expressed, their hugger-mugger mingling of classes, all helped to condemn the theatre in some eyes as a place to be avoided...until the end of the 1850's gatherings of prostitutes in even the legitimate theatres kept many respectable families away. And the link between stage and sin, inherent in plays of any sort, created an insuperable obstacle to theatre going among orthodox Christians throughout the century"*. (Ibid)

It was Gilbert and Sullivan, in the 1870s and 80s, and their operettas and strict control of the morals of their actors and chorus who started to make the theatre respectable again. What was acceptable fare at the theatre was the public lecture. Humphrey Davy, William Hazlitt, Michael Faraday, William Thackeray, J.W. Benn with his "lightning sketches" and George Grossmith, moonlighting from the Savoy Operas, were amongst many on the lecture circuit, earning more money than most actors for their one-man shows.

Crime too would have been on the mind of our spectacle maker, at least as regards avoiding its consequences. The common lodging houses forming many of the "rookeries", apart from being places of degrading poverty and starvation and home to thousands of destitute children, were the breeding ground for crime of all kinds.

Thieves, pickpockets, street robbers, receivers, shop lifters, grave robbers, housebreakers, burglars and murderers lived in the rookeries, passing on their skills, Fagin-like, to the orphans around them. "Garrotting", grabbing the victim by the throat whilst going through his pockets, was so prevalent at one time that a general panic set in, notably in 1849–52, 1856–7, and notoriously in the "garrotting panic" of 1862. As well as garrotting was "bonneting" which was knocking the hat over the eyes of the well-to-do and stripping them of their possessions, which on occasion meant all their clothes. Slowly the rookeries were demolished, moving on the criminals that lived there, though the crimes continued.

As today major crimes, with murders the gorier the better, fascinated the public. The Victorians didn't just read about it in the newspapers, as we do, but went to see exhibitions and re-enactments of the crime, either on stage or at the scene of the crime, with wax figures representing the main players. An exhibition at 17, Southampton Street, where a man had murdered his mistress and her four children, took £50 in a single day. Madame Tussaud's "Chamber of Horrors" opened in 1843, where wax models of the murderer would appear within days of their execution. (1)

If you were reasonably affluent *"Fishing, pigeon flying, watching cricket, or a cheap railway ticket to exotic places or a steamboat down the river. In the evening a meal out in a small chop-house where they could buy a plate of liver and bacon for 10d. (potatoes and bread 2d. extra), gooseberry pie for 5d. and a pint of stout for 4½d. B & B for 2s, gallery ticket at Drury Lane 1s. If on the other hand you were not skilled what were your options? Factory work, children got 5s. a week whilst they stayed fit, climbing boys for chimney sweeps, some children did piece-work at home stitching gloves. In the 1850s about half the children in London between 5 and 15 were at school. There were apprenticeships, the building trade being the favoured one. There were apprenticeships in other trades but they were not as profitable and the working hours longer than those in the building trade, namely 64 hours a week in summer and 52 hours in winter. If you were in domestic service, 121,000 were in 1851, you would expect an 80 hour week at ½d. an hour and your keep. There were costermongers, inordinately proud of their silk neckerchieves. There were sellers of cooked foods and sellers of drink, piemen and muffinmen, spice and rhubarb girls and hot eel boys, mice exhibitors and snake swallowers, penny-gaff clowns and stilt-vaulters, crossing sweepers and scavengers, street mechanics and flagstone artists, reciters and penny profile cutters, rag and bottle men, dog finders, packmen and cheap johns, running patterers and chaunters, old men with trays of cough drops and hot elder wine, old women with pickled whelks and cress, boys with oranges and nuts, girls with boiled puddings, Irish cats-meat dealers, Italian organ boys, Jewish clothesmen, French singing women, Dutch buy-a-broom girls, Highland bagpipe players, Ethiopian serenaders and Sicilian salamanders. There were also bone-pickers, rag-gatherers, sewer scavengers (Toshers), and the mud-larks and dustmen* (Doolittle in *"Pygmalion") and there was work too, in London's docks. Strange to relate there was also money to be had dredging the river for corpses".* (3)

And for the weekend, various sports were getting themselves organised. The rules of football were devised by the London Football Association in 1863. John Graham Chambers drew up more rules for boxing, named after the Marquis of Queensberry, the Queensberry Rules. Athletics, not to be outdone established the Amateur Athletics Association in 1880.

Before we go on to revel in the number of Lord Mayors and Sheriffs to have come from the Spectacle Makers Company in this century it might be as well to bear in mind that, as in later centuries, the Corporation of London came in for heavy criticism in some quarters. There were a number of commissions looking into the affairs of the Corporation, the major criticism being the type of Alderman and Common Councillor. David Owen draws attention to some comments in evidence to the 1854 Royal Commission *"freely charged that both the Court of Aldermen and the Court of Common Council were composed primarily of small-minded tradesmen. James Acland, Secretary of the City of London Municipal Reform Association* (hardly an unbiased witness) *said entertaining the conviction, as I do, that counter transactions in small coins have no tendency to give a man an enlarged view, I think that such men are ill-qualified for the offices they filled"*. Other witnesses backed him up, one claiming *"it was notorious that the higher class of merchants in London keep aloof altogether almost from the corporation affairs leaving them to the smaller shopkeepers who enjoyed having the control of large funds in their own hands"*. Attention was drawn to the fact that very few, if any, of the Aldermen and Common Councillors had addresses within the City, which implied that their real interests lay elsewhere, and were in it for the pageantry and pomp and the generous eating possibilities.

A review of ten years later showed that *"the councilmen were certainly not of the highest commercial and financial classes, but neither were they solely a group of small tradesmen, although such men did appear among their number"*. It was further noted that Liverymen from the Great Twelve *"no longer took any special interest in the government of the City...the Mercers and the Ironmongers had no members at all in the Corporation. Instead, the minor companies had taken over the membership, with a list headed by thirty-seven Spectacle-Makers, twenty-three Loriners and ten Stationers"*. It was suggested that the fairest judgement came from Thomas Dakin (a Spectacle Maker) who *"while admitting that the civic leaders seldom belonged to the princely commercial houses, nevertheless denied that the Common Council was in the hands of small shopkeepers....yet it was true that the Corporation did not consist of City men of the greatest eminence. These, as well as some of their less distinguished colleagues, had other and more demanding concerns."* The arguments around the Corporation have continued to swirl to this day and I must admit, as I have said before, that when I left the service of the Corporation in 1965, to join the Spectacle Makers, I did not consider that the Corporation would outlive my working life. But it still flourishes, far more, it must be said, as a P.R. organisation for the financial city than when I was there. The Corporation has recently done something it would not have contemplated a few years ago in that it has published the accounts of one of its private funds, running into a billion or so, about 10 million of which was spent on "lobbying" for the financial city.

19th CENTURY

JOTTINGS FROM THE MINUTE BOOKS

Before the Court had agreed on a regular meeting place, which may not have been until the 1940s when they moved offices to Apothecaries' Hall, it met in local taverns and inns. Not, I hasten to add, because drinking was of the first importance to our predecessors, but for the mundane reason that it is in these hostelries that rooms were available for hire, and dinner or supper was also obtainable after the meeting. A full list of Court venues appears at Appendix III.

For the first couple of hundred years the taverns and inns in which they met have mostly disappeared, mainly without record. In March 1803, the Court suddenly decided to meet at the King's Head in the Poultry. According to *"City of London Pubs"* (4), it was originally known as "The Rose". The story goes that the landlord's wife, a Mrs. King, was highly pregnant but very anxious to see Charles II's entry into the City. She therefore positioned herself in a chair in front of the inn. Charles, hearing of her loyalty, stopped the procession and went over and kissed her hand. The tavern's name was immediately changed to "The King's Head".

The story does not tell whether, because of the royal recognition, the child was instantly born. Probably all energies were spent on designing, and getting painted, the new sign. No planning permission, or building regulations, to be obtained or satisfied. The big swinging shop signs had been ordered to be removed in 1762, and a sign had to be fixed against the wall with a projection of no more than four inches, a similar edict had been made in Paris a year earlier. (5) Incidentally it is argued that the banning of the old swinging signs brought in house numbering as a means of identification.

**

The Master in 1803-04, and again in 1822-23, was Henry Lawson. Whilst he started out as a practising spectacle maker, having been apprenticed to Edward Nairne, he soon gave that up to scientific study. By 1826, he had equipped his own observatory and, by 1834, had an 11 foot refractor, which Peter Dollond considered as the finest he had made. His written papers on his subsequent observations were published by the Royal Astronomical Society. In 1840, he was elected a fellow of the Royal Society by virtue of his contributions to meteorology and astronomy. Having been left a fortune he moved to Bath (he had resigned from the Court in January, 1824), where he mounted his instruments on the roof. He continued writing learned papers, and invented a reclining medical and observing chair, a thermometer stand intended to standardise shade temperature readings, a "lifting apparatus" for invalids and a "surgical transferrer". His 11 foot telescope was donated to the Royal Naval College at Greenwich, and on his death in 1855, having no children, and his wife having died a few weeks before, his large fortune was divided in his will among some 139 individuals in addition to hospitals and charitable institutions in Bath. His other claim to fame was that one of his probable ancestors was Katherine Parr. (6)

**

On 17th September, 1805, a certain James Christie was admitted, according to the Minutes, by Patrimony. As he was admitted by Patrimony then his father must have been a Freeman, but he does not appear in the Minutes, unless I missed him! However in the

Master and Wardens Accounts for 1801, there is a payment received for the Freedom of a Mr. Christie. Knowing that the James Christie of 1805, was an auctioneer in Pall Mall and that the original James Christie had a son, James, I think we are on safe ground.

The first James Christie was a former midshipman in the Navy who became an assistant to a Mr. Annersley, who was an auctioneer. He established his own business, at first in Great Castle Street, moving in 1767, to an unidentified house in Pall Mall. In 1768 he moved to 83/84, Pall Mall and in 1770, whilst still living in 83/84, transferred the business to 125, Pall Mall, next door to Gainsborough. He auctioned everything *"from chamber pots to sedan chairs, but by the turn of the century his sale rooms had become the fashionable place for art sales, doubtless owing much to his friendship with Reynolds, Garrick, Sheridan and Gainsborough"*. (1) He died in 1803, and in 1823, his son, James, the one we started with, moved the business to King Street. This James Christie was Master of the Company 1818-19. When he resigned from the Court in 1830, the reason he gave was that due to his ill-health he had been *"obliged to avoid exposure to evening air and, above all, convivial meetings"*. The last member of the Christie family to take part in the business was James J.B. Christie, who retired in 1889.

Why an auctioneer should wish to become a Freeman of the Spectacle Makers Company is not obvious, though the Company was beginning to recruit from a different background – it was after all some 4 years before the Livery was obtained. Perhaps the new blood coming in was the reason for the adoption of the Livery at this time.

**

On the 1st February, 1808, the Court admitted to the Freedom, and in due course to the Livery, one William Warriner, Tavern Keeper. They must have been thinking ahead, for in the next year on the 5th October, the Court met for the first time in the George and Vulture, of which Warriner was the tavern keeper. They went on meeting there for the next twenty years when it was considered *"no longer able to accommodate the Company"*.

**

In 1809, comes a major change in the Company's affairs. The Minutes give no indication of why, at this particular time, the Company should choose to approach the Court of Alderman for a Grant of Livery. On the 1st January, 1807, the Clerk is instructed to enquire as to the mode and cost of an application to the Court of Alderman. In December of that year, somewhat arse about face, a Committee is set-up to investigate the Company's power to become a Livery Company. In March of the next year the decision is taken to make application to the Court of Aldermen. By the 27th November, 1809, the Grant of Livery is made, and the initial Liverymen are admitted, all 14 of them, a further 11 in 1810. The Livery Fine was set at £15-15-0d: of that £15 going to the Company 10/- to the Clerk and 5/- to the Beadle. (By 1823 it had already been increased to £20). In 1811, it was agreed that action is to be taken against non-payers! In 1811, Registration of the Grant of Livery was made, at a cost of £100 and legal fees of £18-5-10d, with the Court of Chancery. The Court was no doubt grateful to be advised by the Town Clerk that the Livery Fine could be amended without recourse to the Court of Chancery. That's it, no further information on the reasons for seeking the Grant of Livery. James Boudon was the Clerk from 1800 to 1811, was it he who was the driving force? It's a pity we don't know more for it was the most important step in the development of the Spectacle Makers Company.

In due course the Beadle attended his first Common Hall, no doubt to serve at the Wicket Gates to verify who were Liverymen of the Company, not a difficult task at the time, for which service he was paid 5/-.

**

The quiet waters of the Spectacle Makers Company, after the excitement of the Grant of Livery, were disturbed by a report from the Clerk (quite usual for reports from Clerks to disturb Courts!) at a meeting at the George and Vulture Tavern, Cornhill, on Thursday, 30th December, 1813. You will notice by the date that 19th century Livery Companies did not have long holidays for Christmas, indeed more than one Court meeting was held on the 26th December. What the Clerk had to report was:

"that a Caveat has been entered at the Chamberlain's Office by the Clockmakers Company which goes to prevent the admission of a Mr. Bate, Spectacle Maker, of the Poultry as a Freeman of this Company".

The Master and Wardens were requested: *"to enquire into the circumstances of the Case having communicated with Mr. Bate... take such steps as may appear to them proper".*

On the 29th March, 1814, Robert Brettell Bate, Optician, was admitted to the Freedom of the Spectacle Makers Company by Redemption. At the Court on the 31st March the Master and Wardens reported that having spoken to Mr Bate he:

"had consented to become a Freeman of this Company and had been in consequence sworn in at Guildhall on Tuesday last" they added that *"no further notice was at present at all necessary of the Caveat."*

On the 30th June the Court learnt:

"the Court of Aldermen had passed the Order for Mr. Bate's Freedom, but that the Chamberlain had refused to swear him in

owing to the Caveat of the Clockmakers Company not being removed".

The Master and Wardens were asked to attend at the Chamberlain's Office: *"to arrange the business".* On the 6th October the Master and Wardens report that the Caveat had not been removed: *"but they hope to report at the next Quarterly Court that the matter be finally settled".* Little did they know! In December a summons of the Chamberlain was reported *"respecting the Caveat and also a Memorial of the Clockmakers Company of the 12th October, 1812".* The Master and Wardens were requested to draw up an answer and to summon a Special Court to consider the draft.

By the 19th January, 1815, the Answer and Protest were drafted, agreed and written into the Minutes. After rehearsing the Charter rights, etc., it continues:

"And whereas your present Memorialists having duly considered the matter and not having found any denial of the Chartered Rights of the Spectacle Makers, are on that head so far content, But the claims put forth by the Company of Clockmakers are so extensive as to effect in a collateral degree, not only your present Memorialists, but many other companies and indeed in one view of the case every Company of this City". Amongst other points raised: *"the extensive signification of "Mathematical Instruments" involving in its definition a great variety and number of Mechanical Trades in London, cannot for a moment be supposed to be included in the Rights of the Clockmakers Company... your Memorialists are prepared to prove that as far as the Knowledge and Memory of Man will go, the Trade of Optical and Mathematical Instruments has been united by Custom to that of the Spectacle Makers....the Clockmakers apply to the Spectacle Makers for Optical and*

Mathematical Instruments that may be required in the furtherance of their Trade... every Spectacle Maker carrying on the General Trade and keeping an Open Shop, in taking Apprentices considered it his duty to Teach them the Knowledge of Optical and Mathematical Instruments used under those terms in the Trade, - Whereas it can be safely asserted that no Clock Maker in any branch ever teaches his Apprentices the Art of making such Mathematical Instruments as are made by the Spectacle Maker", that the Clockmakers Company: *"has never molested nor claimed any Person who was a recorded Freeman of the Spectacle Makers Company to which Past Art and Trade that of making Optical and Mathematical Instruments has been attached by assimilation and custom for time immemorial"* and finally: *"your Memoralialists Protest against the unreasonable and unjust claim that the Master and Wardens and Fellowship of Clockmakers have made under the term "Mathematical Instruments" as being indefinite in its signification, hurtful in its effects to the Free Artisans, and Trades of this City, and not consonant with their Charter."*

On the 30th March, 1815, the Master and Wardens reported that they had duly attended before the Chamberlain to hear his decision and: *"with pleasure heard it decided in favour of this Company"*. The Chamberlain stated that Bate was entitled to take up his Freedom in the Company of Spectacle Makers and:

"further, that as the said Person neither makes nor sells Clocks, nor Watches nor professes the Trade of Clockmaking, is therefore not compellable to take up his freedom of the City in the Company of Clockmakers as the Charter of the Clockmakers is confined to the Art of Making Clocks, and Sun Dials".

He went on to add that Bate would have to stop making

mathematical instruments, which in their construction particularly belong to clock making, or become a Freeman of the Clockmakers' Company. So far so good, but the report adds that one member of the Court of the Clockmakers' Company stated that they were not satisfied, and would recommend that the case be referred to the Court of Aldermen. Consternation all round!

The Court of Aldermen duly considered and referred the issue to a Committee which would hear both sides of the case. The Master and Wardens next reported that: *"owing to the Season of the Year* (this is in October) *most of the Aldermen on the Committee were out of Town and there had not been another meeting"*. In December 1815, the Court was advised that: *"pressure of business"* would prevent a further meeting until mid-January. In June, 1816, the Clerk advised the Court that the Committee considering the issue with the Clockmakers had been dissolved, and the issue referred to the Committee for General Purposes. The Court therefore decided to petition the Court of Aldermen. At this same Court the Company declined an invitation to subscribe:

"for a Triumphal Column in Massive Plate, etc., to be presented to his Grace the Duke of Wellington for the Victory obtained on the 18th June, 1815, on the Field of Waterloo".

In October little progress was being made, and it was suggested that the help of an Alderman should be sought who might be able to get a meeting of the Committee convened. Alderman Cox undertook: *"to Pursue the affair as far as in his Power to a Conclusion"*. In January, 1817, (the December Court meeting being adjourned as inquorate, somewhat odd considering what was going on) it was reported that Alderman Cox had so far been unable to convene a meeting but: *"would as soon as in his power attend to the affair"*. In June, 1817, the Clerk reported that: *"Alderman Cox, having declined further to interest himself"* he had therefore written to the Clerk to the Clockmakers, asking their aid in bringing the matter to a conclusion. The Clerk to the Clockmakers, George Atkins, replied, apologising for the delay due to the Chairman of the relevant Committee being "from London a considerable length of time" (No reliable post, no phone, no E-mails, not even, Trump-like, Twitter!). He said that his Company had encouraged the appointment of a Committee of Aldermen who would listen to the arguments. (It is always best to ask the Clerks if you want something done!)

In January, 1818, the Master and Wardens reported that they had had an interview with the Lord Mayor, and as a consequence, were summoned to a meeting of the Committee of Aldermen on the 28th October. But:

"so much business occupied the Meeting, that after being in attendance the whole day, the Hearing of this Cause could not come on".

The meeting was re-convened on the 4th November and both sides being heard, the meeting was adjourned. At a third meeting the Lord Mayor, the Chairman of the Committee, announced:

"their decision to be that the previous decision of his Worship the Chamberlain, against which the Clockmakers Company had appealed, be confirmed and the Caveat is consequently of no further avail".

They added that at a subsequent Court of the Lord Mayor and Aldermen: *"the whole proceedings of the Committee of Aldermen were agreed to and Confirmed".* At long last Robert Brettell Bate became a Freeman of the City of London, recorded as a Freeman of the Spectacle Makers Company.

At the March meeting the Court specifically thanked Johnson Lawson:

"for the Zeal with which he defended the rights of this Company during their long pending question with the Clockmakers Company, and for the Ability with which he Maintained the same, upon the hearing granted by the Lord Mayor and Court of Aldermen".

It would appear that the matter was at last laid to rest. However an Especial Court was summoned at 6.30 o'clock on Tuesday, 2nd June, 1818: *"in consequence of a Bill brought into and now passing through the House of Commons relating to the Clockmakers Company".*

The Bill was entitled *"A Bill for the more effectual Prevention of Frauds and Abuses in the Manufacture, Exportation and Importation of Sundry Wares, and for the relief of distress of Workmen brought up to practise the Manufacture of Clocks and Watches"* - a pretty snappy title! The Court considered that:

"the Clauses, Expressions and Words, in the way inserted in said Bill that relate to Mathematical Instruments and Engraving, would if passed into a Law be very oppressive and hurtful to all such Trades and Workmen as might come under the name of Mathematical Instrument Makers and Engravers, and would not as proposed in that Bill be of any utility to the Public".

A Petition was drafted to the House of Commons. In brief this took no exception to the principle of the Bill as set out in the title but concentrated on the fact that the introduction of:

"Mathematical Instruments and Engraving increased the Charter powers of the Clockmakers Company and would a) be a great infringement of the rights of citizens involved in mechanical trades

b) would be oppressive in its operation c) in many instances scarcely profitable to be complied with and d) not of any service to the Trade or Public in general."

The Petition was sealed and the Master and Wardens given such powers as they required and, additionally, were to obtain an interview with the Members of Parliament for the City, and communicate with any other companies who might also feel inclined to petition Parliament: *"against any infringement of their particular and general rights by the said Bill"*.

It was reported on the 25th June, that the Master and Wardens had attended at the House of Commons to learn the progress of the Bill. They were informed:

"as the Sessions of Parliament would terminate in a few days (namely about the 9th June) that the said Bill had been withdrawn, consequently it became unnecessary (and indeed the time was too short) to present the Petition to the House".

A member of the Court of the Clockmakers Company assured the Master and Wardens that they would be advised if the Clockmakers Company introduced a similar Bill on a subsequent occasion. There the matter rested until the meeting, still at the George and Vulture, on the 30th September, 1819, when the Master and Wardens reported a little primly that:

"they had not neglected to watch the introduction by the Clockmakers Company of any Bill into the House of Commons".

A Bill had indeed been introduced entitled *"A Bill to regulate the Manufacture of Clocks and Watches"*. However the Master and Wardens added that they: *"are happy to inform the Court that there was not any Clause whatever in the said Bill that could in any way affect the Rights and Usages of this Company"*. They went on to add they had spoken to a member of the Clockmakers Company:

"who had declared that his Court had entirely abandoned any revival of the former Bill printed by the House of Commons, 8th May, 1818 – and further did not mean to pursue any more those claims which this Court had resisted".

Thus some six years after the issue had first arisen it was finally resolved in favour of the Spectacle Makers Company. The Court could rightly and with good heart *"adjourn to receive the Livery at Dinner"* – probably their first real "Livery Dinner" - but of that more elsewhere.

*NOTATU DIGNUM

The use of phrases such as "as far as the Knowledge and Memory of Man will go" and "from time immemorial" (usually interpreted as 1189), though they run splendidly off the tongue do not bear too close an historical analysis! The earliest instrument makers were Freemen of the Grocers Company. This Company was predominantly involved in the spice trade. It had also dealt in drugs and tobacco, and became involved in the weighing of all heavy imported goods, hence "Grossers" as they dealt in bulk, which became corrupted to Grocers. In 1447, it obtained a Crown patent to appoint a "garbeller" of spices. His job was to certify that impurities had been removed, or that the amount of chaff was permissible, before the "weigher" bagged the spices. The weigher maintained one of the "King's beam", a steelyard with a graduated scale on a measuring arm. Spices were weighed in hundred-weights but medicinal drugs, which also came under the Grocers purview, were weighed in hundredths of a pound. Mathematical instrument makers were employed to make the scale divisions and supervise the making of the scales. It is this latter point which suggests why instrument makers started with the Grocers Company. Incidentally, when the Apothecaries broke away from the Grocers, taking the drug business with them in 1617, this was a severe blow to the Grocers. This and the Great Fire, which destroyed the Hall and nearly all their rentable property, nearly broke the Company.

Of the fifty-three masters specifically engaged in making or selling optical instruments, other than spectacles, between the early seventeenth century and 1720, 18 were members of the Spectacle Makers Company, 5 were Clockmakers, 5 were Turners, 3 were Broderers, 3 were Merchant Taylors, 2 were Grocers, and one each from the Drapers, Joiners, Pewterers, Stationers, and Weavers. The Guilds of the remainder were unknown. (7) and (8)

**

On the 15th May, 1816, William Naish, dealer in British Wines, was admitted to the Freedom. I had supposed that British wine, after the Romans had left, had rather disappeared until the revival in the 1950s. Obviously not, for on the 10th December, 1847, John Stivens was admitted to the Freedom and his occupation is stated as *"British Wine merchant"*.

**

The world outside does intrude on the Minutes from time to time. The 3rd February, 1823, finds John Hodges starting his apprenticeship with Milton Harsant, a carpenter. Consideration was surprisingly high, at £150. Hodges' father was *"soldier of the 4th Regiment of Foot, killed at Waterloo"*.

**

Robert Brettell Bate was Master of the Company in 1828 and 1829. After his contentious entry into the Company he was legally described as *"a maker of spectacles, but a retailer of other mathematical instruments"*. He continued in this profitable line of business. His father-in-law had had an improved design of a hydrometer adopted by the government excise department for revenue purposes, and the right to supply this instrument passed to Bate, on the strength of which he was appointed mathematical instrument maker to HM Excise. He was later appointed optician in ordinary to George IV, and subsequently to William III and Queen Victoria. He continued improvements to the hydrometer, and was invited to make the models for the recently approved new standard weights and measures, as a result of which he produced hundreds of sets of standards for government and municipal use. He was appointed sole Admiralty chart agent in 1830, and wrote and published many books on navigation. He collaborated with David Brewster on the kaleidoscope, and took out further patents for hydrometers and spectacle frames. He was also involved in the family bank, Bate and Robins, later purchased by the Midland Bank. He died in Hampstead in December, 1847. (9)

**

The expression "Break a leg" is a strange way of wishing an actor well before a performance and it always struck me as odd, however it is TRADITION, and must therefore be alright! This somewhat tortuous segue is occasioned by the fact that the Company Minutes make few references to illness and accident. It therefore came as a surprise to read on the 2nd October, 1817, that:

"the Court was informed by a letter to their Clerk, that William Roles, the Beadle, had met with the misfortune of breaking his leg and that he is otherwise in Consequence in Distress – having taken the same into Consideration it was resolved that the sum of three pounds be given to the said William Roles, to aid him in his present unfortunate situation".

At the Court on the 8th January, 1818, the Clerk reported that he had paid Mr. Roles at the rate of 10s. a week (presumably to guard against the unfortunate Roles spending the whole lot at once) but that, when the three pounds had been expended, Mr. Roles was still in distress. The Clerk, having consulted the Master, had continued the payments which now amounted to seven pounds. The Beadle still being absent from duty: *"from continuance of indisposition"*, his son had stood in for him. The Court then decided:

"That it cannot extend any further relief to William Roles. But in order to express its sense of the good conduct of the Younger Roles, The Court grants the sum of Two Pounds to him by way of encouragement and to enable him to assist his Father, until the latter can resume his Duty as Beadle".

As there is no further reference to the Beadle, until his re-election in October 1818, the extra couple of quid must have seen the family through.

Whilst previous Beadles had been Spectacle Makers, and all but one Freemen of the Company, Roles was not. There was a delayed election for Beadle in 1813, when Roles was chosen over the incumbent, William Arnold (the first non-Freeman to hold that office), though as Arnold was given a £1 as compensation for not being elected there doesn't appear to have been any hanky panky going on. Roles address was 2, Brewers Row, Westminster adjacent to the Stag Brewery subsequently owned by Watney, Combe and Reid. In 1814, a new cloak and staff were bought for him: *"at a cost no greater than ten guineas"*. In 1821, the Court authorised the purchase of: *"a hat with Gold Braid"*, perhaps in connection with the Coronation. He also seems to have been the first Beadle to receive an annual Christmas gift, 7s.6d. in 1814, rising to the munificent sum of 10s. in 1819.

To mark the Coronation of George IV in 1821 Roles: *"being poor"* was given a golden sovereign on a par with the other Pensioners. In June 1825, he was given £4 a year in addition to his *"regular income"*. He died on 23rd September, 1828, apparently his accident had not done him lasting harm.

However he was not done with the Company! His penury, frequently referred to, exercised the Company beyond the grave, for after his death the Court, on 2nd October 1828, was petitioned by his widow, Sarah, for assistance: *"to defray the expenses of her late Husband's funeral, which amounts to about £5-5-0"* which was accepted and paid.

Some Beadles were not such loyal servants, as in 1832: *"the Beadle (George Dixon) was repeatedly intoxicated"* and, as a not unreasonable consequence, was not re-elected.

Not all our Beadles were as lucky as Roles, at least as regards his broken leg. It was reported to the Court on the 7th January, 1836 that:

"the severe indisposition of the Beadle, (William Winter) occasioned by an attack of the Small Pox;- that his Doctor had recommended him Port Wine, but from his circumstances, was unable to purchase same, whereupon it was resolved that Two Guineas be forwarded to him, as a Gift of the Court".

At the next Court it was reported: *"The decease of the Beadle, which occurred shortly after the meeting of the last Court"*. It is not clear as to whether the Beadle was able to drink the port and die a cheerful man or whether it didn't get there in time!

**

Smallpox, after the disappearance of the plague, became the most feared of all diseases, particularly for children in industrial towns. There were 3,500 deaths from smallpox in London in 1796.

In certain cases it was shown that the disease might be prevented, in children and adults, by placing them in contact with a person suffering from it. Experiments with transplanting matter from mildly affected patients to one in need of protection, were first made in Italy and Constantinople. Doctors in London repeated these experiments, using Newgate prisoners (who were promised reprieves for submitting to it) and charity schoolchildren! There were dangers in the method, for the induced disease could take a severe course, and the inoculated person had to be kept in isolation, or the disease was likely to spread. The method was rarely practised after 1728, though many felt that the dangers of inoculation were less to be feared than a severe attack of smallpox.

It had long been known that cowherds and milkmaids appeared to be immune to smallpox. It was a pupil of John Hunter, (whose portrait is in Apothecaries' Hall), one Edward Jenner, who made the final breakthrough. He had been studying the relationship between smallpox and cowpox and had inoculated patients with cowpox, and then inoculated them with smallpox, but no disease followed. He duly published his researches, to be ridiculed by medical men, clergymen, journalists and satirists. But more and more distinguished doctors supported vaccination and the prejudice against vaccination was, in due course, overcome.

Thanks to vaccination the outbreaks of the disease were becoming increasingly less severe. About half the children born in British towns were vaccinated between 1800 and 1870. In 1853 vaccination of infants within four months of their birth was made compulsory. There was a serious epidemic in 1870-72 in which over 40,000 people died, nearly 10,000 in London. In the worst year, 1871, 821,856 children were born in England and Wales and of these nearly 80,000 died before they could be vaccinated, but of the rest 94% were successfully treated. After that epidemic was over the number of deaths from the disease rapidly declined. Unfortunately all this came too late for poor Winter, our Beadle. (3)

**

Now that the Company had become a Livery Company, it was only right that a Livery Dinner should be held. The first "Livery Dinner", as opposed to a dinner to which members of the Livery, or before 1809, the Freemen, were invited to dine with the Court, appears to be have been held on the 30th September, 1819. It started out as a dinner to recognise two distinguished members of the Livery.

In 1818, Lawrence Gwynne, LL.D., was made a Liveryman of the Company. He was subsequently elected Sheriff and 16 members of the Livery attended on 28th September, 1818, when he was duly sworn into office. All 16 also attended:

"the Lord Mayor and the Sheriffs to the Exchequer Court at Westminster to be approved and Sworn in before the Barons". They also *"dined each day at Stationers Hall"*.

In view of the detail given to this election it seems to indicate that Gwynne was this Company's first Sheriff and I have yet to find reference to an earlier one and, with the Company only attaining the Livery in 1809, this seems unlikely.

The year Gwynne was elected as Sheriff, another Liveryman, Thomas Wilson, was serving as a Member of Parliament for the City (the City had its own MPs in those days). The Court decided that our two Liverymen should be honoured by a dinner, and additionally that the Lord Mayor elect, John Atkins, and the other Sheriff, John Roberts, also be invited, the date being agreed as the 28th October, 1818. As this decision was taken at a Court meeting on the 13th October it is hardly surprising that the Sheriffs:

"afterwards found it would be impossible to attend owing to the unusual length of the Old Bailey Sessions at that period, and

personally waiting on the Master and Wardens, begged to be excused".

At the Court meeting on the 1st July, 1819, it was agreed that the Livery of the Company be invited to dine at the next Quarterly Court, 30th September, and that the Court meet again on the 16th September: *"to arrange and give orders for the Livery Dinner"*. Whilst members of the Livery had been invited to dine with the Court in 1812, and the subsequent three years, these were not described as "Livery Dinners", nor such precise orders given. Hence my belief that this was the first real Livery Dinner.

The Court on the 16th September, held as usual in the George and Vulture Tavern:

"having consulted Mr. Warriner, the Landlord, on the subject on what he could provide for the same, and the accommodations for the Company it was resolved that the dinner should be given at the George and Vulture Tavern, Cornhill, and that the Clerk do issue the invitations accordingly, and as soon as answers are received that a list be made out of such gentlemen as can attend". It was further resolved that the Master should ask five: *"friends of the Company as he thinks fit to invite",* that members of the Court be entitled to invite "a friend", that the Clerk: *"do provide proper Gowns for the Master and Wardens, and himself"* (and he only had 6 weeks to do it in!), the Master: *"be requested to engage the attendance of such professional Singers as he may think best for the occasion",* that the Clerk engage: *"John Worton for that day to attend the Master, and receive his orders for the Wine, and other Commands"* and finally the Court to meet at 3.30 on the day to the: *"Dispatch of Business, previous to receiving the Liverymen as they arrive to Dinner".*

At the Court on the 30th December, the Clerk was instructed to enter in the Minutes, and duly did so, the names of those attending. Thirty-nine eventually attended, including Lawrence Gwynne, now a Past Sheriff, and Thomas Wilson, together with four singers. The shape and substance of a modern Livery Dinner can be seen to be emerging.

**

The Court's gift to Mrs. Roles, was an example of the charitable activities of the Company to its Freemen and their relatives. The meeting in March, 1820, was another instance. The Court had wanted to ascertain if their oldest Pensioner, a Mrs. Ann Gass, was in fact still alive, and to make sure that their gratuity was really helping her. Henry Lawson, the Renter Warden, was sent to find out. He reported that:

"he found the said Pensioner alive but very feeble and bedridden in the Poor House in Bear Lane, Christchurch, Blackfriars Road – she declared herself satisfied with the Treatment, and begged to return her best Thanks to the Court for their benefaction. It appeared that the money was well expended in procuring for the poor Old Woman many little Comforts in her feeble state". The Renter Warden recommended continuance of the payment, which the Court subsequently endorsed.

The Gass family had been supported by the Court for some time. Robert Gass had been apprenticed to Thomas Lincoln on the 1st May, 1735. Assuming he was 14 at the time he would have been born in 1721. He obtained his Freedom 30th September, 1742. The first time he applied to the Company for financial assistance seems to have been in December, 1772, when he was given 10/-: *"his wife lying-in of Twins"*. It would appear that the birth of these twins started Gass's financial problems for in April, 1773, he was asking for, and being granted, financial assistance, 10/6d. A Quarterly sum of 10/6d. seems to have continued for several years, until on the 27th March, 1800, he was granted two guineas on account of his: *"great age and infirmities"* he was by now at least 79. This continued half-yearly until his death, sometime around 1802/1803. In 1805, his widow, Ann, was granted a sum of 2 guineas and a Quarterly payment of 10/6d. This was increased in 1810, to £1 a Quarter. She eventually died on 27th April, 1823.

The Company had been providing financial assistance for the Gass family for some 50 years – a good example of putting into action one of the main original aims of the Company, to put part of their accumulated funds to the:

"Relief of the POOR of this Fellowshippe".

**

Another example of the Company's charity was in 1833, when the Clerk received two petitions for help, one from the wife of a well-known Freeman, giving a little insight into the conditions of the poor at this time. What happened to those whose late husbands were not Freemen of a Livery Company? Susannah Bumpus petitioned the Company, her late husband having been a Liveryman:

"who was found drowned in November last leaving her in very distressed circumstances, with a family of six children".

The Court, having checked her statement, and the fact that her husband had been up-to-date with his Quarterage, paid her an immediate £5 and added her to the list of Pensioners, paying her £1 a Quarter.

The Bumpus family became well known booksellers until subsequent takeovers. It appears that our two, John and Thomas, sons of John Bumpus of Lower Swell, Gloucestershire, started the

THE SPECTACLE MAKERS

business. At the time they were with us the address given was 6, Holborn Bars, though subsequent shops were opened. Thomas Benjamin Bumpus, John II's son, whilst taking up his apprenticeship, never seems to have taken the Freedom and is the last in that line to be involved with the Spectacle Makers Company.

The second petition was from a Mrs. Irmima Warden stating:

"herself to be in very distressed circumstances, and that in March 1831, while passing over London Bridge, had the misfortune to fracture her leg, which has, and is, likely to render here incapable of obtaining a livelihood".

She was made an immediate payment of £1 and added to the list of Pensioners at £1 a Quarter. No National Health Service to assist her! No "ambulance chasing" solicitors to hound the local authority for a possible act of omission.

**

Having repeatedly grumbled about the lack of everyday detail in the Minutes, the death of a King only mentioned because the Court meeting had to be deferred, there were exceptions. The Coronation of George IV, 19th July, 1821, was celebrated by the Company in two ways. The Court agreed:

"That the pensioners of this Company be provided with a dinner on the occasion, and that a Gold Sovereign be presented to each of them for this purpose".

It was duly reported on 11th October that the Master and Wardens having distributed the donations the pensioners: *"were extremely grateful for the same and begged to return their humble Thanks"*. It is not recorded whether the Master and Wardens actually went to the poorhouse to deliver at least one of the golden sovereigns, my guess is that it would have been the Beadle!

The Court also celebrated the event with a dinner. Theirs was held at the Star and Garter on Richmond Hill on 22nd August. The principal toast was:

"George the 4th. May his Reign be prosperous and the people happy". The Minute goes on to state: *"To which such Honor was paid as to testify the Loyalty and Patriotism of the Company, and the day was passed to the satisfaction of the Court and the Company present."*

It is perhaps only hindsight which gives one pause as to the terms of the Minute. The enjoyment of conviviality was an understatement as far as George IV was concerned. Gillray depicted him under the title *'A voluptuary under the horrors of Digestion'* "*showing him with his florid face on the verge of apoplexy, his huge belly bursting from his breeches recovering from an enormous meal at Carlton House.*" (10) Leigh Hunt said of him in 1812, on his fiftieth birthday "*A libertine over head and ears in debt and disgrace, a despiser of domestic ties, the companion of demi-reps, a man who has just closed half a century without a single claim on the gratitude of his country or the respect of posterity*". (Ibid) It is now considered that George IV was responsible for the cruel slander of George III's insanity, when he actually suffered from a medical condition. The House of Windsor has little to complain about the media in the light of the above!

Despite all this George IV is more likely to be remembered as a man of style and taste, his "Gothick" restoration of Windsor Castle and the "Oriental" Brighton Pavilion, where the King's personal intervention stopped it short of hideous vulgarity. As George IV had been Regent before his coronation the Spectacle Makers Court cannot have been oblivious to his reputation. To suggest that any of this is represented in the Court Minute is perhaps over-egging it a bit – but then you never know!

**

THE CITY OF LONDON TAVERN,
Bishopsgate Street.

Another of the Court's meeting places was the London Coffee House. Subsequently called the London Tavern, it hosted the Court from 1822 until 1853. It was founded some time before 1731, by James Ashley.

He advertised it as *"Punch House, Dorchester Beer and Welsh Ale Warehouse"*. It specialised in Punch made from Arrack, Rum, and French Brandy, and it sold for 6s. a quart. Punch made from Rum and brandy, on the other hand, was only 4s. a quart. When the house was rebuilt in 1765, a monument dedicated to a Roman soldier by his wife, Claudina Martina, was found, together with a fragment of a statue of Hercules. The dining Room could accommodate 355 people. Charles Dickens presided at several meetings, and it was here in *"Nicholas Nickleby"* that the public meeting *"to take into consideration the propriety of petitioning Parliament in favour of the United Metropolitan Improved Hot Muffin and Crumpet Baking and Punctual Delivery Company"* was held.

The Tavern was within the old "Rules of the Fleet Prison" and juries engaged in the Old Bailey sessions trying capital offences were housed and entertained when such trials were adjourned. The house was at one time kept by both the grandfather and father of John Leech, the celebrated artist of "Punch". (11)

**

One of the Company's well-known Freemen at this time was Charles Chubb. Charles Chubb, having been apprenticed to a blacksmith, opened a business together with his younger brother, Jeremiah, first in Winchester, and then Portsea in 1804. They specialised in ship's ironmongery. In 1818, Jeremiah was granted a patent for his Detector Lock (and a prize of £100 offered by the Government for a lock that could not be opened by any but its own key). If the lock was picked a detection mechanism came into action, and to make the lock work again a special regulating key had to be used. The money was put to the establishing of the Chubb Lock Manufacturers, and a workshop opened in Wolverhampton.

In 1820, with lock making being Jeremiah's responsibility, Charles Chubb left to establish the London office at 57, St Paul's Churchyard. In 1828, he was admitted to the Freedom of the Spectacle Makers Company. In 1835, the Chubbs had taken out a patent on a burglar resistant safe, opening their first safe works at Cowcross Street, just near Smithfield Market, and the manufacture of safes, vaults and safe deposits became as important as lock manufacture. Charles's youngest son, John, had by now joined the business, and after Charles's death in 1846, became the sole proprietor. He obtained his Freedom in 1843, after his apprenticeship with his father. On John's death in 1872, he was succeeded by his three sons, one of whom, John Charles, continued the association with the Company, becoming Free by Patrimony in 1886. The Chubb family remained in the great majority on the board of the Company well into the 20th century.

Chubbs expanded rapidly in the latter part of the 19th century. In 1908, having closed their London safe works, they opened a new factory in Wolverhampton *"for the manufacture of safes, strong-*

room doors, treasuries, strong rooms and safe deposits". The next major change came in the 1940s, with the decision to move away from hand-made locks and to produce *"a range of locks, machine made, designed to offer a high degree of security at a reasonable price"*. There have been many subsequent take-overs and mergers but the Chubb name is still going strong. (12) and (13)

**

We have all heard of the Great Fire of London and are pretty well aware that fire was a frequent hazard in London. But we tend to associate this with the idea of the old houses, lathe and plaster and the rest, of the 17th and 18th centuries. The Court Minutes of the 27th March, 1823, give a different picture. George Dollond is reporting to the Court:

"that the Oak Chest of the Company containing the original Charter, - the enrolled Bye Laws, various Minute Books, and papers, - had long been in his possession: considering the danger of Fire, as some time ago a Fire occurred at a Neighbours by which his House was damaged, and from the frequency of similar accidents, he had consulted with Mr. Sewell, the Clerk, about a safer deposit within Guildhall, such a place being found (called the Book Room of the Chamberlain's Outer Office) the said Chest with its contents have been placed there, of which the Court is hereby informed".

This is almost certainly the same chest which the Past Master, Frank Norville, re-acquired for the Company as previously reported. It is comforting to know that it was put to good use – even though it was not full of the Company's silver.

**

With the expansion of the Freedom of the Company to non-spectacle makers, interesting trades had begun to appear. On the

25th July, 1825, Francis Moore was bound apprentice to his father, also Francis, of St. Martins Court, St. Martins Lane, who was by trade an umbrella maker.

The umbrella was used in the Byzantine Church forming part of the Pontifical regalia, and it became recognised as a symbol of dominion. There are few references to umbrellas in literature until the Parasol comes into use in France and England, probably adopted from China, in the seventeenth century, and was initially used by ladies to keep the sun off. In a dictionary of 1708, an umbrella is described as a *"screen commonly used by women to keep off rain"*, but was still not in general use. Defoe had Robinson Crusoe using one *"I covered it with skins, the hair outwards, so that it cast off the rain like a pent-house, and kept off the sun so effectually, that I could walk out in the hottest of the weather with greater advantage than I could before in the coolest"*. As a result of this description the heavy umbrella was called a "Robinson" for many years in England and in France.

Jonas Hanway, born in 1712, and the founder of the Magdalen Hospital, is generally credited with setting the fashion for carrying an umbrella. He had used an umbrella as a sun shade during his travels in Persia, and returning to London, had braved derision by continuing to carry and use it. Hackney coachmen were particularly derisory, seeing the umbrella as an invasion of their vested rights! At the time of his death in 1786, it was claimed that Hanway had carried an umbrella for thirty years. Whilst initially restricted to London, its use soon spread, the first one appearing in Bristol in 1780, and in Taunton a couple of years later. When silk and gingham replaced the heavy oiled silk, lighter ribs and frames could be used, and with ingenious mechanical improvements made to the framework, chiefly in England and France, the modern umbrella had well and truly taken off. (14)

**

On the 8th June, 1839, John Cooper, pianoforte manufacturer, took his Freedom. His father, John, was also a pianoforte manufacturer and at the same address, Southampton Row, Russell Square. As with many inventions, there tends to be argument as to who made it first. An Italian, Bartolomeo Cristofori, is usually credited with making the first *"harpsichord with soft and loud"*, by substituting hammers for the plucking of quills, he also used an escapement and dampers to achieve the effect, this was in about 1709. His invention did not prove particularly popular at the time, so he went back to making harpsichords. The Seven Years War drove many German workmen to England, among them twelve instrument makers, who became known as the "Twelve Apostles". Amongst them was one, J.C. Zumpe, who became famous for the invention and manufacture of the "Square Piano", around 1760. The pianoforte was probably first heard in England at about this time, with the first public performance at the Covent Garden Theatre in 1767, when it was announced that Dibdin would use in the accompaniment of a song a *"new instrument called a piano-forte.*

The following year saw what is believed to be the first solo appearance of the pianoforte, played in Dublin by Henry Walsh, the second, a couple of weeks later in London, played by J.C. Bach. The first piece of music composed specifically for the pianoforte, as opposed to the harpsichord, was probably a Clementi Sonata of 1773. In 1763, appeared the first advertisement in London for a piano, by Zumpe, for £50. The Square Piano, which was actually an oblong, was greatly improved by John Broadwood, who became Zumpe's partner and then his successor. At the time Broadwood died in 1812, it was reckoned that the London piano makers had become the finest in Europe. By 1830, there were reckoned to be 50 piano manufacturers in London. The Upright Piano, as opposed to a Grand Piano turned on its end, was first made in London, following its invention by Isaac Hawkins, an

Englishman living in Philadelphia, and perfected by Robert Wornum (Junior) in 1829. (15)

**

Occasionally the trade description could be deceptive. John Chaplin, when he became a Freeman in May 1831, described himself as a "Victualler" of The Spread Eagle, in Gracechurch Street. In this he did himself less than justice. The Chaplin family were into coaching in a big way. William Chaplin, his brother, who managed the Swan with Two Necks (or more accurately "nicks"), owned some 68 coaches, 1,800 horses and employed some 2,000. Our John ran the Spread Eagle in Gracechurch street, as can be seen in T.H. Shepherd's watercolour drawing below. Their father, also a John, ran the coaching business from Rochester in Kent. It is said that of the 27 mail coaches leaving London every night, William stabled 14 of them, ten from The Swan. He also managed The White Horse in Fetter Lane. Just to add to the Spectacle Makers connection, John married James Harmer's daughter, Clarinda.

**

The first Livery Dinner menu to appear in the Minutes is that for the dinner of 1832, a year resounding in history, with the Reform Bill and its repercussions, though no allusion to that in the Minutes. It was also noted that Dinners to the Livery were on a triennial basis, this being the fourth.

86 were present at the dinner, including presumably the Master and Wardens and the Court, though not stated, 42 Liverymen, the Lord Mayor and 8 other Aldermen and: *"several other highly respectable individuals"*, as if the Spectacle Makers Company ever had any other! The dinner cost 12/6d a head which included:

"Turtle, Bread, Beer, Dessert, Ice Creams and broken glass (either a new form of dessert or they had a somewhat smashing time) *Wines at bottle prices: Sherry and Port 6s., Champagne 10/6d., Claret 9s., Moselle 7s., Sauterne 7s. and Hock 10/6d. Tea and coffee 1/6d. a head or a 1s taking all who dine".*

The Minute goes on to state that: *"the Amount of Bill for the same was £104-13-0"*. Whilst on the subject of menus the Court also agreed Court Dinner menus at 6s. a head with dessert 1/6d. and Turtle 3s. extra. The Dinner to recognise the Company's 350th anniversary was somewhat more sophisticated, and probably with less broken glass, with the Guildhall a more upmarket address than the West India Dock Tavern, Blackwall, but did the drink flow quite so freely?

**

The first member of the Court of Assistants to be elected an Alderman was James Harmer. Thereafter members of the Court and of the Company became Aldermen, and subsequently Lord Mayor, which Harmer did not, with surprising frequency for a Minor

Company. As this is the first time the Minutes report in some detail.

The Court agreed a resolution at *"An Especial Court"* on the 7th March, 1833, which was to be: *"transcribed on vellum and framed"* and presented to Harmer by the Master and Wardens in person. In view of subsequent events it may be that the Court was mindful of obstructions which would be put in the way of Harmer subsequently becoming Lord Mayor when the resolution was drafted as follows:

"That the Cordial congratulations of this Court be presented to James Harmer, Esq., upon his recent Election to the ancient and honourable Office of Alderman of the City of London, assuring him that while the Court feels peculiar pride and gratification that he, a member of the same, and their late Master (in which capacity his lively anxiety for the Welfare of the Company is gratefully remembered) is thus Elevated to the Magistracy of this Metropolis of the British Empire, the Court in common with their fellow Citizens at large are deeply sensible also of the public advantages which must arise from his long experience and eminent knowledge in the Criminal Laws of this Country, attainments which cannot fail to enable him not only to protect the innocent but overawe the evil-doer, and thereby promote the best interests of this great City" – long sentences were a given in 19th century resolution writing!

In due course Harmer was elected Sheriff. At another *"Especial Court"* in August 1833, it was agreed: *"wishing to pay all due honors to Mr. Alderman Harmer at his inauguration"* that a Banner with the Company's Arms be provided, to join a Committee with the Weavers Company, the Mother Company of the other Sheriff, Alderman Wilson, and to go half shares in the hire of a Barge. The Clerk was instructed in due course to record the names of the members of the Court and Livery who attended the inauguration on the 28th and 30th September – in fact the whole Court attended together with some 7 Liverymen who attended: *"on the special invitation of Mr. Sheriff Harmer"*. In the Master and Wardens Account Book the expenses for the event were set out as follows:

Sashes	19-6
Cockades for coachman and Beadle	2-10-2½
Part hire of Barge	14-5-6
Coaches	16-0-0
Messengers	2-8
Gowns	7-15-0
Banners with Company Arms	18-18-0
Box for same	1-8-0
Total	61-18-10½

The Company got off lightly, as according to the *"London Weaver's Company"* by Alfred Plummer, the Weavers paid £120.7s.11d.!

The Minutes refer to an account from the *"Weekly Dispatch"*: *"pasted on the cover at commencement of this Book"* and there it is for all to see, running to in excess of a column. Whilst the report is largely factual, it has a sting in the tail. It stated that on Monday last, after meeting in Weavers' Hall and breakfasting at the London Tavern, the Sheriffs left about one o'clock (a pretty long breakfast) to arrive at the Mansion House: *"where the Lord Mayor joined them, and they proceeded in state to Guildhall, where several Aldermen and City Officers completed the procession, which then proceeded to Blackfriars Bridge, where state barges were in readiness to receive and convey them to Westminster. On reaching Palace-yard stairs the company landed and walked in procession to the Court of Exchequer. The barges were decorated with several beautiful flags and banners. A band of music also accompanied them, and their embarking and disembarking were, as usual, announced by salutes of guns from a temporary battery provided for the occasion"*. In Westminster Hall the Sheriffs were presented to the Cursitor Baron of the Exchequer for His Majesty's approval.

The report goes on its factual description, after a moan *"the admissions to the Court where the ceremony is gone through are necessarily select, for the place being small, few only can be accommodated, and from the anxiety of many to see the proceedings, the Court Room was crowded."* (today of course all tickets for the public would have been taken by Cooks Tours and the place would be full of foreign tourists! Rather like the Ceremony of the Keys! But I digress.). At three o'clock things got going, though the speeches seem to be a re-tread of what was said in Common Hall, and indeed in the Spectacle Makers Court resolution. The description of Sheriff Samuel Wilson *"who had for many years belonged to that class of which the country had good reason to be proud. He was a British merchant – and by his exertions acquired a competent fortune, which enabled him to retire from business, and devote his leisure hours and the experience he had acquired to the service and for the benefit of his fellow-citizens"* would have gone down well with a modern Tory Conference. After the inauguration there was some more ceremonial, and it was this to which our reporter took exception.

Having reported that, in Westminster Hall *"On the table were laid some horse-shoes of the most antiquated model, a canvas bag containing hob-nails, several small bundles of sticks, a small billhook and a diminutive hatchet"* (Those of you acquainted with modern City ceremonies will already know what's coming) *"the custom of counting hob-nails and chopping sticks was gone through. It commenced by the Crier of the Court proclaiming from the table "That the tenants of land in Salop and Saint Clement Danes must come forward and do the requisite suit and service, or forfeit their title to the same";* whereupon Alderman Winchester, as the senior Alderman below the chair, stepped upon the table and received from the Crier a small bill-hook, with which he cut asunder with one stroke a bundle of small sticks which the Crier held extended between his two hands. A small hatchet was then used for the same purpose with two or three other bundles, and the Alderman performed this duty most dexterously, never having occasion to make a second cut. Several horse-shoes were on the table, and the Alderman being asked their numbers answered six. A quantity of horse-shoe nails were then thrown from a bag upon the table, the number of which the Alderman declared to be sixty-one. This farce being concluded the company returned to their respective barges".

Also stuck to the cover of the Minute Book was a report of the Inauguration Dinner, again held at the London Tavern. The dinner was given *"in a style of splendour"* (perhaps the same reporter?). The Lord Mayor was present, and everyone sat down to dinner at six o'clock (later it is stated that the Lord Mayor and Sheriffs retired at about eleven – 5 hours! If this had been held at the modern Mansion House, lights would have been flashing on and off after about three hours! 5 hours and that Company would not be invited back - ever!). A couple of further points of note in the report the first of which I have to confess I do not understand – no doubt I shall be told. *"the Usual toasts of the King, Queen and Royal Family were drunk with* "three", *an essential improvement to the* "three times three" *for which we have to thank Lord Eldon's* "one more", *a surfeit to repletion".*

The second point is more obviously political points scoring. *"We observed that the Toasts of the King, Queen and Royal Family were drunk with the usual spirit, and that the succeeding toast, "His Majesty's Ministers", was received with an applause greater in the ratio of ten to one. However trivial or superfluous such things may appear, they are indicia of the age – and when the late Sheriffs returned thanks, and alluded to the infrequency of capital punishments, and to hope that they would be yet more* infrequent, the applause of the whole Company was immense. This is one of the very many of the indications of the state of public intellect and moral feeling, and is consolitary to humanity."

The report ends with the words *"The conviviality of the entertainment was remarkably well sustained throughout the evening"*. It had been a long day, whatever time breakfast was taken, and if the reporter had been Pepys he could justifiably have ended, *"And so to bed"*.

**

As James Harmer should have been our first Lord Mayor, a few words about him might be appropriate. James Harmer proved to be an interesting, an important and a contentious character. Even the basic facts about him are contentious. It is normally stated that he was born in London, the son of a Spitalfields weaver. However James himself, in the 1851 census, states that he was born in Norwich. The obituaries also state that he was orphaned at age ten. However only his father dies at that time, for his mother was party to his articles to study law in 1792. There also seems to be some doubt as to whether he was actually born in 1775, again as stated in the obituaries, or in 1777.

What is accepted is that he studied law, even if his studies were somewhat interrupted, as he was forced to transfer his articles to another firm of solicitors as *"he formed an attachment for a young lady, whom he afterwards married."* She bore him a daughter, some 18 months before the marriage, as Clarinda was born on the 28th January, 1800 and the marriage was on the 19th July, 1801. (Allegedly she was married to someone else when Clarinda was born). Whilst this might come within the term "interesting", it hardly makes Harmer "important".

His own law practice started in 1799, and had considerable success. He practised chiefly in the criminal courts, and his experience there made him a *"strong advocate of reform in criminal procedure"*. He exposed the shortcomings of witnesses, and especially the mode of obtaining evidence. He particularly investigated cases where he considered that prisoners had been wrongly committed. He specialised in using points of law to win the case, when the defendant was probably guilty. Perhaps Charles Dickens based Mr. Jaggers in *"Great Expectations"* on him, for Harmer knew Dickens through the Newsvendors Benevolent Institution, of which he was the first president and Dickens the second. It is also possible that W.S. Gilbert used him as a basis for his Judge in *"Trial by Jury"* who, you will remember:

*All thieves who could my fees afford
Relied on my orations,
And many a burglar I've restored
To his friends and his relations.*

By 1819, he had proved so successful that he was appearing as an expert witness before a Parliamentary committee for the reform of the criminal law. His evidence before that committee was declared by Sir James Mackintosh *"to be unequalled in its effect: he was held to have had great influence on both public opinion and parliamentary decision"*. Part of his evidence was later quoted in a case in Australia in the Superior Court of New South Wales, R. v Monkey and others (the defendants were Aborigines), of 1835. It arose on the question of whether speedy trials were fair to the accused, and what was the English practice The previous witness (to the committee) had stated that for the Old Bailey *"he had known one Middlesex Jury convict seventy-three persons at on sitting"*. Harmer argued *"that it was his intention to bring forward the present extremely objectionable practice of trying prisoners against time, before the Court of Aldermen, and if he could not obtain reform there, to carry the subject to a higher tribunal. The system, both at the Old Bailey and at the Middlesex Sessions in all cases except where the Judges preside, was calculated to bring the administration of criminal law into odium. The verdict of the Jury was the mere dictum of the Recorder-hundreds of innocent persons had been transported-females especially. His long experience in the practice of the Old Bailey enabled him to know, that the present system required thorough purgation".* Not a statement designed to endear himself to the Court of Alderman, which may have contributed to his later travails.

Looking to become involved in civic affairs, he was admitted to the Freedom and Livery of the Spectacle Makers Company on the 31st March 1824. He was elected to the Court of Assistants and duly took his place on the 6th October, 1825. By normal progression he became Renter Warden, twice in 1828 and 1829, Upper Warden in 1830 and Master in 1831. To complete his record with the Company he was a regular attender at Court meetings, except in 1848, until his death in 1853. In 1840, he was re-elected as Renter Warden *"as a mark of respect"* (for reasons you will find below) and again served that office the following year, was Upper Warden in 1842 and Master for second time in 1843.

Apart from his civic interests, Harmer involved himself in charitable works. As well as establishing the Newsvendors Benevolent Institution, he was President of the Society for providing asylum and relief for aged infirm Fishmongers and Poulterers and their wives and was Chairman of the first meeting of the London General Institution for the Gratuitous Cure of Malignant Diseases, subsequently known as the Royal Free Hospital.

By 1832, he was taking three partners into his practice in order to give more time to civic work. The following year he was elected

Alderman of the Ward of Farringdon Without, which he had represented as a Common Councillor since 1826. At the time of his election as Alderman he gave up his legal practice, said to be worth £4,000 a year. He was elected Sheriff in 1834. By 1840 he had become the Senior Alderman below the Chair, and would have expected to be elected as Lord Mayor. However he was also the proprietor of *"The Weekly Dispatch"*, which, at the time, was advocating very advanced liberal and independent religious and political views.

To judge the feelings this newspaper and its proprietor evoked, Lord Broughton in 1833, wrote *"Alderman Harmer, the attorney, who sits on the London bench to punish petty larceny, gets £3,000 or £4,000 a year by being the proprietor of the Weekly Dispatch, a paper which thrives on the worst of all crimes, the destruction of private and public character"*. (If that was true, Harmer would have done well in the 21st century). In the House of Lords the Bishop of London, and you should be aware that the *"Weekly Dispatch"* was published on a Sunday, said the paper *"prostituted press, in advocating a system of blasphemous infidelity, democratic plunder and gross licentiousness, the direct tendency of which is to subvert the whole of our social structure, and to revolutionise the property, the laws, the morals and the religion of the country"*. *"The Times"* wrote *"twelve powerful leaders against Harmer, which at once decided the question. This was a great assertion of power, and raised "The Times" in the estimation of all England"*. (16) After that, and a lot more in the same vein, including petitions, and added to the fact that the Tory faction was in power in the City, and Harmer was no Tory, he failed to be elected as Lord Mayor, and he immediately resigned as an Alderman.

In November, 1840, he retired permanently to the country, his wife and daughter having already died, and to the house he was rebuilding at Greenhithe. This he renamed Ingress Abbey, which according to the *"Weekly Dispatch"* of 1842, was *"a fine pile of a building in the Tudor Style of domestic architecture"*. His worth at his death was reckoned to be between £70,000 and £300,000.

He also left behind a little bit more gossip to add to the indiscretions of his youth. Eliza Cook, the Victorian poet, was a contributor to the *"Weekly Dispatch"*, and at one stage sued them for libel, though an apology righted the issue. She did however stay at Ingress Abbey on a number of occasions, sufficient evidence to cause people to speculate that she was Harmer's mistress. As she was a lesbian the explanation that she became firm, but platonic, friends with Harmer's granddaughter is much more likely. As has already been noted Harmer's daughter, Clarinda, married John Chaplin in 1823. (17)

As a footnote even after his death, in 1853, there was still mystery surrounding Harmer. The following notice appeared in the *"Daily Telegraph"* on the 24th April, 1855:

"To the Spectacle Makers Company, Brother Freemen are you aware that by the Will of the late James Harmer the Spectacle Makers Company are entitled to the residue of his property, which amounts to upwards of £100,000.

The bequest states that the amount is to be laid out in erecting such a number of almshouses as they, the Spectacle Makers Company may deem proper for the reception of decayed men and females who have held respectable stations in life, and borne good characters, and to whom pecuniary allowance shall be made, for their maintenance and support.

Brother Freemen – Exert yourselves, and see that your Company take the necessary steps to carry out the benevolent intention of the donor".

As the Company hasn't got, or had, any alms-houses one can only assume that the Freemen did not *"exert themselves"*.

P.S. In 1936, the Company was offered a portrait of Harmer, for

£50, but as they had no Hall in which to hang it, declined the offer.

**

On the 22nd October, 1834, Henry Colwell, truss maker, was admitted to the Freedom. His father was *"Principal Turnkey and Chum Man"*. I have been unable to find out what a "Chum Man" was I am afraid.

**

On the 12th December, 1834, another distinguished name was admitted to the Freedom and Livery, Nathaniel de Rothschild. He duly worked in the family merchant banking firm despite being part paralysed and virtually blind due to a fall out hunting. His interests really lay in wine and in 1853, he bought a vineyard near Bordeaux, which became known as Mouton Rothschild. With his uncle acquiring the neighbouring vineyard of Chateau Lafite, a healthy family rivalry soon developed. Unfortunately there is nothing in the Minutes which suggest that the Company got any discount on any of these wines.

**

Not long after the excitement of the election of James Harmer as an Alderman, and then Sheriff in 1833, came the election, in 1836, of two Liverymen of the Company to be the Sheriffs. John Johnson was already a member of the Court and was indeed the Upper Warden. James Duke, the other Sheriff, was not a member of the Court, though this was rapidly amended with his election in the October of 1836. When James Harmer was elected Sheriff in 1833 the costs of the inauguration were shared with the Company of the other Sheriff, the Weavers. This time all the arrangements, and costs, fell to the Spectacle Makers.

Captain Searle provided the Barge, for £26-5-0d., slightly less than last time. This time there were additional items:

"porterage of dresses (sic) *for the Watermen 6s. and for the*

washing of the same, before return to the Ironmonger's Company, 15s. Men to carry the Colors at 2/6d. each. Mr. Walker of the Blue Anchor, Coleman Street, engaged to provide the coaches at 30/-d. each including the fee to the Coachmen Favors to be provided for the Coachmen and Watermen and scarves for Captain Searle, the Beadle and Mr. Whithear head of Police."

In pencil beside this is written: *"It is usual for the Sheriffs to provide all the Scarfs and Favors"* so some expense was saved. Finally: *"Mrs. Couick, engaged to provide Livery Gowns at 5/d. each".*

The newspaper report, stuck in the Minute book, is this time from the *"Morning Herald"*. I quote it only in that it tells a little more about our two worthy Sheriffs. James Duke was a native of Montrose *"and in early life entered the civil department of his Majesty's Navy. In the year 1809 he served his country, under the command of Admiral Sir Peter Parker; he subsequently served under the command of Sir Richard Keats, Sir John Jones, and Lord Exmouth, and took an active part in those brilliant achievements which distinguished the career of the illustrious names he had mentioned. On the return of peace, Mr. Duke directed his attention to commercial pursuits, and had since that period carried on a successful business connected with the coal trade"*.

John Johnson *"had been equally successful in commercial pursuits, and had by industry, honesty, and integrity in business amassed a splendid fortune. He was the lessee of the celebrated Dartmoor quarries – he was also distinguished by his skill in the erection of several bridges – in the construction of docks – and, above all, in superintending that stupendous structure the Plymouth Breakwater"*. Johnson, when he came to reply, soon dispelled the self-made man bit by disclaiming *"the merit of being the architect of his own fortune – he succeeded to the business of his father, whose honourable exertions obtained for himself and his family an almost unprecedented career of success".*

**

In December 1837, the Clerk reported to the Court that:

"he had received an intimation from the Town Clerk respecting the attendance of the Livery of this Company to view the procession of Her Majesty to Guildhall to Dinner on the 9th November last, but as the Communication came to him so late, in his opinion no suitable arrangements could be made".

Now as John Sewell, the Clerk, worked in the Chamberlain's Office, he must have known all about the arrangements well in advance. Was this umbrage that a Minor Company had been invited so late, or perhaps it applied to all the Livery Companies, or perhaps Buck House were late "intimating" that Livery Companies were welcome.

Anyway feathers can't have been too ruffled as the Company Banners were used to decorate the Guildhall on the occasion. When they were returned they also included, from the Sheriffs:

"the Union Banner, with Pole and Truck, to be presented to the Worshipful Company of Spectaclemakers, in our names, in testimony of the high respect we have for the Members thereof".

**

Whilst it is carefully noted that *"no reporters were present"* for the Livery Dinner in 1837, the *"Morning Herald"* was there for 1839. He doesn't get off to a good start by referring to The Worshipful Company of Opticians but he soon gets into his stride. *"On the arrival of the lord mayor, at half-past five, the banquet was served; and it was equally worthy of the chief magistrate and creditable to the taste of the court of managers of the company. After the cloth was removed, and Non nobis domine was sung"* the speeches and the toasts began. I counted 8 toasts, to some of which there were two replies, the reporter noting *"spoke at some length"* in respect of 5 of the replies!

Eventually *"The Permanence and Prosperity of the Company" was drunk with great applause. Several songs and glees filled up the intervals between the speeches, and although many were present whose politics were strongly opposed to each other, yet the most perfect harmony and good feeling prevailed throughout the whole evening".*

I am at last becoming reconciled to the vast amount of food and drink that appears to have been consumed at these Victorian Dinners, though I appreciate that a diner was not expected to eat everything on the menu, merely make a choice. They needed it to keep going through, what appears to modern eyes, to have been an inordinately long evening. It is also strange to modern ears the reference to politics, presumably amongst the City luminaries. A proud boast of the modern Corporation of London used to be that it is above politics. Apparently not so their Victorian predecessors.

**

Whilst the Company Chaplain is very much part and parcel of the modern Spectacle Makers Company, this was not always so. At the December Court of 1837, it was resolved that:

"the Revd. John Jennings, M.A., Prebendary of Westminster, Rector of St. John's, in the same City, Chaplain to the late Sheriff Johnson (the then Master) *and a Freeman and Liveryman of this Company, be requested to accept the office of Honorary Chaplain to this Company".*

By the next Court, Jennings had replied, thanking the Court for the honour it had done him and:

> *"my honest intentions to do all in my power to contribute to the welfare and prosperity of the Company".*

Jennings had become a Freeman and Liveryman of the Company in 1837, during Johnson's Shrievalty. Presumably Johnson had enlisted Jennings into the Company in view of the fact that he, and others in the Company, would be proceeding to City office, and would require the services of a Chaplain. Jennings certainly became more involved with the Company, presenting his Banner to the Company in 1840, with the words:

> *"that I have performed no service to entitle me to such a privilege – I trust however that you will allow it a place among your splendid Banners, and regard it no less as a small proof of the lively interest I take in the prosperity of the Company, than as a humble tribute of sincere friendship to the merits of your indefatigable Master, on the auspicious occasion of his elevation to the Aldermanic Chair".*

**

The Livery Dinner of 1841, was to be held originally in July, at the West India Dock Tavern, Blackwall, the usual resort at this time. However:

> *"in Consequence of the Disposition of Parliament and the General Election, the said Dinner had by order of the Master and Wardens, been postponed sine die".*

It soon became dated for the 28th September at the London Coffee House, Ludgate Hill, where Court meetings were invariably held at this time.

The *"Morning Sun"* duly reported. Some 200 attended, included amongst whom were the Sheriffs, several Aldermen, *"several Members of Parliament, several members of the bar and a number of gentlemen connected with the arts, science, and literature"*. The report continues *"Sir James Duke made an excellent Chairman, and proposed the various toasts in a spirited and becoming manner, especially those of "Her Majesty" and "Prince Albert and the Princess Royal" so as to elicit very great applause. Indeed it was amusing to observe how cordially the Tories cheered the Queen, for, as a wag observed, "They thought they could now see her through their own spectacles, and she was indeed a Queen!" But politics formed no part of the hilarity of the evening. Every man magnified his neighbour through the medium of good cheer into an equality with himself, and certainly the various toasts were responded to with a cordiality of good feeling which did great honour to a company composed of such a diversity of public opinion*. Of the replies to the Toast *"The Navy and Army"* the one from the Navy which ended *"if war should hereafter arise, the enemies of England would find out that our Ordnance Board had made such improvements in the arts of destruction as would utterly astonish them"* was greeted with *"Great Applause"* and the reply from the gallant Colonel stating that the City of London *"had the distinguished honour of not only doing justice to her brave defenders by sea and land, but of proving her high sense their patriotic services by substantial and encouraging proofs of her good opinion (This expression was so truly correct that it elicited unbounded applause)"*. A jingoistic spirit was much abroad at this time.

The usual toasts followed, Heaven knows what the Toast List looked like, and at some stage a Member of Parliament, in replying to one of a myriad number of toasts, drew attention to the diversity of opinion in the House, which reminded him of *"Cowper's well-known lines on the dispute between the nose and the eyes as to* which the spectacles belonged, and that the question of right or wrong was much the same between the Honourable Members present and himself, for they all belonged to the House of "Ayes and Noes" – (Great laughter). The festivities of the evening terminated in great good feeling."

Maybe the knock-about humour of the evening does not come over so well on paper, or perhaps the wines referred to earlier in the report as *"of the first order"*, were decidedly more potent than those of the 21st century, but it does come over as a very heavy and portentous evening, rather than the riot of mirth implied. Of course in comparison with the modern Livery Dinner there was in the Victorian dinners a profusion of speeches and toasts, the penalty for getting, and enjoying, the food and drink free of charge!

**

The March Court of 1838, had come out with a very firm resolution in connection with the Livery Dinner, due to be held at the West India Dock Tavern, Blackwall in the June:

"That for the future no Servants be allowed to Dine at the expense of the Company, and that the Beadle be allowed 2/6d. of the funds of the Company in lieu of a Dinner."

Had the Clerk, then John Sewell, won the interminable battle, still being waged in the 21st century with places like the Mansion House by Clerks of Livery Companies, to stop the steady accretion of "hangers on" who were expected to be fed and watered by the hirer?

By the time of the next Livery Dinner, 27th June, 1839, the Committee meeting for the final arrangements agreed that:

"the Servants of the Lord Mayor and Sheriffs, and also the Servants of the Master and Wardens be allowed 2/6d. each in lieu

of Dinner".

Why the change of heart? Had the Servants thrown around the costly plate? Had the servants' union won? Or had the Master and Wardens, who formed the above mentioned Committee and who were involved or were about to be involved deeply in City affairs, decided not to rock the boat? We will never know!

**

As it happened the Dinner in 1838 had to be postponed as it clashed with the Coronation - Victoria's since you ask. It duly took place on the 4th July, a clash with Independence Day was at this time irrelevant and probably unappreciated, with Sir Moses Montefiore, one of the Sheriffs and a subsequent Liveryman, being invited. It was for this Dinner that the Court decided:

"having taken into consideration the pleasing circumstance, and being highly gratified that the Sheriffs of London and Middlesex in the past year were selected by our fellow Citizens from this Company of Spectaclemakers, namely Sir James Duke M.P. and John Johnson, Esq., both Members of this Court, and they have throughout their Shrievalty exhibited such superior abilities in the discharge of their duties and effected so much permanent good, particularly in the Metropolitan Prison, that much Honor is thereby reflected on this Company, - And the said Gentlemen, the late Sheriffs, having obtained by their merits deserved applause from the Court of Lord Mayor, Aldermen, and Common Council, as to receive an unprecedented mark of favour being each presented with a splendid piece of plate, with a suitable inscription thereon as a Memorial of their important services" – they loved their long phrases these new Victorians! The point of all this was that the Court wanted to ask the late Sheriffs: *"to Permit their said presents of costly plate to be placed on the Table to gratify their*

Brethren of the Livery with the view of so pleasing a Testimonial of their distinguished merit."

**

The cost of living was also going up in the 1840s. The Company paid 3/6d for each copy of the *"A Present from an apprentice"* given to each new Freeman. But three years later the cost had leapt to 3/9d for each. These little books came from Bumpus the bookseller and, as already noted, a member of the Company.

**

As an erstwhile philatelist, I had been surprised to find in a stamp magazine mention of a member of the Company. This was Robert William Sievier who had been admitted to the Freedom and Livery early in 1831. I only remembered him as, so far as I know, he is the only sculptor amongst our 15,000 odd members, though he did take an apprentice who never completed his apprenticeship, according to our records. Sievier started as an engraver but soon gave this up in favour of sculpture. He seems to have been quite successful producing portrait busts of Lord Eldon, Sir Thomas Lawrence and Prince Albert. He executed a number of memorial statues including those of Edward Jenner, Earl Harcourt and a large number of church monuments. He exhibited at the Royal Academy, the British Institution and at the Society of British Artists for a number of years. In his later years he devoted himself to science, being involved in rubber production and in the early development of electric telegraphy, all this according to Martin Greenwood's article in the *"Oxford Dictionary of National Biography"*.

The reason he was in the stamp magazine was that he had contributed a competition entry for the design of the first postage stamp. Rowland Hill had proposed in 1837, in order to tidy up the enormous anomalies which had developed in the delivery of the post, that the basic rate for letters be reduced to 1d., that letters would be charged by weight, and paid for by the writer and not the recipient. As a method of prepayment Hill proposed *"a bit of paper just large enough to bear the stamp, and covered at the back with a glutinous wash"* - the adhesive postage stamp was born. A competition was held for the design and Sievier's entry, which didn't win, was illustrated in the magazine. I don't know how successful Sievier was but by 1868, his widow, Ann Eliza, was a pensioner of the Company until her death in 1873.

**

On the 27th October, 1841, Edward Lloyd became Free of the Company, and a Liveryman on the 1st December that year, stating his occupation as that of a bookseller, some 34 booksellers and 14 publishers had joined the Company since the Freedom had been opened to all and sundry in the last century. Lloyd's claim to fame was to be as a publisher for he saw a gap in the market for cheap affordable fiction, which he was able to produce by using the recent innovations in printing, including the steam press. In 1835, he started publishing penny versions of the works of Dickens, such as *"The Penny Pickwick"* and *"Oliver Twiss"*. He was soon selling 50,000 a week. Dickens publishers sued him but lost, as Lloyd's defence was that his books were so bad that no one could mistake them for the real thing. The Dickens books were only part of his enterprise for he published a number of 'romances', featuring highwaymen, pirates and vampires aimed at the female market. Among his titles was *"String of Pearls"*, which introduced Sweeney Todd to the world, and these came to be called "Penny Dreadfuls" or "Penny Bloods".

He branched out into the newspaper world with *"The Daily Chronicle"*, and *"Lloyd's Illustrated London News"*, basing it on the success of *"The Illustrated London News"* which cost 6d., whereas his was much cheaper. To avoid the tax at the time it contained no "news" but was fictional or historical. The newspaper tax was repealed in 1855 and by 1896, six years after his death,

"Lloyd's Illustrated London News", now edited by his sons, was the first Fleet Street newspaper to sell more than a million copies.

Whilst Edward Lloyd has a blue plaque, on Water House, Walthamstow, his name is not as well known as Kemsley and the Burnhams, who may well have joined the Company later in the century, knowing that Lloyd was a Spectacle Maker, but his influence on Fleet Street may well have been equally as important as theirs proved to be. (18)

**

Every now and again something turns up in the records to give a Past Clerk pause for thought. In the Master and Wardens' Accounts for 1845, appears for four vocalists £12-12-0, which is fine but *"books of the songs for the Livery"*. It is perhaps unfair to judge just on the face of the evidence but the thought of a couple of hundred or so eminent Victorians, having had a large dinner and no doubt copious wine, all solemnly standing (perhaps not) and singing is just too much to contemplate.

**

For reasons which are not immediately obvious the Court decided in 1847, to hold the Livery Dinner not in the West India Dock Tavern in Blackwall, where they had been held for many years, but in the Star and Garter, Richmond.

The view of the Thames from the top of Richmond Hill was an ideal spot for an hotel. In 1738 the site had been leased by John Christopher from the Earl of Dysart. As the Earl was a member of the Noble Order of the Garter, the Star and Garter was flatteringly chosen as the name for the first inn, a small and unpretentious building. It was rebuilt in 1780, and a large private house was added, which subsequently became part of the hotel. In 1808, the inn being now large enough to provide overnight accommodation, one Christoher Crean, *"sometime cook to the Duke of York"* took over, refurbished the place and overcharged for everything. *"It was said that a visitor paid half a sovereign for the privilege of looking through one of its windows"*. He died in 1815, and his executors ordered the sale of the hotel to pay off the mortgage. With its purchase in 1822, by Joseph Ellis, whose family ran it for the next forty or so years, came real success.

Joseph Ellis ran it as a flourishing and fashionable meeting place. It was described in 1825, by John Evans as *"more like the mansion of a nobleman than a receptacle for the public; looking down with stately aspect from the adjoining valley, and seen to advantage from every point of the horizon. Hither, in the summer season, crowd visitants from the overgrown Metropolis, to inhale the pure air and exhilarate their spirits by contemplating widespreading circumference of rural scenery"*. How could the Court resist such blandishments!

The Assembly Room was the fashionable place to hold wedding receptions and balls. Louis Philippe stayed there for six months after his flight from Paris. Napoleon III had apartments there. Dickens gave a dinner for friends every year in a private room to celebrate his wedding anniversary. By the 1850s as many as 560 dinners were served on Sundays. It was here that the Spectacle Makers Livery Dinner came on the 7th July, 1847.

After that for the Star and Garter it was all downhill. It was purchased by a limited liability company, the then current invention, and was rebuilt in the style of a French renaissance chateau. This did not appeal to at least one correspondent to *"The Times"* who described it as *"gross, pretentious, common, impudently obtrusive, it stood out, a great disfiguring wart or wen on the face of Richmond Hill"*. That letter should have done much for the entente cordiale! Two fires in 1870 and 1888 destroyed what remained of the old Star and Garter. In 1915, the hotel was presented to Queen Mary, then Patron of the British Red Cross, for use as a hospital, but was soon found to be too small and unsuitable for this purpose.

It was finally demolished in 1919, to make way for the present building, the Royal Star and Garter Home for Disabled Sailors, Soldiers and Airmen which was principally paid for by the women of the British Empire who adopted it as their war memorial. (19)

**

The Court kept itself advised of its position in the City World for in 1847, the Clerk paid 4/6d for 11 copies of the *"Sunday Times"* so that members of the Court could read the write-up of the Livery Dinner. Things have no doubt changed, but it was suggested to the Clerks in the 1970s and 80s that they should play down the "eating and drinking" aspects of the Livery Companies, to put the emphasis on any "trade" activity in which a particular Company was involved in the report of a Livery Dinner. This was not well received by all Masters, who like everyone else, wanted their moment in the sun to be registered in all the right places.

**

In 1849, the Court gave Mrs. Shirley and her daughter £10 to start a school in South Petherton. Perhaps the one I attended briefly on being evacuated there?

**

I have commented before on the, to us, useful habit of including cuttings from newspapers in the Court Minute Books, usually stuck in the inside of the covers. The 1843 to 1853 book is no exception.

The Lord Mayor of 1849, the Master of the Company, Sir James Duke, entertained the Livery to Dinner at the Mansion House. The write-up is interesting in two respects. Firstly it is stated that *"covers were laid for 250, and we believe not less than 230 took their places"*. Unless this was the habit of the time, a modern Clerk of the Company would be tearing his, or her, hair out at this waste of money and discourtesy!

More to the point was the opening remarks of the Lord Mayor who in proposing "*The health of the Spectacle Makers' Company*" said " *after expressing his gratification at having been three times elected Master of that ancient company, although it could not, like the Goldsmiths' or the Merchant Tailors, and many other of the companies of the city of London, claim the honour of being possessed of those ancient halls which had, from the earliest history, been transmitted with other important rights and privileges to their present possessors, yet he would venture to say that no company could boast of a more distinguished list of members. Amongst them they had the honour to possess men whose names had been distinguished in the navy and army, in the law, and in the extensive commercial pursuits for which the citizens of London were so celebrated. They numbered in their list the names of Rothschild, of Baring, of Stone, of Mildred, of their esteemed friend Mr. Wilson (who they were all proud to see), and who had once represented the city of London, and of a gentleman who had achieved for himself a European reputation by the erection of their noble Exchange* (he meant William Tite). *They also claimed as one of their members Mr. Cubitt, whose name had been connected with some of the most important works of modern times, and who had only recently served the office of sheriff, with the greatest credit to himself and the city of London".* This is a real indication that, putting aside the puffs, the Company was really coming of age and punching above its weight as a "minor" livery company.

**

There was the odd word of criticism appearing as well, I don't suppose the media has changed that much. In a report of the Livery Dinner at the Castle Tavern, Richmond in June, 1850, the writer, who probably got in free, states *"the livery enjoyed an excellent dinner placed before them; the only drawback being, that it was nearly cold before it reached the mouths of the guests, either from the small number of waiters or their want of tact in distributing it. The mock turtle soup was complained of as not being such as was usually found at the Castle, probably from this cause".*

Mark you today the mere mention of mock turtle soup would have the protesters out in force, be it hot or cold, and no doubt health and safety issues also would be raised, somewhere and sometime. I must be growing old and, breathe it not in Gath, not gracefully!

**

In 1852, a pensioner, Mrs. Jones, was granted £1 to visit: *"her native place in Wales for the re-establishment of her health".*

**

In 1852, a Bill was introduced into Parliament by the Corporation of London, which affected the voting rights of Freemen and Liverymen. The Livery Companies assembled in all their might, led by the Mercers' Company, to oppose. A Steering Committee was established, and in July the Bill was "thrown out" by a Committee of the House. In due course the Mercers asked the Company to sub up for its contribution to the expenses, £15 *"as a Class 3 Company"*, the classification based upon financial means rather than precedents.

At the Court on the 10th January, 1856, a letter is received from George Sutton stating inter alia:

"being unable to obtain a settlement of my Account in relation to the opposition to the City of London Corporation Bill I am compelled to take proceedings to recover the amount", the amount was £1,463-2-0, it was resolved that *"No Order be made thereon"*. The matter was subsequently referred to the Company's solicitors Messrs Palmer, Palmer and Bull. They duly reported that:

"Mr. Sutton has taken no steps towards the Special Case, or even sending us the draft of a Case since the Trial, as the Verdict at present stands against the Company, I do not think it advisable to take any steps to drive him on... in view of fees and other disbursements. we trust we are not asking too much in requesting a draft for about £200 (say £200) on account of costs generally".

I do admire the legal habit of fee charging – work out the figure, add on a profit margin, and then "say" a figure, as if they were doing the client a favour. Rather like the mark-up procedure of opticians – in the eighteenth and nineteenth century I mean of course!

To get back to the issue in hand (another legal cliché), a Special Court was summoned for the 5th November, 1857. As only two members turned up it tends to show how heavily the matter was weighing on the Company's conscience. However, undeterred, the two members prepared a report. It appears that the Bill of Costs amounted to £228-11-6 of which £107-18-8 had: *"actually disbursed out of Pocket"*. They recommended payment of the £200 and: *"with reference to so serious a matter as this action"* that they form a Standing Committee empowered to take action. Two Court meetings later this was agreed, and the payment (of £228-11-6) made. The Clerk had to sell two Exchequer Bills, the investment the Court was currently favouring in lieu of the 3% Consols, to pay the bill.

There the matter appears to have rested. Who delayed what, or was the slow progress at that time standard procedure? I don't think the Minutes give us the whole story. I don't believe that the £1,000 plus requested can possibly have been the costs for the Spectacle Makers only. What about the other Companies? No I haven't done those enquiries just yet – perhaps some time in the future I might get round to it. What's the hurry?

**

In due course, some 200 hundred years too late, a Standing Committee of Finance was convened, which was to provide an abstract of the accounts, to come before each Quarter Court. Its first report was on the 30th June, 1853, covering the period 31st December, 1851 to April 1853. Two small errors noted in five Quarterly accounts: *"show the propriety of a regular Audit"*. The Clerk was acting as Treasurer, collecting and receiving its income, making payments as directed, or at his discretion, and retaining in his hands the balances, until invested by Order of the Court.

"The prosperity of the Company, and amount of its income, as well as its numbers, and reputation, have greatly increased under the zealous, and judicious, management of its affairs by Mr. John Sewell, who has been the Clerk for 44 years."

In 1809, there were 237 Freemen, 24 Liverymen, and the amount of Stock (in South Sea Stock) was £250. The comparisons in 1853, were 1928, 374 and £9,600 (in 3 % Consols) respectively. There was a discussion of saving costs, advertising was £36 and printing £32. It was recommended that advertisements for summoning of Common Hall be discontinued:

> *"except on Special occasions and when one of the Livery is a Candidate for Election there; and in such cases one advertisement in one newspaper only be inserted. It does not seem expedient that such Advertisements should be altogether abolished, as though mere form in most respects they tend to assert and maintain the rightful connection of the Company with the Corporation, in cases where the Company is entitled to take part."* (Such advertising was still going on when I came in 1965).

**

The Standing Committee of Finance also recommended a new introduction:

> *"a rough Minute Book shall be kept in two columns, in which the Agenda for each Court shall be entered, and the rough Minutes of its Orders, Resolutions and proceedings written down, from which the Minutes shall afterwards be drawn out and entered."* (It's a pity that the rough minutes up until 1853, were not kept, as they would make more sense of the highly abbreviated "official record").

These recommendations should not be taken as a criticism of the way that John Sewell had been conducting the business. More of a reflection of the fact that the Company had now grown considerably in number, stature, financial standing and City respect, and required an internal organisation to match.

**

In 1861, John Meyer aged 60, disabled and on hard times, petitions the Company requesting help to open a school in Jersey. Given a donation of £10. When he was admitted to the Freedom Meyer was a wharfinger. I don't how much the donation helped him, as he died in October, 1863.

**

Samuel Smiles was another of our well-known, non-spectacle maker. Not a name to conjure with these days, though he does still have three quotes in *"The Oxford Dictionary of Quotations"*. Smiles was well-known in the 19th century, his influence lasting into the 20th. He was born in Haddington, Scotland, the son of a papermaker, in 1812. Leaving school at 14 he was apprenticed to a doctor, before enrolling at Edinburgh University to study medicine. After working as a doctor for a time, his interests turned to politics, coming under the influence of Jeremy Bentham, Joseph Hume and John Stuart Mill's father, James, and the Chartists in general. In 1838, he moved to Leeds to edit the radical *"Leeds Times"*. After campaigning for parliamentary reform, free trade, extension of the suffrage, and better conditions for factory workers, he became disillusioned with politics and increasingly advocated personal development. He changed careers and became a railway administrator, first as Secretary of the Leeds and Thirsk Railway, before moving to London, to take the same post with the South Eastern Railway, at their offices in Cannon Street. It is here where he becomes involved with the Spectacle Makers Company, becoming Free of the Company on the 24th November, 1854.

In 1859, he published his most famous work *"Self-Help"*. Based on the Victorian values of industry, thrift and personal progress, it was so popular at the time that it had a status second only to the Bible. He used biography as the basis of his book, each chapter giving a potted history of a person, e.g.: Sir William Herschel, who was a travelling oboist before becoming curious about astronomy, and ending up as astronomer to the King; Bernard Palissy, a poor potter who threw his own furniture into the furnace to initially create his enamel ware, ending as potter to the French throne, and Granville Sharp, a clerk who in his spare time began the anti-slavery movement, eventually getting the Courts to recognise that slavery was illegal. The examples were to illustrate how tenacity, industry and endurance were essential to success. In the lives of the artists it was their industry as much as their artistic talent which had enabled them to succeed. Michelangelo was prepared to lie on his back for months on end to paint the Sistine Chapel ceiling, and it had taken Titian 7 years to complete *"The Last Supper"*. What the world proclaims as a "burst of genius" may, on examination, prove to be the end product of hard and laborious graft.

"Self-Help", it has to be admitted, is sexist. There is not a single female mentioned in it, which may account for its waning popularity. (Nowadays of course self-help has been replaced by "someone else has to help me, and take the blame"). Smiles went on to write other books with typically Victorian titles, *"Character"*, *"Thrift"* and *"Duty"*. He also wrote biographies of men who through hard graft had achieved their success, George Stephenson, and Josiah Wedgewood and in 1861, *"Lives of the Engineers"*, all men needless to say.

Smiles lives on in this day and age, if at all, through oft-quoted quotes:

a place for everything, and everything in its place
he who never made a mistake, never made a discovery
life will always be to a large extent what we ourselves make it
the reason so little is done, is generally because so little is attempted
the shortest way to do many things is to do only one thing at once

All so self-evident one would have thought that their author should not so much have obtained fame as the comment "So?" But then at the time of his writing the concept of self-improvement was largely unappreciated. (20)

**

It is not always easy to come across contemporary and informal mention of individual Freeman and Liveryman outside of the Minutes. However Edward Callow in *"Old London Taverns"* mentions a Spectacle Maker who became Lord Mayor, one Sir Francis Moon.

"At the corner of Threadneedle Street, on the eastern side of Finch Lane was the shop of Alderman and sometime Lord Mayor, Sir Francis Graham Moon, Bart, the great print publisher and seller of his time. Alderman Moon was created a baronet on the occasion of the visit of the Emperor and Empress of the French to the City on April 5th, 1855. A portrait of him is to be seen in one corner of the engravings of the 'Waterloo Banquet'".

As he was not at the event he looks very much out of place, particularly as he is the only one in the picture not in uniform of one kind or another. When the painting was first seen by the Duke of Wellington, for whom it was painted, *"he gave vent to very forcible language, and ordered it to be painted out, declining to accept the picture till it was so"*. But Moon had obtained the artist's copyright and published the engraving. Thus all engravings of the painting include this appearance by Moon, though not the original painting.

According to Callow, Moon was the subject of a number of jokes in *"Punch"* for many years, particularly during his Shrievalty and Mayoralty. Callow goes on to write *"I personally knew Sir Francis Moon well. His manner had an air of 'empressement' about it, almost overpowering; he was so extremely bland. He was not a bad sort of fellow altogether, but his effusiveness and conceit were frequently just a leetle 'de trop'. He was appointed printseller to the Queen; and as new works of art were ready for publication it was* his custom and his duty to take them to Windsor or Buckingham Palace, wherever the Court might be at the time, to submit them to her Majesty and the Prince Consort for inspection. Here he was more bland and effusive than ever – polite and deferential he, no doubt, considered it – so much so that the Prince was wont to exclaim, whenever his visits to the Palace were announced, 'Oh that fulsome little man again'". (11) (Now I know from whence Prince Phillip got the idea of how Royal Consorts should act!)

I had wondered why such a distinguished Liveryman had not been invited to join the Court of Assistants, perhaps they weren't so daft after all.

**

The Company was still active in looking after its own. The Court on the 30th December, 1858, considered the petition of Catherine Sarah Benson. She was the widow of a silversmith who had died the previous year insolvent. She had three infant children. In order to make ends meet she:

"opened a small shop in the fancy line at Erith in Kent" in a short time: *"her children were attacked one after the other by Scarlet fever, one of whom has died of it, - this severe visitation has quite ruined her little business, in consequence of the infectious nature of the disease, and being therefore compelled to attend and nurse her children herself".*

The Court having considered the petition decided that because of her age, 27, and the fact that some very respectable friends: *"who have and are likely to continue to assist her, that having lost one of her children, and the other two restored to health, - her business again improving"* they could not offer her a pension, but gave her a donation of £5.

**

1858 is the year of "The Great Stink". This was a steady culmination of a number of causes. Brick sewers had been built in the City since the 17th century, when the Fleet and Walbrook rivers had been part covered for that purpose. Further sewers had been constructed over the years, amounting to some 360, the problem was that they all eventually flowed, or over-flowed, into the Thames. In time the wooden and brick sewers were replaced with iron, which improved the flow. With the increase in population and the introduction of flushing toilets, together with the outfalls from factories, slaughterhouses and other industrial activities, the system eventually just could not cope. Remembering also that London's "improved supply" of drinking water came from the Thames.

This did not go unmentioned. Michael Faraday writing to the *"Times"* in 1855, on an experiment he had conducted of dropping pieces of paper into the river to test its opacity wrote *"near the bridges the feculence rolled up in clouds so dense that they were visible at the surface... the smell was very bad and common to the whole of the water."* Dickens had said that the Thames was *"a deadly sewer... I can certify that the offensive smells, even in that short whiff, have been of a most head-and-stomach-distending nature".* Another writer had noted that *"in parts the deposit is more than six feet deep on the Thames foreshore".* So to all the problem was obvious, the solution more of a puzzle.

In healthcare at this period it was considered that the transmission of contagious diseases was due to the miasma theory, which argued that most communicable diseases were caused by the inhalation of contaminated air. The contamination could come from the odour of rotting corpses, sewage, rotting vegetation and the exhaled breath of the dead. All agree that it was miasma which accounted for the transmission of cholera. London's first cholera epidemic was in 1831, when 6,536 died, in 1848/49, 14,137 died and in 1853/54, 10,738. John Snow, a physician, noted that the incidence of the disease was greater in certain areas which were served by the Lambeth, Southwark and Vauxhall water companies. He suggested that the disease was water-borne, he was ignored. However in 1854, Snow narrowed his research to Broad Street and removed the handle of the local water pump, which resulted in a fall in the number of deaths, bearing out his argument as to the disease being water-borne. It was later established that the well had a leaking sewer running nearby.

By June 1858, the shade temperature in London averaged the mid 30s Centigrade (93-97F) and rose as high as 48 (118F) in the sun, which, together with an extended period of dry weather, caused a drop in the level of Thames water, leaving raw effluent on the banks. Queen Victoria and Prince Albert attempted a trip on the river, which ended after a few minutes because of the smell. The press soon coined the phrase the "Great Stink". The *"City Press"* observed that *"Gentility of speech is at an end – it stinks, and whoso once inhales the stink can never forget it and can count himself lucky if he lives to remember it"*. Up to 250 tons of lime were spread around the mouths of the sewers and on the foreshore. In Parliament the curtains on the riverside were soaked in lime chloride to overcome the smell. It didn't really work, but at last Parliament acted. Disraeli introduced the Metropolis Local Management Amendment Bill and, in opening the debate, referred to the Thames as *"a Stygian pool, reeking with ineffable and intolerable horrors"*. The Bill put the responsibility of clearing up the Thames on the Metropolitan Board of Works, adding that as far as possible the sewage outlets should not be within the boundaries of London, it also allowed the Board to borrow £3 million, to be repaid by a levy of 3d. on all London households.

Fortunately the Board had been giving some serious thought to the problem and the plan proposed by Joseph Bazalgette was adopted. In brief the scheme proposed some 1,100 miles of additional street sewers to collect effluent and rainwater, which would drain into 82 miles of main sewers, which would be gravity fed with the aid of various pumping stations, and onto the outfalls. The scheme included both the North bank and the South bank of the Thames. The North bank development produced the Victoria, Chelsea and Albert Embankments. Bazalgette's first estimate was for £2.4 million but, as with most big schemes, a further £1.2 million was lent to the MBW in 1863. The scheme was eventually finished in 1875, and whilst the stench did not instantly go away at least "something was being done" rather than everybody shaking their heads whilst holding their noses, and conditions steadily improved. (21)

**

From time to time the Court ordered letters to be entered in the Minute Book. These are mostly Petitions from widows in parlous circumstances, which the court regularly supported if the deceased husband had duly paid his Quarterage, and which are appearing with monotonous regularity in the 1860s.

At the meeting of the 3rd October, 1861, a letter from a Mr. W. Winn appeared:

Dear Sir, Last evening I had the pleasure of dining at the Spectaclemaker's Dinner, and for so large a Company I am bound to say it really was a very excellent one, as however I and six or seven of my friends could not without injury to our health, drink Port Wine, I ordered two bottles of claret for which Twenty One Shillings was demanded of me by the Waiter, now as I have not the good fortune at present to be one of the Court, and only get one Dinner a year, I can hardly imagine that the Master and Wardens wish me to pay for my own Wine, when they do honor me with an invite to dine with them, - I beg you will understand that it is not the value of the Money that I ask you to remit me the Guinea, as I shall feel very happy to place it in the Company's poor Box immediately I receive it".

There was a PS to the effect that he was going to Hamburg for a couple of weeks and hoped he would be favoured with a reply on his return. He had written in July and the reply, also entered in the Minutes, is dated October:

"I am directed to inform you that they (the Court) *are unable to make the return required by you, as it would be inconsistent with the usual practice of the Company, to allow any other Wine arrangements than those which have always hitherto been adopted."*

It all seems a little odd that such a letter would deserve immortalising by entry into the Court Minutes. Presumably there was red wine on the menu in any case, and a polite request for a refill should not have been a problem – perhaps deeper waters (wines) here run. I must admit the thought of such a request, and the likely answer from the waiter in the Egyptian Hall these days, gives rise to some wry thoughts.

**

In the newspaper report of the Livery Dinner for July, 1862, Alderman Rose, whilst enforcing my view that it was Sewell, the Clerk, who did most to attract such a powerful Livery, was not above doing some electioneering. He was reported as saying *"that his success in life was coeval with that of the Company, for when he first came as a young man into the City, Mr. Sewell found him out, and induced him to join the Spectacle-makers company, which to the present time, had been a source of unmixed gratification. Before sitting down, he would just say that, having filled the post of Alderman and Sheriff, he was still anxious to fill the higher office of Lord Mayor, and if the citizens did him the honour of placing him in that position of responsibility, he would assure them that they should not have reason to feel that they had made a mistake (Cheers).* He was duly elected later that year, so the point registered with some of the electorate.

In the same report was the reply of a Mr. Chapman to the Toast *"The trade and commerce of the City of London, coupled with the health of Mr. Chapman."* I am not aware of whether the said Mr. Chapman was a known wit, but one hopes so by the terms of his reply. *"Mr. Chapman begged to thank them for the compliment which had been paid him in drinking his health. He never aspired to the honours to which some of his friends did, but to be a respectable and honourable member of the greatest City of the world, was his ambition. They had drunk the health of Sir James Duke, but here was he (Mr. Chapman) without a single decoration, and not even a gold clasp, although he had rendered most important services to his country. (Laughter|) They might laugh, but it was a serious matter, and he hoped they would sympathise with him, when he said that John Chapman was at the Battle of Copenhagen in 1801 with Lord Nelson, and in arms with that gentleman, and yet he had no medal; but, nevertheless, he felt quite rewarded by the sympathy they had expressed towards him this evening, and he asked them if they had not reason to be proud of such a hero as John Chapman, who had come out of such an engagement in the arms of his nurse without a scratch or a wound. (Great laughter)".*

At 150 or so years ago it is perhaps not surprising that the sense of humour may have changed. Rather like someone of my generation trying to find something to laugh at in "Little Britain".

**

Until settling in Apothecaries' Hall in the 20th century the Court meetings moved round various hostelries and function rooms around the City (see Appendix III for a full list). They seemed to have chosen places of which we know little, the Rayne Deare where they first met for example. However the Albion, where the

Court met between 1853 and 1902, we can learn a little about from Edward Callow. (11)

He also mentions, in passing, the importance, or not at that time, of the Freedom and Livery. *"The first time I dined at the Albion was in 1846, when I found it necessary to purchase my freedom of the City of London, and become a liveryman of a city company. From a variety of causes I elected to become a "Plasterer", and the most important part of the ceremony attendant upon my being admitted to the livery, after paying a good round sum for my fees, was my attendance at the court dinner at the Albion"*. So much for the importance of membership of a Livery Company!

The Albion he notes has neither bar nor tap-room and is the dining place for many of the City companies who have no hall of their own *"and of several others who have, but who wisely prefer the comforts and excellence to be obtained at the Albion"*. Many City dinners not held at Guildhall, the Mansion House or at a Livery Hall of one of the Great Companies, took place at the Albion, the East India Company held dinners there for newly appointed Governors of India.

The last time Callow had eaten at the Albion was some fifty or so years after his admission dinner *"and there are few things that better show the progress in the refinement and style of such entertainments, during the long period that has passed, than the difference between these two entertainments.*

At the first dinner the menu was of the same excellent quality, but there was more 'solid' character about it. That there was turtle soup goes without saying – a city feast without it is a poor sort of 'one horse-affair' – fish of the very best, and served to perfection. It was the first time I ever tasted John Dory, and I have never since been surprised that Miss Ann Chovy should have lost whatever part of her that represents a fish's heart, to such an exceedingly nice young fellow. (Callow has that style of humour). *There was also Warden*

Pie. I had read of, but never before partaken of it. Several other dishes, inclined to be substantial as well as savoury, were served, besides joints, poultry, and game. The only wines put upon the table were sherry and port, and the bottles were passed round in the good old-fashioned style, travelling with the sun from right to left, and few there were who shirked filling up their glasses.

At the time it was the fashion to remove the white cloth; the dessert and decanters being set out on the bare, bright, polished mahogany table. In the centre of the table were placed long church-warden clay pipes and brass boxes of tobacco. I forget whether cigars were there as well, for at that time I was not a smoker, and their absence or presence did not attract my attention.

The amount of wine drank(sic) was 'extensive'; and several of the elder Plasterers were in different states of merriment or drowsiness, as their potations affected them. There was some singing by such of the company as could or would oblige, and of course there were the usual toasts and speeches. The Loving Cup was passed round from one to the other, starting from the Master's right hand. The toast given by each one to the other on handing the Loving Cup was the motto of the Plasterers' Company - Let Brotherly Love Continue. Before I left, punch and toddy were brought on, but as I had learned well the lesson of the Irish priest, when giving his parting advice to Charles O'Malley – 'Never sit with your back to the fire – never fight with your face to the sun – and never mix your liquor', I prepared to take my departure after having greatly enjoyed the Albion port.

At the last dinner I attended everything was entirely different and in conformity with the latest fashion of the day – Autres temps, autre moeures. The tables were eloquently laid; and with flowers and dessert looked quite charming. Everything was perfection, and served in smart recherche style, and an unlimited supply of sparkling and light wines was placed upon the table. Port and

Madeira were there for those who preferred them.

After the Loving Cup had passed round, the usual toasts were drunk, and boxes of very excellent cigars were continually handed round by the very attentive waiters. At intervals between the toasts and speeches, professional singers gave a very welcome and pleasing selection of vocal music. 'There were no pipes', and not one of the guests was ineligible to enter a drawing-room and join the ladies, had there been any present".

**

Whilst in the 1850s/60s the Company's status in the City was getting higher and higher, with 12 Lay Sheriffs, and 9 Lord Mayors up to 1870, and a large number of Common Councillors, with highly rated and well attended Livery Dinners, the Company's governance was not receiving such close attention. While there was an established quorum for Court meetings, a number of meetings were postponed as being inquorate, by the 50s and 60s meetings were continuing with only two members present. Admittedly, according to the Minutes, about all that happened in the meeting was the admission of Freemen and Liverymen, the handing out of charity and agreeing the dates for Court and Livery Dinners, so perhaps busy City men had something better to do.

Sometimes it was accident at work. In 1856, there was a motion to increase the number of Assistants, at that time 8 with Master and Wardens making a full Court, but it was correctly pointed out that the Charter would not allow this. It didn't help that within the space of a couple of years there had been 3 resignations and 5 deaths.

**

In 1856 and 1857, Frederick Salmon was Master. The Election Court of 1857, was inquorate and thus the existing officials, which included Salmon, continued in office. Salmon was a rectal surgeon, who had had some difficulty in obtaining a hospital position, so in the end established his own hospital, St. Mark's in London. After his death the British Medical Journal was a bit sniffy, suggesting that as he couldn't find a career in a general hospital the establishment of his own hospital was, *"contrary to the interests of the profession and the public".* As such specialisation as Salmon had pioneered became the norm later in the century, and as St. Mark's was to develop rectal and colorectal surgery and gastroenterology, perhaps he was ahead of his times, and the fact that Salmon made a lot of money with private patients was the real niggle with the B.M.J. (22)

**

The number of Liverymen is stated as 342 in 1852. In April of that year the cab hire to Mercers' Hall and 4 times to the House of Commons was a total of £5.

**

Unless in a particularly cynical mood, one does not normally associate prison with members of the Spectacle Makers Company. However in November 1855, one John Weatherhead, obtained his Freedom of the Company, his occupation stated as "Governor of Newgate". A few years later in 1859, perhaps at the suggestion of Weatherhead, though it is always dangerous to speculate on uncorroborated evidence, George Hicks was admitted, who was the Governor of the White Cross Street Prison. Hicks appears to be a serving officer, a captain, in the Army.

Newgate had a chequered career. It was the 5th gate into the City, and there are records indicating that it was used to house criminals as early as 1218. In 1422, a licence was granted to the executors of Richard Whittington, to *"re-edify the gaol of Newgate".* By the end of the 16th century it had to be *"new fronted and new faced".* It was burnt down in the Great Fire, re-built, and finished in 1672.

One of its famous prisoners, in 1670, was Claude Duval the dancing highwayman. He was renowned for his courtesy and attention to the ladies. Walter Pope describes his most famous exploit where Duval and his gang stopped a coach with a knight and his lady inside.

Duval begged the lady to dance and, to the music of a flageolet, *"they danced and here it was that Du Val performed marvels, the best master in London, except those that are French, not being able to show such footing as he did in his great riding boots"*. Returning the lady to her carriage, he levied a charge on the knight *"for the music."* During his time in prison one report states *"never had a prisoner such a concourse of people come to see him"*. The Old Bailey was packed for the two days of his trial, for public opinion was divided between hanging and clemency. There was a massive crowd at his hanging two days later! (23)

Claude Duval by William Powell Frith.

Conditions in the prison, even by the standards of the day, were atrocious. *"The water supply inadequate, ventilation almost non-existent and the stench appalling"*. Newly arrived prisoners were bullied and robbed, not only by their fellow prisoners but also by the turnkeys, who made big profits from the sale of spirits, candles, food and water. They also charged fees for a number of privileges, including being released from irons. Prisoners who could afford to do so were allowed to sleep in more salubrious parts of the prison. Henry Fielding observed that a London Prison, of which Newgate was the most famous example, was *"both a prototype of Hell and one of the dearest places on earth"*.

Amongst famous names incarcerated during these years were Titus Oates, William Penn, Daniel Defoe, Jonathan Wild and Jack Sheppard, famous for his various ways of escaping from the various prisons in which he found himself. His last escape had been from a cell on the third floor of the 60-foot high tower above the gate that spanned Newgate Street. He had been handcuffed, manacled and chained to the floor prior to his escape! So famous had he become that on his recapture and incarceration in Newgate, people flocked to see and talk to him in the Condemned Hold. Sir James Thornhill, the Serjeant Painter to the Crown, no less, painted his portrait there.

The building from which Sheppard escaped, and from which he was subsequently hanged, was pulled down and re-built yet again, this time from a design of George Dance the Younger and finished in 1778, just in time to be badly damaged by fire in the Gordon Riots of 1780.

Peter Ackroyd (24) states that the Gordon Riots were *"the most violent and widespread riot of its* (London's) *last thousand years.....it started as a demonstration against legislation in favour of Roman Catholics, but quickly turned into a general assault upon the institutions of the state and the city...if ever London came close to a general conflagration, this was the occasion. It was the most significant rebellion of the poor in its entire history ...the firing of Newgate, and the release of its prisoners, remains the single most astonishing and significant act of violence in the history of London"*. Newgate's fate was probably sealed at an early stage of the riot, when a body of Horse Guards surrounded and escorted some of the rioters to Newgate Prison! Four poets witnessed the scene, Blake, Crabbe, Cowper and Johnson, with Charles Dickens writing vividly, though at a later date. Thirty-six major fires were started the same night, leaving as well as Newgate, the Fleet, Kings Bench and the Clink, in flames. There is no lack of literature on the subject for those of you particularly interested in the Gordon Riots as such, but my concern here is Newgate.

It was eventually completed in 1785, Lord George Gordon, who was held responsible for the riot, was admitted and died there of gaol fever in 1793. The rebuild of 1785, left a large area free in front of the prison, so the place of execution was transferred there from Tyburn. Enormous crowds assembled to watch executions (it was estimated that 100,000 were present when a certain Henry Fauntleroy was hanged for forgery in 1824), all available windows with views being full, many people paying high prices for the privilege (in this century no doubt it would have figured on "reality TV"). From 1868, the "entertainment" afforded by executions was curtailed as hangings then took place within the walls of Newgate.

In 1856, the prison had been remodelled inside to reflect the "penitentiary system" (the concept of imprisonment as a punishment only came along after about 1840). Badly damaged again by fire in 1877, it was rebuilt, finally being demolished in 1904 to make way for the new Central Criminal Court, still popularly known as the Old Bailey.

Newgate was the principal prison for London and Middlesex and housed all manner of prisoners, of both sexes, including those remanded in custody, and prisoners awaiting transportation or execution, and those imprisoned for debt. *The Central Criminal Court Act, 1856*, permitted prisoners from anywhere in the country accused of a very serious offence to be tried at the Old Bailey. This allowed the accused some hope of a fair trial, free from local prejudice, Palmer the Poisoner was the first to benefit, if that is the correct word. After the *Prisons Act* of 1877, Newgate was used only for those awaiting trial, and prisoners sentenced to death awaiting execution. Between 1783 and 1902, there had been 1,167 executions, 20 men on one day in February 1785.

It was the conditions in Newgate Prison in the early part of the 19th century that so appalled John Howard and Elizabeth Fry. Fry when she visited found the "Female Quarter" crowded with half-naked women and their children, lying on the stone floor without bedding. The women were waiting for transfer to the prison ships that would take them to the Colonies, sometimes having to remain in Newgate weeks and months before a ship was available. *"As cheap gin was available in the prison many of the women were drunk and many more clearly deranged"*. If they could not afford to pay the Keeper of Newgate for "easement" they were kept in leg irons. Slowly conditions improved and, by the time "our" John Weatherhead came on the scene, were a little more humane.

John Hicks, at the White Cross Street Prison, had very different inmates. For centuries debtors had been put in prison along with "ordinary" criminals, albeit in better conditions, if they could afford them. The separation did not come until early in the 19th century when prisons specifically for debtors began to be built, in 1838 there were 5 Debtors Prisons in London. The Corporation of London built White Cross Street Prison in 1813/15, as *"a place appropriated exclusively to those who are debtors to society"*. It was divided into three parts (not unlike Gaul, according to Caesar). The Ludgate side was for Freemen of the City of London; the London side for persons within the jurisdiction of the City: and the Middlesex side for those arrested in the county. It was by far the largest of the London Debtors Prisons. *"The number of persons annually committed is* supposed to be very nearly 2,000; and the average number of persons always confined in it exceeds 470". The reason for its size was "accounted for from the fact that the majority of those ordered for imprisonment by the Courts of Requests are sent to this place. And such is the facility of the debtor and creditor law in consigning human beings to prison, that a person has only to go and swear a debt of a shilling or sixpence against any other party, before the City Court of Requests, to have that party, if unable or unwilling to pay the debt, shut up in this prison for twenty days".

In the Queen's Bench Prison (and presumably much the same in White Cross Street) there were "state rooms set apart for the better class of prisoners". They paid half-a-crown a week for the privilege, for other rooms the charge was one shilling a week, but inmates had to provide their own furniture. In addition to these rooms "there are a coffee house and public kitchen, and a public-house. At one end of the prison there is a kind of market, consisting of several sheds, occupied by butchers, poulterers, green-grocers, etc, each tenant paying a weekly rent of one shilling". These fees along with other perks went to the Marshal "whose emoluments are usually, or were lately, after deducting drawbacks, worth nearly £3,000 a year".

White Cross Street Prison was closed in 1870, when imprisonment for debt became rare and was finally abolished. (24, 25, 26 and 27.)

**

At a Court meeting in January, 1858, Sir George Carroll read a letter addressed to the Clerk with the following sad tale:

"You will be surprised to receive a letter from me addressed from this place (Hesse Hamburg, Germany) the said causes of which I will detail, - for some years past I have found very great difficulty in providing for the wants of a very large family of ten children all too young to help themselves, the elder ones being Girls, - this

circumstance has made me listen with a credulous ear to any prospect of large profits out of the ordinary channels of business, I unfortunately fell in with some men connected with mines who made some most specious representations to me of the enormous profits to be derived from a mine called "Chollucott Consols", if money could be found to work it, they shewed me specimens of valuable ore to be found on the surface alone, after exhausting every effort to find funds for this seemingly most desirable object, I was at last induced to accept Bills for a large amount, which were to be paid by the first sale of the Shares, the parties in whom I trusted turned out swindlers, they got the Shares on the Market for a time and sold as many as realized a thousand pounds, passed my Bills into the hands of some friends of theirs, strangers to me, and gave me nothing to meet them, to avoid the consequences which my credulity had entailed upon me, and the hope of effecting some settlement with the wretched people, I left England for Frankfort about three months since with my two little Boys, - since this my wife and children have had their furniture seized, and turned out of their home, and are for the present existing on the kindness of friends, the small means I started here, have been for some time exhausted, and I am utterly helpless, - It is with the greatest grief that I ask you if there any funds at the disposal of the Spectaclemakers Company from which I might hope for temporary assistance, I am staying here, lodgings being very cheap, if I had small means at my command I might do a little business in German Wines for England, as I am considered an excellent judge, every effort is being made to effect a settlement with the people who have so grievously wronged me, but in the mean time I am literally without the means of paying for my daily support. I am my dear Sir, Yours very truly, Henry Cremer."

N.B. When Cremer became a Freeman in 1833, his occupation was that of bookseller at 19, Cornhill. His father had been a surgeon in Chelmsford.

The Court in considering the letter had the advice of Sir George Carroll that Cremer, whom he had known for many years, was a: *"very respectable Man in business"*. The Court decided upon a donation of £10. Quite generous considering their average support for a widow, whose reason for asking for help was the death of a husband not his stupidity and ambition, was £1 a Quarter.

**

In 1861, William Tite was elected Master. Tite was born in February 1798, in London, the son of a Russian merchant. His interest in architecture started at an early age and in 1817, he was involved in the re-building of the church of St. Dunstan-in-the-East and ten years later in the design of the London and Westminster bank in Lothbury. His greatest claim to architectural fame was the rebuilding of the Stock Exchange, opened by Queen Victoria in October, 1844. He also designed a number of railway stations in England and Scotland including Vauxhall, Southampton, Carnforth and Carlisle, stations between Yeovil and Exeter, the majority of stations on the Caledonian and Scottish Central railways, including Edinburgh and stations on the line from Le Havre to Paris. He also became involved in the design of cemeteries, including that at Brookwood near Woking and West Norwood, where he was later buried. He retired from architectural activities in 1853, after a grave illness. He then became Member of Parliament for Bath, as a Liberal, which he continued to represent until his death.

He had been admitted to the Freedom of the Company in January, 1829 and to the Livery in October, 1839. He became an Assistant in October, 1859, though he was not present at the meeting, and at the same meeting was elected Renter Warden, they didn't waste time in those days! He duly served as Master in 1861/62. However his Westminster responsibilities caused him to resign in 1863. His lightning acquaintance with the Company, he only attended 9 Court meetings, did not end his interest, as at the end of his Mastership he gave the Company a gift of £1,000, a lot of money at this time, to provide pensions for 4 widows of Liverymen (naturally invested in railway stock - all the rage at the time). Tite's Gift was still in existence, and being used, when I joined the Company in 1965, and has subsequently been subsumed into a new Charity Fund. His generosity to the Company has not been exceeded until very recently. Tite lived on until 1873, being knighted in 1869, was a member of the Metropolitan Board of Works, advised on the construction of the Victoria Embankment and continued an active citizen. Tite Street, off the Chelsea Embankment, named after him, is his National recognition, as his Gift to the Company is his Company memorial. (28)

The Royal Exchange, 1895.

**

The Lord Mayor in 1860/1, and indeed in 1861/2, was William Cubitt. Whilst he became a Freeman and Liveryman of the Company in October, 1847, he did not become a member of the Court of Assistants. He had joined his more illustrious brother to form the building firm of W. Cubitt and Co., who carried out a vast amount of building in and around the City and elsewhere. They built Fishmongers' Hall for instance. He gradually withdrew from the firm to enter politics at both Westminster and the City. The year he was admitted to the Freedom and Livery, he was elected as a Member of Parliament for Andover and as a Sheriff of the City, duly becoming Lord Mayor, as has been stated, in 1860. Unusually he was re-elected for a second term. It was generally considered that this was a consolation prize for failing to be elected as one of the City's M.P.s, though he had proved to be a popular Lord Mayor. (29)

**

Every now and again the Court Minutes give an indication of hard times. In the 1860s the number of petitions, the method of asking for assistance, increased and, by and large, if the deceased husband had paid up his Quarterage and the widow was not of an age when employment was a possibility, the Court would either make a donation or add the applicant to the Pensioners List.

One petition from Anne Durrant, who signed her Petition with a cross, not unusual at this time, added that after looking after her husband for two years, with no money coming in:

"in extremely necessitous circumstances having spent her entire substance as well as her health" she was asking if assistance was available, or placing on the list of pensioners: *"Your Petitioner had only one dry bread and a little tea to exist upon the whole of last week and she is afraid unless some help can be afforded her that*

she will be turned out of her little home this Christmas" this came to the Court at its meeting on the 27th December. The Court gave her an immediate £1 whilst they looked further into the application. Having looked they gave her a donation of £5 with the somewhat unusual proviso: *"that no further application for relief should be made by her"*.

At the same Court came a further application, all the way from Paddington, nr Sydney, New South Wales, Australia. Mrs. Eleanor Tanner appeared to think that as she was now 60 she might: *"have a claim on the Charities of the Company"*. The Court considered that as her husband, who was a Liveryman, had paid his: *"Livery fine and also his Quarterage till the time of his departure from England that a Donation of £5 be forwarded"*.

I am not sure how easy it was at this time to forward money to the Colonies, but the Court stuck to its principles, even though a polite decline would no doubt have been the easier course of action. The Clerk reported in June 1867, that he had received an acknowledgement.

**

In June, 1863, George Joachim Goschen was admitted to the Company. Through, no doubt, no fault of his own, he was to be one of those distinguished members who may have been recruited for his name rather than his presence in the Company. Despite serving as Renter and Upper Warden and, in 1878 as Master, he attended only six meetings of the Court, three of those when he was Master. The year of his admission he was elected as one of the four Members of Parliament for the City of London, at the time he was a Liberal. He was soon appointed Vice President of the Board of Trade and Paymaster General. The following year he became Chancellor of Lancaster, which entitled him to a seat in the Cabinet. During his time in office for the Company he was at the same time dealing with the Khedive of Egypt, who had suspended payments on foreign loans in relation to the purchase of the Suez Canal.

He suspected that City voters would not continue to support him and prudently moved to the safe seat of Ripon, which he later lost. He subsequently served as Chancellor of the Exchequer (where he converted the National Debt, reducing £600 million of debt from 3% to 2½% and where he pressurised the Governor of the Bank of England to set up a fund which subsequently saved the failing bank of Baring Brothers), and later First Lord of the Admiralty. In the meantime he had turned down invitations to be Viceroy of India, Speaker of the House of Commons, and turned down the War Office. He was involved in a number of election battles, not all of which he won. He converted to Home Rule for Ireland in 1885, which infuriated Queen Victoria. He was made Viscount Goschen 1900, though it is said he preferred an earldom. (30) It is quite understandable that he was able to spend so little time on Company affairs, but should the Company have recruited somebody just for the name on the notepaper?

**

At a Court meeting on the 6th October, 1864, Charles Palmer, who was to be Master a couple of years later, presented to the Company a Silver Staff head: *"engraved and chased with the Company Arms"*. I presume that this was the head which was subsequently, a hundred or so years later, made into a Mace for the Spectacle Makers Society.

**

The Master in 1865, was Alderman Thomas Dakin, by the time he was again Master in 1876, he had become Sir Thomas Dakin, having served as Lord Mayor in 1870. His claim for a mention here rests on the fact that he adopted his old family arms, and with it the motto "Strike Dakin – the Devil's in the Hemp". Perhaps he was able to answer the inevitable question as to what it meant.

**

Poor attendance caused strange anomalies. The afore-mentioned Charles James Palmer was elected Master (in his absence) in October 1866, but did not attend the next three Courts. In June 1867, the Clerk received a letter from Palmer offering his resignation, due to ill health, which had kept him in doors for seven months or so, but as: *"a Member of the Court"*, no mention of being elected Master. The Court declined to accept the resignation and sent a deputation to Palmer's house, 46, Portland Place: *"to administer the Oath of Office as Master of the Company"*, which they duly did on the 4th July. The next Court meeting, the only one which Palmer attended as Master, was held at his house on the 2nd August. The sole purpose of this meeting was so that Alderman Benjamin Samuel Phillips could take his Oath of Office as Renter Warden, for the year 1865/66, and Upper Warden, for the year 1866/67. Phillips had only attended 4 meetings since his admission to the Court in 1864, and is taking the Oath of Office for Upper Warden in 1867!

Of course it probably didn't help that 5 members of the Court during this time were Aldermen, holding office as Sheriff or Lord Mayor. Later in the century, in 1874, the Court was to rule that there should be no more than six Aldermen on the Court at any one time.

**

There was the odd office cock-up which was reported in the Minutes. For example it was reported to the Court October, 1867, that the keys to the Poor's Box had been *"mislaid"*, and at the Court on the 15th January, 1868, lock picking was authorised. The eventual sum was £12-5-0d.

I suppose contributions to the Poor's Box over the years give some idea of the change in value of money or, perhaps, the change in status of members of the Company. The amount donated was first reported in 1808 when it was 2/6d. whereas in 1875, the last time it was reported, the amount was £27.

**

The Master in 1867, having been Lord Mayor in 1865, was Alderman Sir Benjamin Samuel Phillips, the second Jewish Lord Mayor. Incidentally by 1867 the limit of 400 Liverymen had been reached.

**

The Court in October, 1868, was asked to consider a letter from a Liveryman, A.I. Vieweg, which, apart from the charitable proposal, throws some light on costs at the time:

"As a member of the Spectaclemakers Company I had the pleasure last night to see you (he is referring to Alderman Benjamin Phillips) *in the Chair and as your position as Master and in the Corporation is of great influence allow me to suggest to you to propose at a Special Court Meeting of the Company to use all your power and influence that in future the usual expense of the annual Dinner be paid for the maintenance and education of as many Orphans as the amount will allow. On the Orphanage on Ashley Down, near Bristol, the cost of an Orphan per annum is about £12 – and as I heard from the Beadle* (no Beadle had been appointed for several years since the death of John Wood) *last night that about 160 members were present I suppose the Dinner will cost about £150 – for which we could maintain and educate 12 Orphans 12 months which when they leave the Orphanage can be replaced by others of which there are many in our Country.*
I think most of the members will agree to this proposal rather than be taken away from their business or home at 4 o'clock to eat a Dinner from 6 to 8 o'clock which being out of their regular time to most of them only occasions uncomfortableness, loss of business or absence from home I am sure if you will exert yourself to carry such a motion many a poor Orphan will thank you and bless you

and your family all their life time, my or your children might be helpless Orphans let us therefore strive to benefit our poor needy fellow creatures with the money which is of no benefit to us so as to glorify God who made the Orphans like ourselves for the purpose that we might be like him take care of them with the means he in his mercy has entrusted to us.

I trust you will pardon the liberty I have taken your position and feelings for our poor fellow beings, has induced one to do it."

The Court considered the letter and the Clerk was instructed to reply:

"to thank Mr. Vieweg at the same time inform him that the suggestions contained in his Communication could not under present circumstances be agreed to".

**

At the Court meeting on the 31st of December, 1868, it was proposed, perhaps still filled with the Christmas spirit, that a gold badge or medal bearing the Arms of the Company be provided for the Master to wear on official occasions, at a cost not exceeding £100. Three designs were received and that of Mr. Benson accepted, at £49. The Master, Alderman Andrew Lusk, was duly invested with the new Master's Badge by the Senior Past Master, at the Court on 1st July, 1869.

That Master's Badge was *"destroyed by Enemy Action"* in July, 1941, for which compensation was paid. It was replaced in 1951, at a cost of £200, this time in 9 carat gold. This, too, was superseded in the early 1990s with a new badge, the old reverting to the use of the Immediate Past Master.

**

Somewhat oddly in 1871, the Court decided:

"on financial as well as other grounds it had been thought desirable not to name either day or place for the Livery Dinner".

**

The Master in 1869-70, and again in 1890, as noted above, was Alderman Andrew Lusk. Sitting on the Bench he was obviously ahead of his time, as he is reported in the *"News of the World",* in a case involving the theft of five handkerchiefs, worth 1s.6d., by a lad of 13, *"Sir Andrew Lusk said he did not like to send so young lad to prison, and he thought it far better that he should be birched and allowed to go home with his parents than that he should be further contaminated by association with thieves in gaol. He therefore sentenced him to receive nine strokes of the birch rod, a punishment which was at once administered in the cells of the Court in the presence of his father".*

**

In 1871, after the death of the sitting Sheriff, one of our Liverymen, John Bennett, was elected as Sheriff in his stead. Bennett had been admitted to the Freedom on the 31st October, 1849, and Livery on the 24th June, 1865. He was a goldsmith, watchmaker and politician, according to Richard Harvey's entry in the *"Oxford Dictionary of National Biography".* He had the distinction of going to the same school as I did, Colfe's Grammar School in Lewisham. (For the record I should add that, following modern educational practice, the school is now known as "Colfe's" and is co-educational!). He promoted his business by advertising extensively, including in the catalogue of the Great Exhibition, and by the use of a time ball operated electrically from Greenwich, and a public clock with the figures of Gog and Magog. A lot of his work was done with the Royal Observatory until the Astronomer Royal, George Airey, is alleged to have said *"I will have no more to do with him"*. This was not his only rejection for he stood as an Alderman and, though successful in the Ward Election, three times, the Court of Aldermen rejected him on each occasion (not the only Spectacle Maker to be so treated). The reason may have been in part because, having married Agnes Willson in 1843 and having three children by her, he started a long relationship with Aimee Guilbert, with whom he was to produce seven children between 1866 and 1884, his wife not dying until 1889. May also have been pure jealousy *"Bennett was a flamboyant personality who seems to have aroused in his contemporaries varying degrees of ridicule, hostility, and admiration…his flamboyance extended to his dress and public appearances: he used to appear in the Lord Mayor's Show mounted on a white horse and dressed in a black velvet jacket and broad-brimmed hat, to applause which sometimes exceeded that for the Lord Mayor"*. He is also alleged to have had *"a pronounced cockney accent, employed in the promotion of his business and himself"*.

**

The very last entry in the Court Minute Book of 1872, of a meeting in October, is as follows:

"A suggestion as to the desirability of the encouragement of the trade of the Company was agreed to be discussed at the next Quarterly Court".

At a Court meeting in June of the same year, a representative had been appointed to a committee, called by the Lord Mayor, not for once a Spectacle Maker, to consider technical education. Was this to be the first stirrings of a return to spectacle making by the Company or just a response to the great Victorian interest in all things "technical"?

**

Unusually for the 19th century, Richard Septimus Wilkinson, J.P., served the office of Master for seven years. Also unusually the Court, after his second term, started giving an annual vote of thanks for his services. Perhaps this was to encourage him to continue as Master, for all the members of the Court of Assistants at that time had already served as Master, and most of them had served, or were about to serve, as Lord Mayor. Despite this many of the Aldermen put in regular appearances at Court meetings, even when serving the office of Lord Mayor. Alderman Sir Nicholas Fowler attended eight of the nine Court meetings during his two spells as Lord Mayor. For whatever reason the Court were grateful to Wilkinson and the Votes of Thanks drew particular attention to:

"his able, kind and courteous services together with his generous hospitality as Master", *"unremitting and unwearying attention to the finances of the Company"* and *"zeal and integrity, coupled with great liberality on many occasions"*.

It may also be that he had reduced the number of Court meetings, in one year to two in the year! He turned up, together with the Clerk, at the missing Quarterly Courts, in order to pay the various pensioners. The Court did get one thing wrong though, in the penultimate Vote of Thanks it was stated that:

"been re-elected for the seventh consecutive time, an unprecedented circumstance in the annals of the Spectaclemakers Company".

I am afraid that this Archivist has to note that way back in 1722, one George Wildey (also spelt Weldy, Welldy, Weildy and Willdey) started on his term of eleven consecutive years as Master. Perhaps he served under various of these aliases, thus fooling the Court. On the other hand as his address at one time was "The Great Toy, Spectacle and Print Shop" he may have been considered as the Court Jester??

**

As readers will appreciate, over the centuries members of the Worshipful Company of Spectacle Makers, be they Liverymen or Freemen, have not all been makers of spectacles. For a hundred and fifty years or so non-spectacle makers were in the ascendancy. It was not until the introduction of the examinations in 1898, that members of the trade, and subsequently the profession, started to join the Company in great numbers until, in the early part of the last century, they were in a majority and have continued so to this day. Even so it was not until 1965, when Bill Hardy became Master, that a qualified optician, an F.S.M.C., had held that office since the early part of the nineteenth century.

But the Company did invite those peripheral to the trade, as it were, to join. One such was George Biddell Airy, Astronomer Royal. (The Company subsequently approached several other Astronomers Royal to join.) Whilst he was writing technical articles on optics, and making use of the products of the spectacle maker, Airy was not one himself. He knew enough, however for *"His eyesight was peculiar, and required correction by spectacles the lenses of which were ground to peculiar curves according to formulae which he himself investigated: with these spectacles he saw extremely well, and he commonly carried three pairs, adapted to different distances".*

Airy was born in Alnwick in Northumberland on 27th July, 1801. His father was *"in the Excise"* and largely self-educated, but nevertheless had a large number of books, which were therefore available to Airy from his early days. In October 1819, he went up to Trinity College, Cambridge. His fame had gone before him in that the papers of the examinations he had taken to obtain entry had been sent onto Cambridge *"Where I found long after that they excited so much admiration and were long preserved".*

During his time at Cambridge he became an Exhibitioner of the Worshipful Company of Fishmongers, worth some £20 a year. Airy came top in the First Class of the Freshman's Year, a habit he seems to have continued throughout his time at Cambridge. He duly obtained his B.A. in 1823, coming first in these final examinations as well. In 1824, he was elected a Fellow. In 1826, he was elected Lucasian Professor, with Isaac Newton as one of his predecessors. In 1828, he became Plumian Professor to which was attached the care of the Cambridge Observatory. Before accepting the post he made it clear that the salary (about £300) was not sufficient for him.

In 1824, Airy first met Richarda Smith, it was love at first sight and Airy had made her an offer of marriage within two days of their first meeting. *"Neither his means nor his prospects at that time permitted the least idea of an immediate marriage, and Mr. Smith would not hear of an engagement."* Eventually, nearly six years after his first proposal, he finally married her. They were to enjoy some 45 years of married life.

In April 1834, came the invitation to accept the office of Astronomer Royal, and after there had been some negotiations as regards a pension, Airy accepted, and remained as Astronomer Royal until he resigned in August 1881, due to ill health. His working life at the Observatory was strenuous to say the least. He was to write some 518 published papers and 11 books. Airy's interests and concerns were extremely wide. Advice was required on the growing number of British and Colonial Observatories; keeping in touch with Continental Observatories; the geodetical survey work; the establishment of time-balls; longitude determinations; observation of eclipses; the determination of the density of the Earth; the correction of compasses in iron ships; the Railway gauge Commission; the Commission for the Restoration of the Standards of Length and Weight; the Maine Boundary; Lighthouses; the Westminster Clock; the London University; Tides and Tidal Observations, Clockwork; the strains in Beams and Bridges; astronomical lectures and the popularising of science in general.

In 1875, during the Mayoralty of Alderman David Stone, a Spectacle Maker, Airy was offered the Freedom of the City of London by Presentation *"in recognition of his indefatigable labours in Astronomy and of his eminent services in the advancement of practical science, whereby he has so materially benefited the cause of Commerce and Civilisation"*. At that time it was necessary that a Freeman should belong to a City Livery Company, and the Clerk, Davies Sewell, suggested that the Spectacle Makers Company would be appropriate. At a Special Court held in Guildhall on Saturday, 8th May 1875:

"It was Resolved Unanimously That the Freedom of this Company be presented to Sir George Biddell Airy, K.C.B., M.A., LL.D., D.C.L., F.R.S., F.R.A.S., the Astronomer Royal as a token of the high estimation entertained by the Guild for one who has made such able use of the Instruments the manufacture of which is so identified with this Craft."

Airy took the Declaration on 27th May and was also presented with a gold medal engraved with the Company's Arms. A special dinner was arranged to be held at the Albion in Aldersgate Street, the Court's then current venue, on 6th July.

The City Freedom was presented on the 4th November in Guildhall, and during the familiarly florid speech from the

Chamberlain, he mentioned that it *"was the first occasion on which the Freedom had been conferred on a person whose name was associated with the sciences other than those of war and statecraft"*. Airy, in his reply, said that he regarded the honour as the greatest and proudest ever received by him. Airy, his powers fading, retired from office, after further discussions of a pension, on 15th August, 1881. He died peacefully, with his six surviving children at his bedside, on 2nd January, 1892. (31)

P.S. – his after-dinner speech must have been forceful for on the 7th October the Court Minutes state:

"It was resolved to specially consider the remarks of Sir George B. Airy at a dinner held in July last on the manufacture of mathematical instruments at the next Quarterly Court" – but that is another story.

P.P.S. An article in the *"Daily Telegraph"* of the 2nd of December, 1909, under the headline *"A modernised Guild. Scientific Sight-testing"* claims that Airy *"discovered a mechanical defect known as astigmatism in the organ of vision"*. Neil Handley at the College of Optometrists, suggests that Airy *"is believed to have been the first to produce spectacles for its correction (in himself)"*.

I am indebted to Past Master Frank Norville for the picture of Sir George Airy *"wearing his cylinder 4.50 specs. self-refracted and lenses "created" by craftsman Fuller of Ipswich"*.

At the Court meeting on the 13th January, 1875, it was agreed to pay the pensioners: "an extra 5s. in consideration of the severity of the weather". According to the weather records *"it was an amazingly snowy winter",* falls in excess of two feet being the norm, with snow falling on seven successive months.

**

Whilst the Charter makes reference to a Company Hall, there is no record of the Company owning any property at all until 1877. The Company purchased 19, Lincoln's Inn Fields for £8,835 in December, 1877. They had been looking for property to acquire as an investment for several years. The accommodation, which was on four floors, was to be used solely as offices.

As landlords they had the usual problems of repairs, lettings, painting, the drains, and the employment of a housekeeper, etc. One, to us, unusual request from the tenants was for the installation of electricity, a proposal with which the Company was happy, providing that the tenants paid for the installation.

After the First World War the Court pondered the sale of number 19 and, having taken professional advice, originally agreed to go for auction, and then accepted a private bid of £13,000 from the Equity and Law Life Assurance Society in March 1921. Of present interest the charges the Company had to pay were £284-10-5 to the Surveyors and Auctioneers and £80-12-0 to the Solicitors. They may have obtained "old boy rates" but they sound pretty good.

So ended the Company's brief life as property speculators. Could they have foreseen the astonishing rise that was to come in property values in London over the next 90 or so years their decision might have been different.

**

At the Court in June, 1878, it was agreed that both the Summer Court Dinner and the Livery Dinner were to be held in the Crystal Palace, Sydenham.

In the 1850s Great Britain was happy with the idea of being considered the leader of the industrial revolution, of being economically and militarily superior, and of having a German consort for their Queen. Public content was such that *"in the mid-1850s the word "Victorian" began to be employed to express a new self-consciousness, both in relation to the nation and to the period through which it was passing".* The time was ripe for some public statement of the country's, and indeed its colonies', achievements.

The idea of the "Great Exhibition" was conceived by Prince Albert and held in Hyde Park in a specially constructed "Crystal Palace", so named by *"Punch".* It was important that the building to act as the showcase, should be grandiose and innovative. It was designed by Joseph Paxton (whose previous claim to fame had rested on greenhouses) a huge iron Goliath with over a million feet of glass. Within this building were housed 13,000 exhibits from all round the world including India, Australia and New Zealand from the new empire. Over 6,200,000 visitors, including no doubt many spectacle makers, came to be marvelled by, amongst other things, the evidence of the industrial revolution which was propelling Great Britain into the greatest power of the time. The profits allowed the foundation of public works such as the Albert Hall, the Science Museum, the National History Museum and the Victoria and Albert Museum. But all good things had to come to an end, even the Great Exhibition, the doors closing for the last time in October 1851.

Exterior of the Great Exhibition of 1851.

It had already been agreed that Hyde Park would be returned to its original state and Paxton, foreseeing trouble, had thoughtfully set up The Crystal Palace Company under Royal Charter, in advance. A site was chosen of 389 acres on land on Sydenham Hill consisting of woodlands and grounds of the mansion known as Penge Place, owned, as it happened, by a friend of Paxton, Leo Schuster. The old building was bought for £70,000 and, at a time of high unemployment, was to provide employment for 7,000 workmen. The new building had a floor area twice the size of that in Hyde Park, with three storeys, and north and south transepts. There were also two brick water towers at either end, 46 feet in diameter and 284 feet high designed and built by Brunel, when Paxton's design had failed (should have built them of glass?) The original had cost around £150,000 but the new building was to cost nearly £1,300,000, raised by various share issues, some £800,000 over budget, and this was never recovered, for the new building was only to make the smallest of profits and that infrequently. Shades of the Channel Tunnel? Who says history does not repeat itself, in financial terms, monotonously frequently.

The building had a series of courts around the outside illustrating a particular period in the history of art. To Pugin's original Mediaeval Court was added Egyptian, Alhambra, Roman, Renaissance, Chinese, Pompeian and Grecian art, peopled by plaster casts of the best statuary from around the world. The gardens included an Italian Garden and fountains, consisting of nearly 12,000 jets, water temples and cascades and three lakes to feed them, the Great Maze and the English Landscape Garden. The fountains (which opened two years late!), needed some 7 million gallons of water for one display and were too costly for regular display, so were used only on special occasions. Incidentally the south basin was converted to a football stadium in 1895, and was used for F.A. Cup Finals until 1914. Plants and ferns were provided for the buildings and grounds at prodigious expense and the first life-size models of extinct animals, including dinosaurs, were constructed.

The building was eventually opened by Queen Victoria on the 10th June, 1854, the delay being partly due to *"the fact that dozens of male statues throughout the building had to have their private parts removed and replaced with fig leaves. This did not satisfy all the delicate Victorian sensibilities so all statues in the building had to be inspected and draped where required. This work went on for the rest of the year."* I had to quote this part verbatim in case you thought the Eldridge sense of humour was at work.

The Sydenham Crystal Palace was nicknamed the "Palace of the People", the world's first theme park, which, for a few pence, offered a whole day's entertainment and education, though not in anatomy. Because of the powerful Lord's Day Observance lobby, the buildings and grounds were not open on Sundays, except to shareholders. The effect being that the ordinary working man, the bulk of the population, could only visit on Bank Holidays and evenings. Despite this some 2 million visited each year between 1854 and 1884, so many in fact that a new railway station, called by our current younger generation for some reason a train station, had to be built by the London, Chatham and Dover Railway.

The Palace of the People came to be used for multifarious purposes. Shows and exhibitions, flower, pigeon, poultry, goat, rabbit, cat, dog, cattle and bird shows, electrical, art, aeronautical, mining, photographic, and transport exhibitions. Meeting places for the National Temperance League, Scottish Athletes, German Gymnasts, Salvation Army, Police, Army, Firemen, Oddfellows, Foresters, religious organisations and thousands of others. There were concerts, massed bands, circuses and pantomimes. Handel Festivals with a concert room with over 2,000 seats. In the central transept was the 4,000 piece Grand Orchestra built around the 4,500 pipe Great Organ.

A microcosm of Victorian interests and ambitions.

In 1868, it had the first public showing of moving pictures, using a Zoetrope, and every Thursday night a Brocks benefit firework display, on the occasion of the Grand Display 5 tons of material were used. The standard price of a ticket was 1/- but on special occasions it could be as much as half a crown (2/6d) or a guinea (£1-1-0d). But still it made a loss. The last big show was for George V's coronation – The Festival of Empire – in 1911, but despite thousands of visitors from all over the world it didn't solve 60 years of financial problems, and the Crystal Palace was declared bankrupt and put up for sale. There were many meetings to save the palace, including several by the Lord Mayor, but it was Lord Plymouth, then mayor of Cardiff, who put down a deposit of £20,000 and later signed a contract to pay the balance of £210,000.

The Lord Mayor of London set up an appeal to raise money to relieve Lord Plymouth of his financial responsibilities, and in 1913, the Palace became the property of the nation, and a charitable trust was formed. During the First World War it was used as a Royal Naval Shore Station. The trust was beginning to turn round the affairs of the old Palace with John Logie Baird opening workshops, a television studio and manufacturing plant in the grounds. By 1934, Baird had 4 fully equipped television studios and by 1935, was transmitting 120 line pictures, and a high definition picture of 500 lines. By 1938, Baird had demonstrated colour television using a radio link from the South Tower to the Dominion Theatre in London, giving a clear picture on a screen 12 ft. by 9 ft.

In November, 1936, the greater part of the Palace was burnt to the ground, despite the efforts of 88 fire engines, 438 officers and men from 4 fire brigades and 749 police officers. (My parents lived in Blackheath at this time and I have a distinct memory of being taken onto the heath to see the Crystal Palace on fire. As I was only

3 in 1936, it was more likely a subsequent fire, in 1938, which I can remember.)

Whilst other activities have taken place on Sydenham Hill subsequently, including motor racing at the then fantastic speed of 57 m.p.h. and athletics, the great days of the Crystal Palace were over. In 1951, the Crystal Palace Trust was dissolved and responsibility for Crystal Palace Park passed first, to the London County Council, then to the Greater London Council and after that, in 1986, to the London Borough of Bromley. (32)

**

The one thing our London centred spectacle maker would have encountered was fog. By 1880, a serious attempt was made to rid London of its thick, all-enveloping FOG. It was caused initially by the effect of sea coal, added to the natural mists in the London Basin. Even by 1228, there was a street called "Sacoles Lane". Queen Elizabeth had found herself *"greatly grieved and annoyed with the taste and smoke of sea-coales"*. John Evelyn had famously complained about it in *"Fumifugium or the Inconvenience of the Aer and Smoake of London Dissipated"* of *"Clowds of Smoake and Sulphur, so full of stink and Darkness"*. But it was in the 19th century that the London smoke, not yet a "fog", became more dense and more frequent.

The reason being that there had been a rapid increase in the quantity of pollutants in the air, particularly smoke from coal fires, with the expansion of London, and sulphurous emissions, as a result of the Industrial Revolution, trapped under cold air above the City. E.F. Benson's description was *"of swirls of orange-coloured vapour were momentarily mixed with the black"* and *"all shades from the deepest orange to pale gray of dawn succeeded one another."* By the 1840s the name "pea-souper" was readily used, followed by "London particular" and later "Smog", borrowed from the Americans, though this was more particularly applied to emissions from vehicles as much as coal.

In the 19th century it slowly became appreciated that health was at risk from the pea-souper, as much as the inconvenience to all and sundry. Various commissions and committees were established to investigate the problem. In evidence to one committee in 1845, Abraham Booth, a chemical engineer stated *"in a district of about two acres there are about 25 chimneys attached to different furnaces... there are two breweries, two shot manufactories, six sawmills, one black-lead factory, one engineering establishment, two connected with Lambeth Waterworks, two boiler mills, one emery manufactory, one India rubber manufactory, two glass manufactories, two coke ovens, one lime-kiln, and one hat manufactory".*

It wasn't only human beings who suffered respiratory problems due to the London fog. In the 1860s Smithfield Market was re-built as a dead-meat market, the livestock market was moved to the Royal Agricultural Hall in Islington, thinking to avoid the fog. In December 1873, came the worst fog in living memory. Mark Twain, who was in London doing a reading tour, wrote *"The cattle are choking and dying in the great animal Cattle Show, and today they had to take some of the poor things out and haul them around on trucks to let them breathe the outside air and save their lives"* It was not entirely successful. Some 90 cattle had been removed at the request of the owners and of these at least 50 were slaughtered or died in the vans taking them away. The *"Daily News"* reported that after examination of the slaughtered animals they had died through suffocation *"their lungs being found gorged with black blood"*. The British Medical Journal ran a series of reports from London hospitals to assess the impact of the fog. At last some serious attention was being paid to the pea-souper and its causes. But there would be considerable opposition from the owners of the industrial polluting chimneys, not to mention the domestic fire issue.

The fog of December, 1879, was reported as the densest yet. The Registrar-General of Births, Deaths and Marriages recorded a 200% increase in mortality during the foggy period. It was noted in 1892, that the number of foggy days per year in London *"had increased from an average of 36 in 1871-1875 to 43 in 1876-1880, 55 in 1881-1885 and 63 in 1886-1890."* The expansion of Greater London was continuing apace and nearly all dwellings had coal fires as a method of heating. Add to this the development of the docks to make it the largest seaport in the world which *"brought a vast increase in atmospheric pollution, as ever more factory chimneys and home fires, steam engines, merchant ships, and steam cranes belched their smoke-laden fumes into the air."*

The 1880s saw the beginning of a serious campaign to deal with the causes of the London particular. Ernest Hart, an eye surgeon, and Octavia Hill, a social reformer, started a campaign to clean up the air of London and founded the Fog and Smoke Committee in 1880. The committee appointed a number of inspectors who, with the introduction of new and more accurate instruments, were better able to measure the pollutants in the atmosphere. The problem with domestic fires was also approached for the first time. The committee decided that Parliamentary action had not produced many results in the past and so utilised publicity to draw attention to the problems, including a Smoke Abatement Exhibition which displayed, amongst other things, smoke-reduction devices for domestic fires. Public opinion, however, was still reluctant to accept the higher cost of anthracite, to be used instead of coal, and the interference of inspectors in their own homes. There were always the objections of the railway companies, the Chambers of Commerce and the gas and electric generating companies to be taken into consideration. The Public Health Act, 1891, added to the pressure, with inspectors reporting more and more *"emissions of black smoke for more than ten minutes in the hour"*, which resulted in more successful prosecutions, with the Coal Smoke Abatement Society being able to enforce the 1891 Act.

The Meteorological Office was able to report that the number of foggy days had been declining steadily since 1890, which was attributed to the work of the Coal Smoke Abatement Society, and to the fact that many homes had fitted better grates or stoves, and that penny-in-the-slot gas cookers had spread, rapidly replacing coal fired kitchen ranges. More and more homes had been supplied with gas heating, and gas ovens and hobs were becoming ever more efficient, easier to clean and more attractive. Industry was beginning to move out of central London and electric motors began to replace coal-fired steam engines.

The fog was also declining in intensity. An article in the Lancet in 1899, noted that the latest fog had *"but a slight approach to the proverbial pea-soup hue, and the Egyptian darkness in which on such occasions London had been invariably plunged was conspicuous by its non-occurrence."* The battle was not over yet, for though the fogs were much less frequent, those that did blow in were almost as intense, as happened in late November 1921, which, according to *"The Times"*, was *"the densest fog for Years"*. By 1920, it was possible to measure the density of fog by scientific means and it was concluded that *"domestic smoke is responsible for about two-thirds of the smoke problem."* Unfortunately this discovery did not lead to any kind of action to abate the nuisance, despite valiant attempts. Londoners seemed loathe to get rid of what they considered "their special fog". Legislation to include central heating in all new houses was opposed, partly on the grounds that the housewife preferred her bright open fire.

Things really began to change with the fog of December 1952, which turned out to be one of the greatest fogs and also one of the last. The fog belt according to The Times, *"extended for about twenty miles from the centre of London in all directions .... The fog had caused widespread interruption of road, rail and air services, and brought shipping in the Thames to a standstill."* It was later reckoned that this "worst ever" fog had caused some 12,000 deaths, and 100,000 were affected with respiratory problems.

Piccadilly Circus – December, 1952.

At last enough was enough. Fleet Street was unanimous in demanding that "something must be done". A committee, inevitably, was established, the Beaver Committee, which to everyone's surprise, not least that of the Government, came up with firm conclusions, which the Government did not immediately implement, instead issuing advice to householders as to what to do during foggy weather.

Gerald Nabarro M.P., and a larger than life character, led a vigorous campaign to put a "Smoke Act" on the statute book. In 1954, he was first in the ballot for a Private Members Bill and proposed a "Clean Air Bill". Duncan Sandys, Minister of Housing and Local Government, asked Nabarro to withdraw his Private Members Bill, as it could not include financial provisions, on the understanding that the Government would introduce a Clean Air Bill. In case the Government hesitated there was a *"frightening darkness caused by a smoke cloud that passed high over London on January 16th 1955, in the early afternoon. Darkness was intense in places, coming rapidly but lasting only a short time...the total width was estimated to be at least 20 miles, and at its densest some two miles deep."* It provided sensational headlines and even though there was a General Election in the Spring, the returning Tory Government duly passed the *Clean Air Act* in July, 1956.

"Its major innovation was its focus above all on domestic sources of smoke pollution, it provided a scientifically measurable definition of "dark" rather than the old "black" smoke... it gave industry seven years to comply with the relevant provisions...and it provided for the creation of smokeless zones in the city." Smokeless zones had first been suggested in 1935, by a Manchester lawyer, and Manchester had established its own smokeless zone in 1946. The City of London had followed and, despite objections, the whole of the City of London (effectively the old city within the walls) became a smokeless zone on the 2nd

October, 1955. Naturally, being good publicists, the City trumpeted this advance with the Lord Mayor, not a Spectacle Maker on this occasion, Sir Seymour Howard, writing that *"this city has ever been in the van of all wise and beneficent movements, and I hope our neighbours will soon follow our lead",* which in due, though in not over hasty time, they did.

There were still smogs. That in December, 1957, was partly responsible for the Lewisham train crash, in which 90 people were killed and 109 injured. I well remember it as my father was on one of the trains involved, though he was himself uninjured. He was in a part of the train where, according to him, he hardly felt anything, climbed out of the train and got on with his journey. My fiancée and I had been to the theatre at Streatham Hill, (Gilbert and Sullivan naturally), and came out into the murk to find no trains running and a difficult journey back to Sevenoaks. I can still well remember the smell, the taste and the eerie, clammy silence which the "smog" produced, together with the feeling that one was totally cut off from the world.

There was one more severe fog in December 1962, which lasted five days and which the press reported in sensational terms where it was described as *"a choking, chemical-laden smog settled over Greater London for four days this month and created a major medical crisis."* The reporting here drew attention to the level of sulphur content, the major enemy now being sulphur dioxide. In London smoke control orders were quickly extended which helped, but it came to be realised that hydrocarbon pollution, from the increasing number of motor vehicles was exacerbating the problem. The introduction of catalytic converters and low emission zones helped, but by now this sort of pollution was affecting all big cities around the world and it was no longer a London particular. *"Foggy London Town is no more, and the pea-souper has, both in reality and in fiction, been consigned to the past."* (33)

**

1884, and still problems with money, for in order to pay for the Livery Dinner of that year the Company had to sell £300 worth of 3% Consols.

**

At a Court meeting on the 31st December, 1886, it was reported that the General Insurance Company had paid out £*100:*

"for the loss of the Banners of this Company at the premises of Messrs. Bishop".

Nothing extraordinary in that you might think, except that the minute went on to explain that this was a voluntary payment: *"notwithstanding the policy of insurance did not cover the risk there"*. Today it is alleged that insurance companies wriggle if the articles are specifically covered, let alone not covered.

It doesn't state how many of the banners were destroyed, or whether they were specifically only the Company's, or banners of various members donated to the Company. It seems to have been a Victorian habit to donate a banner to the Company on becoming Sheriff or Lord Mayor, or indeed taking Company office. In 1886, the Company had some 33 banners in its possession. Those of you who have been to Apothecaries' Hall will have seen an example of the type of banner under discussion, displayed high on the wall in the hall.

**

The Lord Mayor in 1885/86, George Swan Nottage, was one of that distinguished group of Liveryman who have attained the office of Lord Mayor without having been Master of the Company. Nottage has two other claims to fame. He founded, with Sir David Brewster, the London Stereoscopic and Photographic Company which in due course, 1862, undertook the largest contract then known in connection with photography, buying the exclusive rights for producing and selling photographs for the Great International Exhibition. The company had agencies in various parts of the world and was awarded medals at international exhibitions in Vienna, Paris and Berlin for their work.

His second claim, which he did not seek, was that he died in the Mansion House, in the April of his year of office, which had not happened for just over a hundred years.

**

To those of you who wrote with an ink pen, the name of *"Stephens Ink"*, and it's "logo", would have been well-known. It was Dr. Henry Stephens who, in 1832, invented the famous *"Blue-Black Writing Fluid"* which was later developed into ink. The family firm manufactured the ink and various other accessories, which laid the foundations for the family fortune. It was under his son, Henry Charles Stephens, that the firm flourished. He was admitted to the Freedom and Livery on the 19th January, 1888. Henry, a Member of Parliament, was one of those active Victorians whom the Spectacle Makers Company seemed to attract at this time. His activities were such that, because of his family firm, he became known as "Inky". In the mid nineteenth century Stephens, along with Arnolds, dominated the American market.

In 1874, Inky bought Avenue House in Finchley, had it extended, and built a laboratory where he carried out his experiments on writing fluids. Henry also had the grounds laid out, which, after his death in 1918, were given in his will together with the house to the people of Finchley. It now houses the Stephens Collection, which is open to the public, free, three days a week. (34)

**

The rush and hurry, the mobile phone, the internet, Twitter, have hastened our world considerably from 1888. Nowadays everybody is busy and the Lord Mayor has a full diary well before he even takes office.

At a Court meeting in February, 1888, which was held at the Albion, Aldersgate Street, it was announced, with great sadness, the death of Alderman Sir William McArthur, a late Lord Mayor, Past Master and member of the Court of Assistants. The terms of the report indicate that the death was unexpected. The very next Minute elects the Right Honourable Polydore De Keyser, the Lord Mayor, to fill the vacancy on the Court. The minute continues: *"was informed of his election and attended, made the Declaration"*, etc. The idea that someone, probably the Acting Beadle, could just nip out and ask the Lord Mayor to come along now to join the Company, is strange to say the least.

Admittedly it was not unusual for the Court to arrange a dinner, either for the Court or the Livery, a couple of weeks in advance, and still expect their distinguished guests to be free to accept. In some ways the duties of the Clerk may have been easier but he had no email to send out these invitations, and probably not even a typewriter upon which to type them, though he may not have had to resort to a quill pen.

**

In June, 1889, Frederick Dallas Barnes, J.P. became a Freeman and Liveryman, his occupation was stated as Managing Director of the Peninsula and Oriental Company (well that is what the Minute says). P & O started from a partnership in 1822, between Brodie McGhie Wilcox a shipbroker, and a Shetland-born former Royal Navy clerk, named Arthur Anderson. They concentrated on business with the Iberian Peninsula, hence the name Peninsula Navigation Company. Their ships went as far as Chile and during the Portuguese and Spanish Wars in the 1830s they *"ran guns, raised loans and chartered steamers as warships for the legitimate heirs to both thrones"*. Their peacetime cargoes included, at one extreme, machinery for minting money to, at the other, giraffes for London Zoo.

In 1835, they joined forces with a Captain Richard Bourne, a Dublin ship owner, and began regular trade between London, Spain and Portugal. In 1837, Bourne signed a contract with the Admiralty for carrying mails by sea, for a weekly service between Falmouth and Lisbon, Cadiz and Gibraltar. This laid the financial foundations of the Company and continued to be its major source of revenue until the Second World War. The first contract run, with one of the largest steamers at the time, nearly ended in disaster when, on the homeward run, she foundered in fog between Gibraltar and Cadiz, but Anderson, who happened to be on board, made sure that the mails were saved. Its reputation grew and in 1840, it received a contract for a monthly run to Alexandria. On the profits of this the Peninsular and Oriental Steam Navigation Company was incorporated by Royal Charter and remained for many years as one of the few commercial concerns not to have been incorporated under the *Companies Acts.*

Over later years P & O acquired a number of other shipping companies and the combined fleet grew to a peak in the 1930s, with five hundred ships of many different kinds. By the 1970s the group had owned every kind of merchant vessel, and completed the hand in 1990, with the purchase of an icebreaker, the research vessel the *Aurora Australis*. Concentrating on large, fast passenger and mail steamers the Company's ships were much used during both World Wars, a number were sunk, 85 were damaged in the First World War and 179 in the Second.

In the 1980s it was P & O who pioneered the biggest change in cargo shipping with the conversion of all its dry cargo liner routes to container operations and by the establishing the necessary on-shore infrastructure required of a container port. (35)

**

On the 18th June, 1890, one Augustus Henry Glossop Harris was admitted to the Freedom and Livery. The reason for his seeking admission at that time was that he intended to stand for Sheriff. I think it safe to say that he was not your traditional spectacle maker. Born into a theatrical family he was soon gaining experience as an actor, though he had greater ambitions. Passing the empty Drury Lane Theatre one day in 1879, though penniless, he applied for the lease, badgering his friends for the necessary funds, £2,750. *"Harris had a straightforward management policy: to gauge public taste precisely and satisfy the demand"*. He needed spectacular and lavish productions to fill the vast theatre. This he did by having a pantomime season as the money-maker, preceded with a season of melodrama and followed by a season of "highbrow" productions, all paid for from the pantomime profits. Harris's first melodrama was *"The World"*, which he co-wrote, staged and acted in and *"although the plot was baffling, audiences (though not every critic) were enthralled and almost overwhelmed by the stupendous staging and effects"*. Other melodramas followed and *"First nights, often four hours long, became attractions in themselves: the complex staging often resulted in confusion and disarray... nevertheless virtually all were successful"*. The pantomimes were equally successful and introduced future music hall stars such as Little Tich, Marie Lloyd, Vesta Tilley and Dan Leno. A hallmark of these pantomimes was enormous processions involving five or six hundred performers, and for one of these he invited a certain Major Kitchener to supervise the marching scenes.

He introduced seasons of opera including the first English performances of *"Die Meistersinger"* and *"Tristan und Isolde"* with Hans Richter conducting, and encouraged the Carl Rosa Company. His success enabled him to tackle Covent Garden, where in the first season, 1888, he introduced Nellie Melba and bought *"The Sunday Times"* to retaliate against the criticisms of other newspapers. He produced operas in their original language, introduced Emma Eames and Emma Calve, encouraged Adelina Patti to give her final performances, whilst Leoncavallo, Mascagni and Puccini visited, and there were two Royal Command performances. He also had time to be a member of the L.C.C. and a Sheriff of the City. But all this labour and enthusiasm came at a price and by 43 he died of exhaustion, diabetes and cancer in 1896.

"A genial, gregarious, man Harris had the knack of surrounding himself with clever assistants and friends. His spectacular Drury Lane productions had become legendary and he rejuvenated Covent Garden, making it a world-class opera house". (36)

**

"The cup that cheers but does not inebriate". Could this be anything else but tea? Well yes it could, but not in this case. Frederick John Horniman was admitted to the Freedom and Livery of the Company on the 30th January, 1891. His father, John, was a Quaker who started business as a tea merchant in 1826, with a

warehouse just north of the City. The story is that he was one of the first merchants to have the idea of selling tea in packets in guaranteed quality and weight, which completely revolutionised the sale of tea and made Horniman's the only name in tea for many years.

His slogan *"We undertake to supply the public with unadulterated teas sold in sealed packets"* seems to have gone down well at the time, though to the modern ear has perhaps not the snap required of sound-bite advertising. The tea warehouses were moved from 28 to 33, Wormwood Street and young Frederick John, who was born in 1835, joined when he was fourteen and spent the next forty years there. It must have been well-known tea for it gets a mention in a work by Sullivan, but not with Gilbert, namely *"The Zoo"*, where Edith laments that:

You've had four tarts and a couple of pears,
You've had three buns that were meant for the bears;
Two bags of nuts instead of the apes,
Ten biscuits of various sizes and shapes,
Three packets of superfine lollipops.
One ounce of the very best pineapple drops,
The largest cake you ever did see,
And a half pound packet of Horniman's tea.

His great interest, apart, presumably, from tea, was entomology and collecting. He had amassed *"a vast collection of butterflies, moths, insects of all kinds, as well as a vast collection of birds' eggs"*. He married when he was twenty-four and settled at Surrey House, Forest Hill. Though he apparently did not go abroad himself until he was sixty, he collected avariciously *"curios and specimens of insect life"* and his interests became known to other travellers, who bought specimens home for him from their travels. So great

was his collection that he started opening rooms in his house so that members of the public could view his collection, first one day a week and then on to three. Not surprisingly his wife is eventually supposed to have said *"Either the collection goes or we do"* and they duly did, to Surrey Mount in 1890.

In the course of his eventual travels Frederick John visited Egypt, India (where he first saw a tea plant at the age of 69), Ceylon, Burma, China, Japan, Canada and the United States of America. He amassed *"large collections illustrating natural history and the arts and handicrafts of various peoples which either appealed to his own fancy or which seemed to him likely to interest and inform those whom circumstances prevented from visiting distant lands"*.

The Horniman Museum opened on the 24th December, 1890, three days a week without charge. An extension was opened in 1893, and the gardens opened to the public in 1895. Frederick John decided that a new building was required, the old building was demolished in 1898. The North and South Halls of the present museum were built in 1898. In 1901, the gardens and the museum were offered to the L.C.C. as a gift to the people of London on condition that responsibility was accepted through a Board of Trustees. This was agreed and the plaque at the entrance records *"This building and its contents, being a portion of a gift from Frederick John Horniman, M.P., to the London County Council as representing the people of London, are dedicated to the public for ever as a free museum for their recreation, instruction and enjoyment"* and they still are, being taken on by the Greater London Council.

To complete the picture, Frederick John in his spare time was a member of the L.C.C., a Member of Parliament (for Falmouth), *"a builder in the sense that he donated money and supervised the erection of buildings of all sorts – churches for various denominations, halls, clubs and so on"*. He attributed his obviously vast energies to eating a rice pudding every day. When he visited his constituency in Cornwall he took rice puddings in hay boxes to last the journey! (37)

**

The Master in 1891, Sir Polydor de Keyser, whom we have already encountered, was a little out of the norm for Spectacle Maker Masters. Firstly he was Belgian, or rather was born one. His parents came to England where, in due course, his father established the Royal Hotel at the corner of Victoria Embankment and New Bridge Street, just round the corner from Apothecaries' Hall, in 1845. By the time it was finished it was the largest hotel in London with a total capacity for 480 guests. Polydor was going to be a surgeon, but instead he joined his father in running the new hotel.

He soon entered local activities becoming a Freeman of the Company in 1862, a Liveryman in 1873, a Common Councillor in 1868, and Alderman in 1882. He eventually became Sheriff, having overcome objections that as an alien and the holder of an innkeeper's licence he was ineligible for the office. In 1887, he was elected Lord Mayor, the first Roman Catholic to hold the office since the Reformation. Not unnaturally, he paid a state visit to Belgium during his mayoralty. His public efforts did not end there for in 1889, he presided over the organisation of the British section of the Paris Universal Exhibition of that year, with no little success. He was also a founder of the Guildhall School of Music. Though I don't believe in this particular multiplicity, for the record he was a Liveryman of the Loriners', Butchers', Innholders', Poulters' and Wyre-Drawers Companies. He died in January, 1898. (38)

**

If you happen to be involved in amateur choirs, or operatic societies, then you will know that not only are men in short supply, but tenors particularly so. This must have been the thought in 1892, when the Court agreed to give ten guineas for three years for a scholarship at the Guildhall School of Music (as it then was). Not just any old scholarship but *"for a Tenor"*. I don't yet know whether the Company money was to unearth a Victorian Pavarotti, if such a person could exist. It will be a case of watch this space, and if it was going to be Pavarotti, it will be a large space.

**

In 1893, the Court was asked by the Lord Mayor, not a Spectacle Maker, to provide prizes for a forthcoming Workmen's Exhibition at the Agricultural Hall, Islington. It was agreed that:

"a sum of £10-10 be divided into Prizes at £3-3 - £2-2 and £1-1 should be offered to encourage emulation in Spectaclemaking by British Workmen".

At the next Court Mr. Thornthwaite announced that the exhibition had attracted: *"50 or 60 Exhibits of exceptionally excellent character and the Judges recommended Additional Prizes to the amount of £3-3"* which was duly agreed.

At the October Court the Immediate Past Master, Lt. Col. and Alderman Horatio Davies, reported that:

"the Prizes awarded at the Competitive Exhibition of Spectacles held in July last had been presented by him on the 27th September at a Dinner to which all the Exhibitors and many of the Employers were invited which Entertainment had given great satisfaction in the Trade"

and a good time was had by all (No the report didn't say that, I made it up, this was after all Victorian England, nobody had a good time!). The dinner was duly reported in *"The Optician"* of the 5th October, 1893.

The review is enthusiastic, though it has to be borne in mind that the magazine claimed that it had been agitating for such an exhibition for some two and a half years but, *"we cannot, nor do we wish, however, to claim for ourselves the entire credit of this great event in the history of Optics"*, it modestly adds. In the event some 130 people turned up *"a most representative company of Opticians, mechanics and members of the Press"*. As a side issue the menu reads more like a Livery Dinner. Soups: Hare and Julienne. Fish: Turbot and Lobster Sauce. Poultry: Roast Fowl, Boiled Fowl and York Ham Joints: Roast Beef, Boiled Leg of Mutton, French Salad, Vegetables in variety. Sweets: Lord Mayor's Pudding, Cabinet Pudding, Noyeau Jelly, Italian Cream, Maids of Honour, Cheese, Celery and Dessert. *"Champagne and other wines were served throughout the repast"*. There were the usual flowery Victorian style speeches. The Master, in one of his several speeches, summed up the Company's reasons behind the exhibition *"In organising the prize-giving to the toilers and workers they had had no selfish motive, their one object, in fact, being to endeavour to improve those who worked at spectacle-making and at optics generally"*. Mr. Watson, in replying for the guests, referred to *"the pleasure the trade felt in being brought together. In all his experience he did not remember such hospitality being extended to the trade as a trade. He thought it tended to strengthen the bonds of friendship between the trade which had hitherto been weak owing to the members never having had a chance of coming together"*.

**

At that Court in October, 1893, no less than four Manufacturing Opticians were admitted to the Freeedom and Livery (quite often the two ceremonies were taken at the same Court meeting), namely George Culver, William Curry, George Paxton and James Joseph Hicks, at least three of the names have come down to us in optical history. Either the Company's growing interest in optics, for Thornthwaite was now on the Court, indicated by the prizes awarded, was having an effect, or the industry was realising that there was a Livery Company who could share their trade involvement. Maybe a bit of both.

In December of that year the Court was asked to call a meeting of:

"such members of the craft as belonged to the Spectaclemakers Company for the purpose of considering a matter now being publicly agitated likely to affect persons engaged in the Optical Trade". To which the Clerk was instructed in a rather lordly manner to state that: *"the Master and Upper Warden would be present on Thursday 25th January for which day a meeting should be called at Guildhall to discuss the matter"*.

At the next Court the Master reported that *"a Meeting of the Trade had been held with no practical result"*. Plus ça change!

**

I would love to be able to tell you about the Livery Dinner of 1894, which was held in June that year. The only reference in the Minutes is that: *"a Gratuity of Ten Guineas (£10-10-0) was voted to the Clerk for his extra services in connection with the recent Livery Dinner at Grocer's Hall"*. As his annual salary at that time only amounted to £100, there must have been a lot of "extras". The mind boggles, but the truth might be a lot less interesting than the speculation. Rather like reading modern newspapers. Perhaps he just had to go and rescue three of the Company's Banners lent for the Antwerp Exhibition.

John Salmon, my immediate successor as Clerk, sent me this picture and asked, in short, what is it? It turns out to be the Company "float, or "car" as they were called, in the Lord Mayor's Show of 1894. The Lord Mayor was a Spectacle Maker that year, Sir Joseph Renals, Bt.

According to the programme of the Show the general theme was a display of the trades of the various companies. The Company's car *"was to be emblematic of the craft of the Company, with carriage groups illustrating subjects such as Archimedes, Galileo, Newton, Jansens and Captain Cook and also workmen employed in making gold and steel spectacle frames and a London apprentice engaged in grinding and fitting the lenses"*. The report in the *"London Daily News"* of the 10th November, 1894, was a little down market saying *"Some of the mystic emblems on this palace of science on wheels were hard to guess at without the printed descriptions"* though it did recognise workmen making gold and steel spectacle frames and the apprentice grinding lenses.

"Reynolds Newspaper" of the 11th November on the other hand presumed the display was *"supposed to illustrate the planetary*

theory of the ages, Newton was seeking the secret of gravitation, Galileo was busy with his telescope, and Captain Cook was troubled over the sextant" but considered that the historical group depicted would not be understood *"by those who were without the programme"*. Either a pitch to sell more programmes on future occasions or a low appreciation of the intelligence of the Show watchers.

"The Times" report of the 10th November was somewhat longer, and I will quote from it to indicate how little the Lord Mayor's Show has changed over 120 or so years. In a report running to some 12,225 words they covered the procession, the ceremony at the Law Courts and the Lord Mayor's Banquet together with the history and purpose of these various events over seven centuries and more.

As to the procession the report remarked on the large crowds it had always attracted - *"Dense masses of humanity throughout the way, well-filled balconies and roofs, more or less ambitious decorations here and there, and, above all, that wonderful sea of faces in front of St. Paul's Cathedral-it is precisely the same old story that has to be told again."* The procession was shorter this year but included four cars as opposed to the two of the previous year, the Fire Brigade was notable for its absence, though there were plenty of bands *"including the pipers and drum-and-fife band of the Gordon Boys' Orphanage who presented a pleasing appearance in their distinctive dress"* and the usual array of City dignitaries (as would be recognised in a 21st century procession). The cars were emblematic of the trade of the three Companies, the Tinplate Workers, the Spectacle Makers and the Gardeners, the last which took the form of *"a huge basket of flowers, with Flora holding a wreath, a gardener at work, and a nymph scattering artificial flowers"*. The female figures were not of the human variety but *"in wood or papier-mache. It is a pity that they could not have been prevented from wobbling about in a decidedly undignified fashion"*. The fourth car combined the three Companies to which the Lord Mayor belonged.

The Procession halted when it arrived at the Ward of Aldersgate for a cordial address from the inhabitants, to which of course the Lord Mayor replied. Through all *"this the behaviour of the crowd seems to have been particularly good"*. The report considered that *"the decorations in the City, on the whole, were anything but of an elaborate kind....the gloom of Gresham Street was relieved by means of a graceful arch. Aldersgate Street was a mass of variegated colour, and between Long Lane and Barbican a handsome cupola of flowers had been suspended overhead by garlands from several points."* Thence to the Law Courts for more history and a precise description of how many times the Lord Mayor raised his hat during the ceremony. The banquet in Guildhall started with a reception from 6 until 7, followed by the meal itself, catered by *"Messrs J. Lyons and Co. (Limited) the service was well organised considering the very crowded state of the room"* and the speeches, of which I counted 14, were reported, apparently verbatim. After the Lord Mayor left *"dancing commenced in the library, and a band of lady harpists, under the direction of Miss A. Arnold, performed a selection of music in the Council-chamber"*.

The previous evening *"through the liberality of the Lord Mayor and Sheriffs some 2,000 of the poorest persons in the East-end were entertained to a banquet at the Great Assembly Hall, Mile-end-Road. Tickets were distributed by the City missionaries and at the hall each recipient was supplied with a bag containing a substantial meat pie, a roll, 1 lb. Cake, and two apples"*. This time there were only *"short addresses"*, five this time, and *"an entertainment was also provided, and the Crusaders' brass band was in attendance"*

As to our distinguished Lord Mayor for that year, Joseph Renals was born in Nottingham on the 21st February, 1843. He went into partnership with his brother in the bleaching business, which was so successful that he retired after a few years and decided to move to London. He then became engaged in the lace trade, and when he comes to be admitted to the Spectacle Makers Company he calls himself a "manufacturer" As a Liberal he remained a staunch upholder of the civic rights and privileges of the City. He was active in Freemasonry and in the city guilds. Apart from the Spectacle Makers he was a Liveryman of the Fruiterers (and became Master), the Gold and Silver Wyre Drawers, and was later admitted to the Framework Knitters. He was admitted to the Freedom and Livery of the Spectacle Makers Company on the 21st November, 1885, the same year he became a Common Councillor for the Ward of Aldersgate, which he held until 1888, when he was elected Alderman of the Ward. He became Sheriff in 1892 and, as already mentioned, Lord Mayor in 1894-95. He died on the 1st November, 1907.

His election as Lord Mayor was not straightforward in that it was *"severely contested"*. For the first time in the history of the Corporation a one-day poll was taken, as a result of the *City of London Ballot Act, 1888* (which had also abolished open voting), in which Renals got 1,462 votes, as opposed to Faudel-Phillips, also a Spectacle Maker, who obtained 1,360. Whether it was this election which caused the problem or whether, as some suggest and as quoted in his obituary in *"The Times"*, he innocently incensed the Court of Common Council by giving a banquet in the last week of his term of office to a Jewish capitalist, Barnett Barnato, the Common Councillors refused to award him the customary vote of thanks at the end of his mayoral year. The *"City Press"* in their obituary refer to *"a disturbed year of office"*. During the course of his year he made a *"state visit"* to Bordeaux and Paris, where the French President conferred upon him the distinction of Officer of the Legion of Honour, which it is suggested helped to found the *"entente cordiale"*. He was knighted to commemorate the wedding of the Duke of York in July, 1893, and became a Baronet in September, 1895. (39)

**

Towards the end of the century the City was beginning to realise the importance of technical education. A meeting of 16 Livery Companies in 1876, not as it happens including the Spectacle Makers Company, though we did have a representative on the subsequent Committee, led to the foundation on the 11th November, 1878, of the City and Guilds of London Institute for the Advancement of Technical Education. It initially had difficulty in finding a suitable site within the City and then went to Exhibition Road in South Kensington, with evening classes in Cowper Street in physics and chemistry for those who wished to continue their education after working hours, but with its headquarters in Gresham College. Still looking for a substantial site, and after a tie up with Finsbury Technical College, a site of some eighty-seven acres in South Kensington was obtained from the 1851 Exhibition Commissioners, and the Central Technical College was established. In 1907, the Royal School of Mines and the Royal College of Science, who were sharing the site, were incorporated into the Imperial College of Science and Technology, the City and Guilds of London Central Technical College was renamed the City and Guilds College.

And things were moving elsewhere in the City. The Northampton Institute was founded under a scheme of the Charity Commissioners, whereby two existing institutes, Birkbeck and the City of London College, were affiliated into a new institute in Clerkenwell, on land given by the Marquis of Northampton, hence the adopted name. The first part of the technical education started in September, 1897.

For its part the Company, as has already been mentioned, had been reminded of its history on the occasion of Sir George Biddell

Airy's, the then Astronomer Royal, admission to the Freedom of the Company in May, 1875, when he had thrown out a remark on the subject of technical education. It was picked up, as no doubt was the intention, at the Court meeting in October when:

"it was resolved to specifically consider the remarks of the Sir George Biddell Airy on the manufacture of mathematical instruments at the next Quarterly Court". At the next Court meeting: *"three members of the Company being practical opticians"* were invited to submit their views to the Court. I can find no further reference to this initiative.

In 1880, Gladstone appointed a committee to enquire into the working of the Livery Companies. The report, when it was published in 1884 showed, to many people's surprise, that the guilds were managed with more economy than was expected, and that only a small part of their money was expended on "wining and dining" and much on charitable and educational activities.

The Company had been considering: *"the desirability of encouraging the trade"* in the 1870s, but nothing had come of it. An exhibition with the same objective had been contemplated in 1890/91, but again no progress made. As referred to above the Court, in March, 1893, did agree to award prizes in the Society of Arts Steel manufacture examinations. It has to be remembered that there were very few opticians among the Freemen and Liverymen at this time, and none on the Court. From the Minutes at any rate, there was no demand for action from Freemen, though, as we have already seen, there was a meeting of Liverymen who were manufacturing and wholesale opticians, to discuss matters affecting the trade on the 28th December, 1893, but it was reported in June of the following year: *"that there was no practical result"*.

The Company was returning to the trade upon which it was

founded, the trade of spectacle making, rather than the growing "professional" activity of sight testing. With the election on the 17th July, 1891, of William Henry Emilien Thornthwaite to the Court of Assistants, the Company's attention became more directed to the "professional side" of optics. The optician at the end of the 19th century was still considered a tradesman, which attitude probably didn't change until the establishment of the General Optical Council in 1958.

Thornthwaite was an interesting character according to his obituary in the report of the 89th A.G.M of the Royal Astronomical Society. Born in 1850, he soon showed *"practical ability in the art of optical science in his father's workshop...he was not merely a master of his trade, but a practical and even eloquent exponent of it, being possessed of the happy gift of imparting knowledge and of interesting students in details...to these advantages he added a genial manner and a persuasive tongue"*. He became Master of the Company in 1898, amidst a plethora of future Lord Mayors, and *"in this position he brought his influence to bear in furthering and completing the scheme initiated by the Guild for the technical education of rising opticians... in 1897-98 he was Chairman of the Board of Examiners and so highly were his services appreciated, and in his zeal for the scheme in general, that his fellow Liverymen, and a large number of members of the optical industry, joined in presenting him with an equatorial telescope made by Sir H. Grubb. This instrument he lent to the Northampton Polytechnic... he was also a keen entomologist and possessed a representative collection of British Lepidoptera... he was a skilled musician... he was widely known and respected, and the news of his sudden death was received with feelings of great regret"*.

Reverting back, Thornthwaite waited until he had his feet comfortably under the table before, as Upper Warden in October, 1896, he: *"gave notice of his intention to bring forward at the next*

Court a motion upon the presentation of Optical Diplomas". At the Court meeting on the 15th February, 1897, he moved a resolution:

"that it be referred to a Sub-Committee of the Court to consider if it is desirable that the Spectacle Makers Company should grant Diplomas to Members of the Optical profession and if so considered, then to report to Court on the best methods of carrying the same into effect – powers to be given to the Committee to expend an amount not exceeding £50 on expert opinions or otherwise" which was agreed. At the July meeting the matter was adjourned as the report was not ready.

At a Special Court meeting, held at the Mansion House, the Lord Mayor being a Spectacle Maker, Alfred Newton, the report was: *"considered at considerable length"* and was carried nem. con.:

"that this Court whilst regarding with favour the proposition of the Upper Warden are not disinclined to try his Scheme for a period, adjourned the settlement and requests him to consult as far as possible the Oculists and Members of the Trade and to report the result to the next Court".

Thornthwaite in his report said: *"...the aim of the Company is now to offer advantages which will induce all craftsmen to become members. Amongst those now to be inaugurated will be Lectures, Exhibitions, and Meetings for Scientific Discussion and Social Intercourse, as well as Classes and the holding of Examinations, which will entitle those who pass to receive a special diploma of Membership, from which the public may see that, in dealing with a qualified spectacle maker it is consulting an optician of proved ability and experience. No other title than that of a Freeman or*

Livery of the Company will be conferred. Members will especially be taught to immediately know when a customer should be advised to consult an oculist before spectacles are adopted, and also how to execute the most intricate prescription which may be ordered. The relations between the oculist and the optician will thus be maintained on a mutually satisfactory and profitable basis. Members may also be examined in the theory, manufacture, and adjustment of any scientific instrument, and have their qualifications inscribed on their diplomas."

On the 11th January, 1898, the Court duly considered the proposed: *"Professional Craft Regulations"* and agreed unanimously that: *"the Scheme contained in the Report ...be adopted for a period of one year on trial"*. Thus started the Company's involvement in optics and opticians which would last until 1980, with the establishment of the College of Optometrists.

The British Optical Association had started examinations in January, 1897, in Liverpool with just three candidates. It held a second examination in London in July of the same year with many more candidates. The very first B.O.A. "examination" was actually held in March, 1895, *"when five candidates drawn from the founder members examined each other orally 'in full council'"*. Included in their number were two from London, one being John Browning, so the B.O.A. was far more national from the outset whilst the S.M.C. tended to be London based. There was already "competition" between the two bodies, still simmering when I got involved in 1965. I am indebted to Neil Handley for the details on the B.O.A. examinations. He goes on to add *"the London venue was the Masonic Rooms at Anderton's Hotel. This reinforces a view I have long been generating that the link between the B.O.A. and Freemasonry was significant.... almost as a conscious alternative to going down the guild/livery company route. It was these wider ties of brotherhood that gave the B.O.A. its early strength and influence".*

By April, 1899, the Master was able to tell the Court that the Certification Scheme was being carried out with considerable energy: *"and up to now had been received both by the Trade and the Public with marked favour"* two examinations had been held and: *"a large number of Opticians certified"*.

For some years afterwards the suggestion had been around that the B.O.A. had been founded by disgruntled Freemen of the Company, whose request to the Company to establish examinations for opticians had fallen on stony ground. This is not justified from the Minutes of the Company. Of the nine "founding members" of the B.O.A. who had met at Ridler's Hotel in 1895, none were Freemen of the Company. However by the end of 1898, seven had become Freemen *"thus all except two of the founders of the B.O.A. became S.M.C. members before the first written examinations were started by both bodies in 1898."* This is stated by Roland Champness in a letter to the *"Ophthalmic Optician"* in March, 1965. (I have been unable to establish whether this letter was actually published.) He went on to state that *"Dissatisfaction and criticism of details of the scheme under discussion were expressed in some outside quarters and the Court of the Company arranged a conference with the Council of the B.O.A. on the 11th February, 1898, to try to smooth out difficulties. Had this succeeded there might have been a joint examination, but the parties failed to agree and went their respective ways".*

In 1898, the Optical Committee, which had been established with the Scheme, made use of the Mansion House again, yes the Lord Mayor was a spectacle maker, Sir Horatio David Davies, to organise an "Optical Exhibition". The main driver of the exhibition was H.C. Kemp, *"well known in the Optical Trade"* and highly active in many Company activities. It was held in the Old Ballroom at the Mansion House and seems to have been well received, if only because it was unlike any previous trade exhibition in that there was time and room to study the various exhibits, at least according to a report in *"The Optician and Photographic Trades Review"*. In July, 1898, the Optical committee proposed that a teacher of Optical Science be nominated to the Northampton Institute at a salary of £32-10-0d. per annum: *"to instruct the classes about to be formed for visual optics at that Institute"*, which was agreed, and they also suggested that a sum not exceeding £100 should be granted for the purchase of optical instruments for use at these classes, also agreed. In March, 1900, the Court was receiving a Deputation of Liverymen which recommended, amongst other things, the appointment of a Consultative Committee for the Diploma Scheme, a suggestion the Court declined in the July when it was decided that: *"the management of the examinations will be undertaken by the Court"* and a Consultative Committee would be considered only when: *"a question arises which may make the advice of the trade desirable"*. It had been reported that two examiners had resigned, the reason being as medical men, that they had been threatened with disciplinary action by the B.M.A. if they should take part in such examinations, a recurring problem which anonymity did not entirely answer. In 1898, Thornthwaite had proposed a subscription to 5 London ophthalmic institutions, perhaps foreseeing the problem. At the same meeting he had proposed that representatives be invited from the Pharmaceutical Society and the Watchmakers and Jewellers Society to serve on the Optical Diploma Committee considering the Scheme. In November, 1901, Lionel Laurance was appointed under the Scheme as *"Official Instructor without emolument"*.

Despite the Court suggesting that no alterations to the Scheme were expected for some time, by January, 1903, they were being urged to include sight testing in the examination (the B.O.A. was already doing so). The Court initially declined but in April of that year they received a Memorial from nearly 70 Freemen *"holding the*

Diploma of proficiency as Craftsmen" to the same effect. In June, a Memorial of 150 Freemen, 90% of whom were Diploma holders of London, was received, urging the Committee the Court had established, to look at the first Memorial to *"consider the desirability of examining candidates in sight testing....we desire to emphasise the necessity that still exists for establishing a standard of skill in or knowledge of the art of sight testing, if considering this matter simply on the ground of public policy. The protection of the public from imposition was one of the principal objects for which the Guild was founded by Royal Charter, and there is surely no means by which this object can be furthered more than by an Examination fully covering the work in which practically all opticians are engaged... while it is true that the present examination to a certain extent covers the ground indicated, since the existing syllabus includes much of the required knowledge of theoretical optics, it stops short of examination in the practical routine of sight testing"*. In October that year some heavyweight Liverymen, including Lord Kelvin, Sir R. Bell, and Sir William Crookes, weighed in on the same issue. In January, 1904, the Court accepted the advice of their Committee and Sight Testing was added to the Company's examinations.

Again in 1904, in view of an application from the Society of Chemist-Opticians and the Editor of the "*British and Colonial Druggist*" exemptions from certain parts of the Company examinations were allowed to those who had qualified, or part qualified, through the examinations of the Pharmaceutical Society of Great Britain or the Pharmaceutical Society of Ireland.

On the 19th January, 1905, it was reported:

"that there is every probability of my (The Renter Warden) being able to report to the next Court that the diploma scheme is, for the first time, paying its own way".

Whilst examination results were regularly reported to Court, it kept out of the day to day running of the examination scheme, save for major changes, like the introduction of drugs to the syllabus, an Opticians Bill, or, much later, the joint examinations with other examining bodies, particularly in the 1980s. (I got caught in the cross-fire between the Advisory Board, of which I was Chairman, and the Court, over progress on joint examinations, and argued the case so vigorously in Court, which resulted in my no longer being Chairman of the Advisory Board!) There was occasional interface as when in 1901, it was agreed that the Master and Wardens, formally gowned, should open the written examinations, which can have done nothing for the candidates' nerves. Or the arranging of a conversazione at Carpenter's Hall for Diploma Holders in 1902, which was declared a *"complete success"*. Noted in the Warden's Accounts were the expenses for the event: *"Ladies' Band, Pierrot Troupe, Band and Exhibition cost £105-2-10d."*

**

As we have seen the Master in 1897, was, in full, Colonel and Alderman Sir Horatio Davies, he was Lord Mayor the same year. In the 1870s, together with his brother-in-law Frederick Gordon, he entered into the arena of businessman's restaurants. They started by acquiring the London Tavern, Pimm's Oyster Bar, Crosby Hall and the Holborn Restaurant. Frederick Gordon went on to establish the Gordon Hotels group. Our interest is with Pimm's Oyster Bar.

James Pimm, the son of a farmer from Kent, became the owner of an oyster bar in the City of London in the 1820s. He thought that his customers needed aid in the digestion of their oysters. He offered them a gin-based drink containing a secret mixture of herbs and liqueurs, served in a small tankard and called "No. 1 Cup". By 1851 he began large scale production, selling commercially in 1859. It didn't really take-off until, after several take-overs, the business, and the right to the name, came into the hands of Horatio Davies. Davies started bottling "Number One Cup" and by 1887, he had franchised a chain of 5 Pimm's Restaurants. He also built up the export trade and by the time of his death in 1912, Pimm's cocktails were known internationally, especially in the Empire.

Over the years Pimm's extended their range until by 1960, "Pimm's No.1" had gone as far as "Pimm's No. 6". It was all the rage for many years, mainly in the soft south of England and, for some reason, in the Universities. Next time you are invited to *"It's Pimms O'clock"* remember with fondness one of our past masters. (40)

**

Horatio Davies had, as one of his Sheriffs, another Liveryman of the Company in Thomas Robert Dewar. He was the son of John Dewar who had established the firm of John Dewar and Son. On his father's death, Tommy, as he soon became known, along with his brother John, built the family business by blending whisky to make it more appealing for the international market. Tommy was the salesman par excellence, and in the space of two years, had visited 26 countries and sold the Dewar blended whisky worldwide. He was admitted to the Freedom and Livery in 1897.

Egypt, Dewar in one of the 26 countries he visited.

Apart from being a salesman Tommy Dewar was by way of being a philosopher, preaching that success in life can be attained, admittedly through hard work, but without compromising the joy in life. He wrote a number of well-known thoughts and philosophies, too many to set out here, but some caught my attention: *sometimes doing nothing is doing something; if you think you know it all, you are missing something; when a man says his word is his bond – get his bond; yesterday's success belongs to yesterday; life is a one-way street and you are not coming back; of two evils, choose the more interesting one; we have a great regard for old age when it is bottled; minds are like parachutes, they only function when they are open; if we are here to help others, I often wonder what the others are here for,* and lastly, *don't question your wife's judgement, look who she married.* He never married, he was knighted in 1902, later became Lord Dewar and died in 1930. (41)

**

I have written before of the well-known names who have joined the Company from time to time, but the 25th March, 1899, was exceptional, even for the Spectacle Makers. No less than four eminent scientists joined that day: Lord Kelvin, Sir William Christie, William Abney and the Earl of Rosse.

Lord Kelvin was born in 1824, in Belfast and by the time he became a Freeman had made his name as a mathematical physicist, engineer and leader in the physical sciences in the 19th century. He did important work in the mathematical analysis of electricity and thermodynamics, and did much to unify the emerging discipline of physics in its modern form. He developed the Kelvin scale of absolute temperature measurement. A bit of a tempestuous figure, his work as a telegraph engineer brought him into the public eye and ensured wealth, fame and honour which his early work might not have achieved. The first successful transatlantic submarine cable was laid in 1866, and William Thomson as he then was, became involved in many other submarine cables of the time. (42)

Sir William Christie was the second Astronomer Royal to be admitted as a Freeman, following George Airy. A complete opposite to Kelvin, Christie *"was unobtrusive in manner and personality"* but *"it may be said in truth that in during the last fifty years no person has had more influence directly or indirectly on British astronomy"*. So said his obituary from the Royal Astronomical Society.

Born in 1845, the son of a Professor of Mathematics, his greatest achievement was perhaps the resuscitation of astronomy from the rather low level that Airy had left it, and a greater emphasis on astrophysics. *"The Times"* said that *"Greenwich owes its largest extensions in buildings and instruments"* to William Christie, and a doubling of its staff. One of his changes was, in 1893, the replacing of the old dome with a new onion-shaped dome, still a distinctive feature. A sound but not brilliant mind had contributed more to the development of astronomy, and astrophysics, than his better known and more extrovert contemporaries. (43)

The onion domes, Greenwich Observatory, from a contemporary postcard.

William Abney, or to give him his full title, Sir William de Wiveleslie Abney, was an astronomer, chemist and photographer. Born in 1843, after a few years in the Royal Engineers he went to work at the Chatham School of Military Engineering, where he developed the Abney level, a surveying instrument used in military reconnaissance. In 1881, he was appointed an inspector of science schools for the Department of Science and Art at Kensington. Though his methods were criticised, by the time he retired in 1903, there were 1,165 school laboratories recognised by the Board of Education, as opposed to a mere handful when he was first appointed. He was a pioneer of several technical aspects of photography and photographic developments in astronomy. The author of a number of books on photography which became standard texts he was, again unlike Kelvin, modest of his achievements. In 1874, he developed a dry photographic emulsion which he used to photograph the transit of Venus across the sun. Amongst his new types of photographic paper was a formula for gelatin silver chloride paper. He conducted early research in the field of spectroscopy and was a pioneer in photographing the infrared solar spectrum. He also investigated the sensitivity of the eye to light and colour, as a result of which he introduced his own system of colour photography. He died at Folkestone in 1920. (44)

The Earl of Rosse was the son of a famous father, the 3rd Earl, who built a 72 inch telescope at Barr in Ireland, which was for 70 years the largest telescope in the world. He, the father, carried out pioneering astronomical studies discovering the spiral nature of nebulas (now known as spiral galaxies) and getting into fierce arguments with John Herschel. The son suffered from the fact that if Lord Rosse was referred to, it was inevitably his father, though in his own way he pursued pioneering astronomical observations, particularly of the Moon and its radiant heat. His estimates of the temperature of the moon's surface, though somewhat ignored by the scientific world, were proved to be accurate in 1958. He also took an interest in the development of the steam turbine, which had been invented by his brother, through the Parsons Marine Steam Turbine Company, Parsons being the family name. (45)

All of these four had reason to thank, in some way or another, the help of the optician and of the scientific instrument maker, and thus would be led towards the Spectacle Makers Company. (All four subsequently petitioned the Court for the introduction of sight testing examinations.) It may, on the other hand, be the influence of Thornthwaite, or the Company's burgeoning interest in the trade. Whichever, surely a clutch of scientists of which the Company could be rightly proud.

**

So ended a tumultuous century for the Company. It had finally become a Livery Company in the full sense of the word. Its Freemen and Liverymen, steadily increasing in number, had begun to play their full part in the running of the City of London. A return to the "trade" had been established, making a firm base for further expansion. Its finances had been put on firmer foundations, though not exactly flourishing. It could look forward to a secure future though, in truth, perhaps the 19th century would prove to be the Company's high point.

**

References:

1. Jerry White *"London in the nineteenth century"* Jonathan Cape 2007.

2. *"The Times History of London"* ed. Hugh Clout Times Books 2007.

3. *"The English. A social history 1066-1945"* by Christopher Hibbert 1987, Book Club Associates.

4. *"City of London Pubs"* by Timothy M. Richards and James Stevens Curl David and Charles 1973.

5. *"Sign Boards of Old London Shops"* by Sir Ambrose Heal, Batsford 1957.

6. Incorporates text from A.M. Clerke's article as revised by Anita McConnell in the *"Oxford Dictionary of National Biography"*.

7. *"Scientific Instrument Makers in London during the seventeenth and eighteenth centuries"* Mary Robischon.

8. *"The Spectaclemakers' Company and the origins of the Optical Instrument-making trade in London"* Gloria C. Clifton.

9. Incorporates text from Anita McConnell's article in the *"Oxford Dictionary of National Biography"*.

10. *"The lives of the Kings of England"* – ed. Antonia Fraser, Weidenfeld and Nicolson.

11. *"Old London Taverns"* Edward Callow 1899.

12. Taken from the Chubb Archive.

13. Further information from *"A Gazetteer of Lock and Key Makers"* by Jim Evans.

14. *"Umbrellas and their history"* by William Sangster.

15. Information taken from *"The UK Piano"*.

16. *"Old and New London"* Edward Walford.

17. The Harmer Society.

18. Based on an article by Joy Vick which appeared in *"From the Master and Wardens"* of November, 2015.

19. London Borough of Richmond upon Thames – Local history notes *"Richmond and its vicinity"* – John Evans 1825.

20. Information taken from the BBC History and Butler-Bowdon web sites.

21. *"Big Stink"* incorporates text from Wikipedia.

22. Incorporates text from Lindsay Granshaw's article in the *"Oxford Dictionary of National Biography"*.

23. Based on John Sugden's article *"The merry dance of the Highwayman"* in *"History Today"* March, 2017.

24. *"London the Biography"* Peter Ackroyd, Chatto and Windus.

25. *"The London Encyclopaedia"* Ben Weinreb and Christopher Hibbert.

26. *"Sketches in London"* James Grant 1838.

27. *"Newgate Prison"* Richard Clark.

28. Incorporates text from S.P. Parissien's article in the *"Oxford Dictionary of National Biography"*.

29. Incorporates text from Hermione Hobhouse's article in the *"Oxford Dictionary of National Biography"*.

30. Incorporates text from Thomas J. Spinner's article in the *"Oxford Dictionary of National Biography"*.

31. *"Autobiography of Sir George Biddell Airy"* edited by Wilfrid Airy, Cambridge University Press 1896.

32. This article is based on information from the Crystal Palace Foundation and the Victorian Station web sites.

33. Largely taken from *"London Fog"* by Christine L. Corton, the Harvard University Press, 2015.

34. Based on information provided by the Stephens Collection.

35. Incorporates text from *"P and O Heritage"*.

36. Incorporates text from the article by J.P Wearing in the *"Oxford Dictionary of National Biography"*.

37. Information provided by the *Horniman Museum*.

38. Incorporates text from Anita McConnell's article in the *"Oxford Dictionary of National Biography"*.

39. The information for this article was kindly provided by the London Metropolitan Archive from the Lord Mayor's Day Book.

40. *Wateringbury Local History Society* 2013 and Wikipedia.

41. Incorporates text from Ronal B. Weir's article in the *"Oxford Dictionary of National Biography"*.

42. Incorporates text from Crosbie Smith's article in the *"Oxford Dictionary*

of National Biography".

43. Incorporates text from A.J. Meadows' article in the *"Oxford Dictionary of National Biography"*.

44. Incorporates text from the article by Peter J.T. Morris in the *"Oxford Dictionary of National Biography"*.

45. Incorporates text from the article by I. Elliott in the *"Oxford Dictionary of National Biography"*.

20th CENTURY

PRELUDE

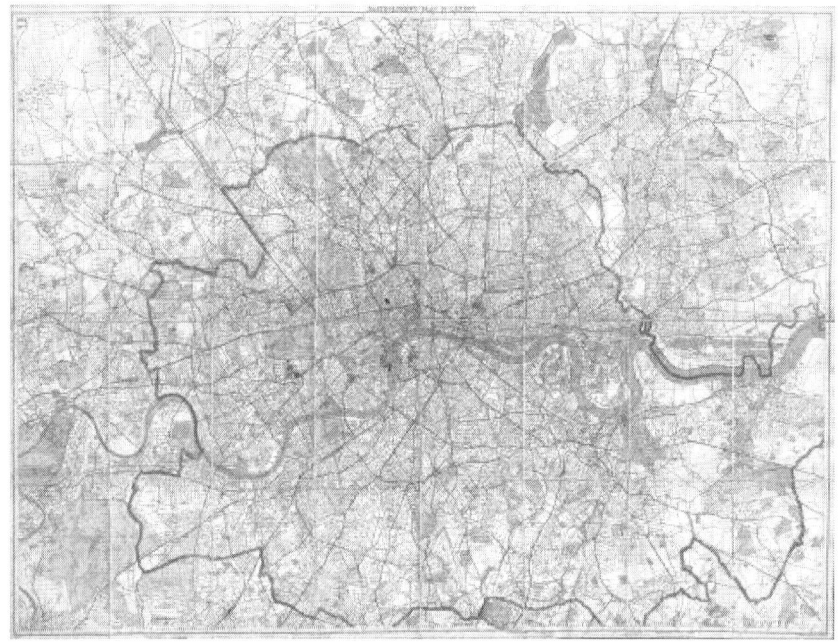

Bartholomew's Map of London c1900.

I am going to find this part difficult to write. I lived through two thirds of the century – it can't possibly be HISTORY. I'm not history – yet. It was an astonishing 100 years with two world wars, which actually involved a large part of the world, previous wars had been little local struggles, three depressions and men landing on the moon. Medicine had improved beyond recognition, a distinguished Apothecary had been heard to say in the 1980s that all the important advances in medical science had taken place within his lifetime. By the end of the century there was talk of extending life and "slowing" ageing, strangely enough this was taken as an advance, yet the world was rapidly becoming overpopulated as it was. As to the provision of medicine, the National Health Service, founded in 1948, revolutionised the receipt of medical care "free at the point of care".

The N.H.S. was introduced by the Labour Party, itself not much more than just a gleam in the eye in 1900. The House of Commons went on its traditional way, though frock coats and top hats were not so much in evidence. The House of Lords went unreformed, despite threats and the creation, from time to time, of sufficient new peers for the Government of the day to get its way.

The population had become more prosperous, women had begun to obtain some parity with men, but there was still a long way to go. In Britain de-industrialisation was taking a grip, with the rapid decline of mining, shipbuilding and textiles and Globalisation, with the transfer of many jobs overseas, was causing as yet unanswered problems. With the end of factories and the introduction of robots, jobs for the "semi-skilled" would be at a premium. Homes were better furnished, electricity and gas were universal and equipment, like washing machines, fridges and microwaves, affordable for most. In the middle of the century, more people owned their homes, though by the end, renting, the European norm, was taking over.

The diet of the average Briton improved with food becoming cheaper and more available. Convenience food appeared, along with "take-aways". The hamburger came to Britain and the fish finger. By the end of the century scientists were genetically modifying food. The supermarket arrived, along with credit cards, and shopping on the internet eventually became available, all threatening the end of the local shop. Clothes became more informal and a hat, or cap was no longer considered an essential for either sex. Sex was also discussed openly, and some would say endlessly. The currency was decimalized by 1971.

The car appeared in the previous century and thoroughly took over. By 1940, about one in ten families owned a car, by the end of the century most families owned one, and in some cases, one each, causing the introduction of motorways, somewhat late as most of Europe had had them before Britain. The plane, after the Wright Brothers initial flight, developed such that by the end of the century almost everyone who wanted to could have cheap flights, and cheap holidays, to places barely known at the beginning of the century. Holidays were now written into the law for almost every employee.

Warfare advanced rapidly with gas, the tank, submarines, Zeppelins, and that was just in the First World War, the war to end all wars remember? By the time of the Second World War, aircraft were fully utilised, pattern bombing involving non-combatants for almost the first time. The V1, and V2 rockets, the atomic bomb, the hydrogen bomb and nuclear powered submarines as a means of delivery and, of course the drone, a coward's weapon, as the firer of the guns or bombs on the drone was a few thousand miles away in a safe spot. The invention of nuclear weapons produced peace, of a sort, for the rest of the century, as no one wanted to be the first to use it.

Broadcasting began in the 1920s by the B.B.C, to be followed by television, and by 1952, about a quarter of households had a T.V. Then came commercial television and by 1964, 90% of households had a television set. It was supposed to kill off the cinema which had developed from jerky black and white, through the "talkies" to colour, Todd AO and other wonders. The blockbuster and endless sequels may be more likely to kill off the film rather than T.V. Records had changed from 78s, to 45, then 33 then onto CDs. The massive computer, taking up a basement or so, morphed into the personal computer, laptop, etc. and by the 1990s the internet arrived.

As to London itself, it continued to increase in size, though at nothing like the speed of the previous century. With the Company, the introduction of non-spectacle makers, followed by the introduction of the examinations, Freemen and Liverymen came from far afield and were not centred on London, though the main membership was still in London and the south east. London was bombed in the First World War, at first by Zeppelin and then by Gotha biplanes, but this was as nothing compared to the Blitz in the Second World War, which lasted for almost a hundred continuous days, leaving the City a flattened and smoking ruin in places, giving unexpected views of buildings left standing with their neighbours obliterated, as shown in the view from St. Paul's.

View from St. Paul's across towards the Old Bailey.

20th CENTURY

JOTTINGS FROM THE MINUTE BOOKS

The Master in 1900/01, was The Rt.Hon. Sir William Hart-Dyke whose family seat was Lullingstone Castle, Eynsford in Kent. He was a politician but, to humanise these distant characters, he was an excellent rackets player who, in 1892, defeated the professional and holder of the world rackets championship "easily". He started the public schools' racket championship and was one of the originators of lawn tennis. In 1873, he and two friends *"laid out a tennis court at Lullingstone Castle and played one of the early recorded games a year before Major W.C. Wingfield took out a patent for 'Sphairistke'.* (1)

**

In December 1908, the pensioners were sent their money by post, they normally had to collect in person, due to a severe snowstorm.

**

In the latter part of the nineteenth century, and the earlier part of the twentieth century, the Company attracted a number of newspaper proprietors as it had earlier in the century (see Edward Lloyd on Page 192). This seems to start with the admission of Edward Levy to the Freedom and Livery on the 20th October, 1893. He was the son of Joseph Moses Levy who had acquired the *"Daily Telegraph"* in 1855, shortly after its founding. He may well have joined through George Faudel-Phillips, who had married Edward

Levy's sister. Our Edward Levy complicated matters by assuming, under Royal Licence, the additional surname of Lawson. Edward had worked in newspapers *"He had personal knowledge of almost every department of a newspaper: he could set type; he had "handled" copy; he could turn a neat paragraph and dictate a telling leader... long before his father's death in 1888 the principal direction of the paper had been in Levy-Lawson's hands; he had indeed been managing proprietor and sole controller since 1885. He was never formally its editor, but he directed the day-to-day content of the paper"*. The *"Daily Telegraph"* became the best-selling newspaper in the capital. Feelings in politics ran high in those days and a disagreement with the radical Henry Labouchere *"led to fisticuffs in the street"*. Always interested in politics Levy-Lawson led the paper away from the Liberal Party and *"Gladstone gave Levy-Lawson a baronetcy in October, 1892, but it was not enough to win him back"*. He was raised to the Peerage, as Baron Burnham, in 1903, before he became Master of the Company in 1905. He had effectively retired from day-today involvement with the paper to be succeeded by his eldest son, Harry, as proprietor. (2)

Harry Lawson Webster Levy-Lawson, was admitted to the Company on the 13th January, 1903. Harry was an active Member of Parliament, on and off, between 1885 and 1916, had a distinguished record in the First World War, ending as Lieutenant-Colonel. He was Master of the Company for two years, 1909-10. On the death of his father in 1916, he succeeded to the titles of Viscount Burnham, and the baronetcy, and took his seat in the Lords. He had become proprietor of the *"Daily Telegraph"* in 1903 *"Lord Salisbury, ruling that his father's elevation to the peerage was incompatible with continuing to run a national newspaper. He was not wholly successful in the role.... He lacked the business and journalistic talents that had made his father so spectacularly successful"*. The *"Daily Telegraph"* was losing the circulation battle against both the *"Daily Mail"* and the rejuvenated *"Times"*. In 1928, he sold the paper to the Berry Brothers and Sir William Illiffe. To be fair, Harry was highly active, and perhaps most effective, in spheres other than the newspaper world, chairing public bodies nationally and internationally. Most memorably, so far as the modern generation is concerned, chairing the Standing Joint Committee on teacher's pay, later known as the Burnham Committee, which established the Burnham Scales. On his death there was no surviving male heir, the Viscountcy became extinct and his younger brother succeeded to the baronetcy as the 3rd Baron Burnham who, perhaps surprisingly, did not join the Company. (3)

However his son, Edward Frederick Lawson, was admitted to the Freedom and Livery on the 19th January, 1922. Edward, after Oxford, joined the *"Daily Telegraph"* as a reporter, at first in Paris and then New York. He came home to fight in the First World War. He served with distinction rising, at 26, to the rank of Lieutenant-Colonel, with the Royal Bucks serving with the Desert Mounted Corps in Palestine, where his regiment was lent to T.E. Lawrence, helping to complete the destruction of Turkish Fourth Army. He was awarded the D.S.O. and the M.C. and mentioned three times in dispatches. After the war he returned to the *"Daily Telegraph"* as second-in-command to his uncle. As already reported this was not a good time for the *"Daily Telegraph"* and Lawson was annoyed as he felt he could have raised the necessary funds to "save" the paper. Sir William Berry considered that *"if he had succeeded to control instead of his uncle, I doubt very much if the "Telegraph" would* have reached the position where a sale was desirable or necessary". It is alleged that the retention of Lawson was a condition of the sale going through, and Berry backed his views by appointing him general manager, where he proved himself as a moderniser and negotiator, installing new printing plant and negotiating the takeover of *"The Morning Post" i*n 1937.

The Second World War saw him back in action at Dunkirk earning a C.B. for distinguished service in the campaign, and promotion to Major-General. On his father's death he became the 4th Baron Burnham and the 4th Baronet. He returned to the *"Daily Telegraph"* at the end of the war as managing director, where he remained until his retirement in 1961. Amidst all this he was Master of the Company on three occasions, 1926-27, 1932 and 1943-44. (4)

To complete that family's association with the Company, though not the newspaper business, I would like to mention Gerald Coke, even though this is outside the scope of this book. His mother was the only daughter of the 1st Viscount Burnham, Harry Levy-Lawson. He was admitted to the Freedom and Livery on the 5th May, 1936. He had worked in the haematite iron-ore mining industry before service with the Scots Guards in the Second World War, rising to the rank of Lieutenant-Colonel. After the war he became a director, and later vice-chairman, of S.G. Warburg and Co. and a director and later chairman, of Rio Tinto-Zinc Corporation. His interests were many, but gardening, music and scholarship occupied much of his time. His transformation, together with his wife, of Jenkyn Place in Hampshire, both house and garden, attested to his gardening skills. The Spectacle Makers Fellowship, as it then was, enjoyed several visits to both garden and house. As to music, he was Chairman of the Glyndebourne Arts Trust for twenty years, a director of the Royal Opera House, Covent Garden and of the Royal Academy of Music, and established the Gerald Coke Handel Foundation, to which he donated his considerable collection. He was the treasurer and benefactor of both the Bridewell Royal Hospital and King Edward's School, Witley. He was a Governor of the B.B.C. and had an outstanding collection of porcelain. He also made time to be Master of the Company on two occasions, 1945 and 1957-58. (5)

To bring the Company's association with newspaper families up-to-date, though taking us beyond 1929, I had mentioned in passing another of the Company's newspaper families, namely the Berrys. James Gomer Berry was admitted to the Freedom and Livery on the 18th February, 1932, not long after he took over the *"Daily Telegraph"*. One of three brothers who all attained high honours, the eldest became Baron Buckland, the middle brother Lord Camrose and Gomer Berry, Viscount Kemsley. He started working for local papers in Wales before coming to London, and with money from his eldest brother, started the *"Advertising World"*, and went into partnership with his other brother. The brothers saw an opening for magazines on sport and leisure and set about expansion, Gomer's part was to generate sales and sell advertising space. Between them they were very successful, buying the struggling *"Sunday Times"* and the St. Clement Press, and with it, the *"Financial Times"*. In 1924, they founded Allied Newspapers, along with Sir E.M. Illiffe, taking over the Hulton Newspapers from Lord Rothermere and a whole swathe of local papers. They purchased the Amalgamated Press from Lord Northcliffe's executors and obtained one of the largest mills in the world.

The 1927 acquisition of the *"Daily Telegraph"* was almost the height of their success, but eventually, in 1937, Allied Newspapers was dissolved, the three families taking equal parts. Gomer became chairman of Kemsley Newspapers, the largest newspaper empire in Britain, which included his favourite paper, the *"Sunday Times"*. Gomer's strength lay in his financial ability, whereas his brother had the newspaper flare. Gomer's autocratic manner *"the stiff manner and equally stiff collars, the bespoke suits and silk ties, the private lift to the top-floor, the chauffeured limousine, and the white-gloved flunkeys all signalled a creaking, old-fashioned newspaper operation. Kemsley's sons, three of whom worked on the "Sunday Times", enjoyed the same privileges as their father".* The total opposition to the new Labour government, a more competitive newspaper climate and, finally, the defence of Eden over Suez, led to the sale of Kemsley's, (he had become a Viscount in 1945) holdings to Roy H. Thomson, a Canadian newspaper and television proprietor. Ironically Kemsley had opted out of the consortium awarded the first I.T.A. franchise for weekend television in the Midlands and the North. He was Master of the Company in 1934-35. (6)

Geoffrey Lionel Berry, his eldest son, was admitted to the Freedom and Livery on the 6th January, 1944. He served in the Grenadier Guards in the Second World War, being invalided out in 1942. He was managing editor of the *"Daily Sketch"* and later Deputy Chairman of Kemsley Newspapers. He succeeded his father as the 2nd Viscount Kemsley on his father's death in 1968. The newspaper business having been sold off, Lionel Berry played no further part in it. He had been elected an M.P. in 1943, as a Conservative, but lost his seat in the 1945 election. When he went to the House of Lords he continued his allegiance with the Conservative Party. At Court meetings he had the habit of idly flipping the sides of his spectacles, the speed of the flip indicated his interest in proceedings. A fast flip indicated an imminent entry into the discussion! I came to value the shrewd advice he provided to the Clerk from time to time, sometimes privately, sometimes sotto voce, but sometimes not. He was Master on two occasions, 1949-50 and 1959-60. (7)

To complete the family connection with the Company, Lionel Berry's second daughter, Jane, they had no sons, married Nigel

Mobbs and on the 10th February, 1977, the Court was delighted to admit him to the Freedom and subsequently the Livery, to continue, at one remove as it were, the family connection with the Company. Mobbs, after an unsuccessful academic career, he didn't get his Oxford engineering degree because he found it "extremely boring", got his grounding in the property world before following his father and grandfather into Slough Estates, which his grandfather had part founded in 1920. He duly became Chairman and Chief Executive, in 1976, where he showed his considerable expertise in the property world for the next twenty years. He took direct and active management of Slough Estates and proved astute in the acquisition of other property. When he eventually retired from Slough Estates their properties were estimated to be worth £1.8 billion. His "feel" for business soon became appreciated elsewhere and over the years he was involved with Barclays Bank, Charterhouse Banking Group, the retailer Kingfisher, Bovis Homes, Cookson and the Howard de Walden Estate. He was also Chairman of the Conservative Party, vice president of the Association of British Chambers of Commerce and Chairman of the Historic Royal Palaces He was once compared to *"a slightly lumbering but affectionate and appealing Great Dane"*. It was at his insistence that the term of office of the Master and Wardens was reduced to one year and not the two year period it had been for many years. He was strongly of the opinion that if the Company wished to continue to attract the best people, both within and without the profession, a two year period, effectively six years, over the three offices, was too much to expect in modern times. He was the first Master, in 1989, to serve the new one year term. (8)

This all strikes of nepotism and jobs for the boys in Livery Companies. It wasn't really a problem with the Spectacle Makers Company, though when a son joined a father on the Court one Liveryman was sufficiently irate as to write to the Lord Mayor about it. I duly got a call from the Lord Mayor, oh yes they do take notice, or did, along the lines of "And what's all this about". Having explained the position he laughed, "Have you looked at the Mercers Court recently" he asked. Having taken the hint I did look, and at that time that Court consisted almost entirely of members of the Watney family. As it happened our family doctor was a Watney and when he retired, so I heard, the head of the family said "Right now it's your turn to come on the Court", so he did.

**

All the Minutes have so far, up to 1909, been hand-written in various degrees of legibility. For the 31st March, 1909, the Minutes of a Special Meeting, convened by the Master at the offices of the *"Daily Telegraph"*, are typed on flimsy paper – and what a meeting!

The Clerk: *was "permitted to be present"* but the Assistant Clerk, who never seems to have been officially appointed as such: *"was requested to stay in an adjoining room"*. The Clerk was invited to make a statement, the basis of which was that irregularities had occurred in respect to the Diploma Scheme. The Clerk had been invited to go to see a solicitor, who had in his possession a number of letters written to the Clerk and marked "Personal", which had not been delivered because the solicitor had been advised by the Assistant Clerk, one J.W. Forster, that: *"the Clerk had had a stroke of paralysis and it was undesirable that he should see a letter"* the solicitor added that there were 24 other letters from members of the Industry *"complaining of the way in which they had been treated with regard to Diploma matters"*. The Clerk then took the: *"whole of the active conduct of the Diploma Scheme out of the Assistant Clerk's hands"*.

The Clerk added, that the Assistant Clerk had disposed of one of the Clerk's typewriters without permission: *"and other acts of misconduct and insubordination were referred to"*. The Clerk therefore gave Forster notice that his services would be no longer required personally by the Clerk. Account books were then requested and: *"the Clerk was then asked to retire. The Assistant Clerk was then called in and remained with the Master and Wardens for a considerable time: eventually being also requested to withdraw"*. The meeting then: *"remained in deliberation for another considerable period"* at the end of which the Clerk was asked to summon a Special Court Meeting at the *"Daily Telegraph"* office on the 28th April, using a special agenda: *"To consider the question of the organisation of the office of the Company"* – this, incidentally, is pinned onto the Minutes scrawled by the Master on an old envelope! What drama! Or a storm in a teacup?

The meeting on the 28th April proceeds with the payment of Court attendance fees, the acceptance of a revised examination syllabus, and a further proposed improvement to the sight testing examination, by the Clerk. One would normally expect such a meeting to stick to the main subject alone. However, things warm up with the Clerk, replying to a question from the Master, informing the meeting that *"he intended after Saturday next having his son who was relinquishing a very good position in the North in order to assist his father the Clerk of the Spectaclemakers Company"*.

In reply to a question from the Upper Warden: *"the Clerk stated his opinion that he considered three months the proper notice to give Mr. J.W. Forster to terminate his Assistant Clerkship to this Company and it would be desirable the notice should be on the same lines as which he* (Sewell) *gave Forster in February last when taking action to part with him as his* (Sewell's) *private Secretary in February last."*

The Clerk was eventually asked to withdraw, but before doing so, emphatically expressed to the Court his unqualified objection to Mr. J.W. Forster serving any longer with him as Assistant Clerk to the Company – for reasons partly explained to the Master and Wardens on the 31st March. Mr. Foster was then called in, and shortly afterwards the Clerk was requested to return, when the Master informed him (the Clerk): *"it had been decided to hold the Adjourned Ladyday Quarterly Court on Thursday 13th prox. at 2.30 of the clock in the offices of the Daily Telegraph the same as today"*.

Perhaps I am reading the runes wrongly, but if I had been the Clerk at this time, with all this huffing and puffing, I would have expected the Court to have given Forster notice. But they apparently didn't. At the May Court meeting, after the normal discharge of business and just before it was agreed that the July Diploma examinations be held, for the first time, at the Northampton Institute, it was reported that: *"Mr. J.W. Forster the Assistant Clerk having offered to resign the Court in consideration thereof agreed to vote him thirty guineas as recognition of his past services"*.

If half of what Sewell had alleged had been true the Court ought to have sacked Forster, and there was no modern wrongful dismissal procedures to worry them. Had Sewell over egged it all, after more than 40 years service were his faculties failing? Or had the Court talked Forster into a resignation, rather than a sacking, for forms sake, if so why make him a payment. We shall never know, but it did liven the Minutes up considerably from their normally straight-laced and brief description of quite important matters.

It is not clear from the handwritten part of these various Minutes referred to who actually wrote them. The handwriting changes for the 28th April and 13th May meetings, and changes again for the following Court. Somebody wrote up just the two Court meetings. It could be Peel, the Master, but as we don't, for various reasons, seem to have his signature anywhere, it is difficult to know. Perhaps Sewell himself wrote them, and not other Minutes, which would account for the reporting of his *"emphatically expressed"* views.

It is unusual, in my experience at any rate, for the Clerk being asked to withdraw, except on matters concerning his own salary. The only other time I can remember being asked to withdraw, was when the Master of the day was going to get it in the neck from the Court! I know this only because after the meeting various members of the Court came across the Courtyard and told me what went on, and then the Master came over to the Office and gave me his version. Needless to say none of this was minuted, a pity it might have cheered up a future Archivist's reading.

**

Another well-known Liveryman at this time was Albert Walter Gamage, who became a Freeman and Liveryman of the Company on 8th October, 1904. He was the seventeenth child of a Herefordshire plumber and glazier, and was born on the 14th July, 1855. Several of his brothers and sisters established a draper's and milliner's shop and, though too young to have taken much part in the early days of the shop, he helped out from time to time, and obviously learnt something of the art of window display, which was to stand him in good stead in London.

Albert was apprenticed to a London draper and subsequently to the wholesale drapery warehouse run by Hitchcock, Williams and Co. in St Paul's Churchyard. By 1878, he went into partnership with a colleague, Frank Spain, and they sunk their savings into leasing a small, the front was just 5 feet wide, watch repair shop at 128, Holborn, on the strength of the advice of a local trader that *"Holborn lacked a decent hosiery shop"*. Arthur's first action was to hang his motto over the doorway *"Tall Oaks from Little Acorns Grow"*.

He and his partner slept in the back of the shop and allowed themselves 14 shillings a week for their living expenses. Another of his mottoes was *"Always be satisfied with small profits"* and to that end they bought up some special hair brushes and sold them much more cheaply than their competitors. Though the area was considered unfashionable, the crowds began to come, and after the first year of trading they had made £1,632. By 1881, he had bought out his partner and set about reorganising the business in order to sell a wider range of goods.

He searched far and wide for new products, travelling extensively in Europe and North America. On his travels he called on Frau Steiff's teddy-bear factory in the Black Forest, and became the greatest importer of her teddies. He hit on the idea, as had others who were to run department stores, of buying in bulk and selling at a low profit. In 1885, after the new safety bicycle was introduced, Albert arranged for bikes to be built under the Gamages' label.

With more stock Albert obviously needed more warehouse and shop space, so he started acquiring adjacent properties and managed to put together about two acres of floor space, most of the area between Leather Lane and Hatton Gardens, in front of which he had constructed an impressive neo-Gothic façade, which he called the *People's Popular Emporium,* and he took a full page advertisement, the front page, of the *"Daily Mail",* to announce it. With such higgledy piggledy acquisition, despite alterations, the place became a veritable rabbit warren of rooms, passages, ramps, steps and stairs. Those of a similar age to the venerable past Clerk no doubt have vivid memories of trying to find things in Gamages, and the excitement of going into the unknown. A bit like buying books at the old Foyles in Charing Cross Road.

Gamages was not directly aimed at the lady shopper, but more at the City gents who worked in the Square Mile south and east of Holborn. But then at the weekends these self-same gents would return with the family, clever marketing! At Christmas time it was a child's dream, full of toys, many of which Albert had uncovered.

Albert was an innovator in that he forged links with companies who made goods just for Gamages, so that he could avoid using firms which objected to his pricing policy. Anything new was rapidly adopted. When cars came to be in demand he sold them under his own label and opened a special motoring department in the shop. At the same time he added large zoological and toy departments. He was the first in this country to produce a huge mail-order catalogue. That for 1911, 900 pages of it, had 49 pages devoted to bicycles, motor-bicycles and cycling equipment. But haberdashery, furniture, sporting goods, gardening supplies and utensils, camping equipment and clothing were also to be had. He built up the outdoor side of the store which was much to his own liking. He became president of a number of athletic clubs, and the donor of endless challenge cups and shields. Gamages in due course became the official outfitter for the Boy Scouts. Albert Gamage died in 1930 when tradition has it *"that he lay in state in the cycle department with a guard of honour made up of members of his staff"*.

The premises eventually closed in March 1972, to be replaced by a massive redevelopment scheme, perhaps not the *"tall oaks"* Albert originally had in mind. (9)

**

In 1909, another Liveryman with a still well-known name, who had been admitted to the Company some 2 years before, was setting out to become a Sheriff, Ralph Slazenger. Born Ralph Slazenger Moss in 1845, he had initially joined his father in the tailoring business which had expanded into a general outfitters. In 1885, Ralph, leaving the Northern business in the hands of his brothers, came to London and set-up a new business at 56, Cannon Street *"manufacturing indiarubber goods for the growing enthusiasm for middle-class sports"*. Having left his old haunts behind, he also left off the Moss bit of his name. Not least because he had married a rich New Zealand widow, his business grew rapidly, becoming a leading manufacturer of balls and other equipment for golf and tennis. On the tennis front the publicity which came from providing balls to the All England Tennis Club, with Wimbledon, Eastbourne and other events that they arranged, was the great prize.

Slazenger had a manager, Archdale Palmer, whose sharp practice engineered the All England contract. At a cost, for the firm *"was dragged into a scandal and allegations of attempted bribery at Wimbledon in 1905. This did not, however, harm the firm's reputation or growth and Palmer continued to work for Slazengers"*. Slazenger, up-to-date as usual, moved the firm away from manual manufacture to machine production and, on the basis of continued success, floated the business on the Stock Exchange.

While the firm was flourishing Slazenger became involved in the corporate life of the City of London, becoming a member of 6 other Livery Companies as well as the Spectacle Makers, a Common Councillor, and duly made Sheriff in 1909, though he was defeated in an Aldermanic election. He died in October, 1910 and despite his wishes for a non-religious cremation his wife arranged an Anglican service. After a number of mergers during the Second World War Slazengers was eventually sold to Dunlop Rubber in 1950, though the sale did not include the brand name. (10)

**

The first Spectacle Maker to hold a V.C. was Major Edward Browne-Synge-Hutchinson, who became a Freeman and Liveryman on 3rd February, 1911. He was the son of Major David Brown of 7th (Queen's Own) Hussars. He obtained his commission as a Lieutenant in the 18th Hussars in 1883, becoming a Captain in less than 5 years. It was during his service with the 18th Hussars in South Africa at the action at Geluk that he won the Victoria Cross.

His action was gazetted as follows: *"On the 13th October, 1900 when the enemy were within 400 yards, and bringing heavy fire to bear, Major Brown, seeing that Sergeant Kersey's horse was shot, stopped behind the last squadron as it was retiring, and helped Sergeant Kersey to mount behind him, carrying him for about three quarters of a mile to a place of safety. He did this under heavy fire. Major Brown afterwards enabled Lieutenant Browne, 14th Hussars, to mount, by holding his horse, which was very restive under the heavy fire. Lieutenant Browne could not otherwise have mounted. Subsequently Major Brown carried Lance Corporal Trumpeter Leigh out of action."* It was not mentioned in the official account that the horses of three other men were held by Major Brown, as they were in difficulties with them, and that one of the animals had run away and had to be caught and brought back! He was the last officer of the British Regular Army to win the Victoria Cross in the life-time of Queen Victoria.

He was mentioned in Despatches a number of times and commanded the 14th Hussars. He was promoted to Colonel, became a member of the Central Executive Committee of the St. John's Ambulance Association and was created a C.B. all in 1911, the year he obtained His Freedom and Livery of the Spectacle Makers Company.

**

For a "Minor" Livery Company, which only obtained its Livery in 1809, the Company has produced some 32 Lord Mayors from amongst its ranks, an extraordinarily high number. (See Appendix I) Of that number 20 were also Masters of the Company. The reason for this glut of Spectacle Makers as Lord Mayor, and to that number should be added a further 35 who became Sheriff, must, I think, stem from the fact that all three Clerks to the Company in the 19th Century also served, as their day job as it were, in the Chamberlain's Court. These potential Lord Mayors would have to be Free of the City before their admission to the Livery, and this freedom was of course via the Chamberlain's Court. What would be more natural, should the question of an appropriate Livery Company to join been raised, than that the Clerk to the Spectacle Makers would suggest the Spectacle Makers Company. Once a pattern of members of this Livery becoming Aldermen, Sheriff, and subsequently Lord Mayor became established, around the late 1840s, then it would be even more likely that aspiring Lord Mayors would head towards the Spectacle Makers. Particularly as, like London buses, there were no Spectacle Maker Lord Mayors and then three came along in four years, John Johnson 1845, Sir George Carroll 1846 and Sir James Duke 1848, and there would have been two others if Alderman James Harmer had not upset the

City, and had Alderman John Lainson become Lord Mayor.

James Boudon, who was Clerk to the Company for 11 years to 1811, and who was later invited as a guest to a Livery Dinner, no hint intended, was in the Chamberlain's Office from 1809 to 1831. It was his name on the Guest List quoted in the Court Minutes which started me on this line of research. James Sewell, Clerk 1811 to 1866, was elected Clerk of the Chamber in 1842 to 1866. Col. Thomas Davies Sewell, Clerk to the Company from 1866 to 1916, was Clerk to the Chamberlain's Court from 1867 to 1901. Thus there was only a few years in the 19th Century when a Clerk to the Spectacle Makers Company did not hold this office!

After the 3 Lord Mayors in four years in the late 1840s they came in "clumps" if such a word could be used for such elevated persons as Lord Mayors. 6 between 1860 and 1874 (7 as one, William Cubitt, served for 2 years), 7 from 1880 to 1887 (8 as Sir Robert Fowler served a second term on the death of George Nottage in office, another Spectacle Maker), 5 between 1894 and 1902 and finally, 5 between 1915 and 1924. I doubt if this Company will be as well represented again, and I doubt if any other "Minor Company" can make such a claim.

Of course not all these Lord Mayors had the Spectacle Makers as their "Mother Company". It has to be appreciated that when an individual first becomes a member of a Livery Company this is then his "Mother Company". It remains so despite any later Companies he may join, unless he asks to change his Mother Company, which is usually agreed, the official description being "translated". Such translations are often from a Minor Company to one of the self-elected "Great Twelve". Up until 1740, the Lord Mayor had to be a Liveryman of one of the Great Twelve, so such translations were not rare. Since that date the greater percentage of Lord Mayors have come from the Minor Companies, the Liverymen of the Great Twelve having become more involved in national and international trade rather than the trade of their Company, or in the affairs of the City of London. When a Liveryman takes office as Alderman, Sheriff or Lord Mayor, his Livery is naturally stated as that of his mother Company whatever other Companies he, or she, may belong to.

Of the 12 Liverymen of the Spectacle Makers who became Lord Mayor but did not become Master of the Company, four have the Spectacle Makers as their Mother Company. Of these four, Sir Henry Knight, who was Sheriff in 1875/76 and Lord Mayor in 1882/83, was actually translated to the Fishmongers Company in 1887, after he had been Lord Mayor. During his Mayoralty he dedicated two open spaces, Burnham Beeches and Coulsdon Common, as recreation grounds. He was also the last Lord Mayor to be sworn in at Westminster, for the new Law Courts in the Strand were opened during his year of office. Since then all Lord Mayors have been sworn in at the Law Courts in the Strand, which is why this is the half way mark in the Lord Mayor's Procession, from whence it returns to the Mansion House.

The second was the unfortunate George Nottage. He had started work at sixteen in his uncle's iron foundry in Glamorgan. He became interested in photography and when he came to London, he founded the London Stereoscopic and Photographic Company, which was a pioneer in photographic work. The third was Sir Joseph Renals whom we have already met. Last, and by no means least, Sir Frederick Hoare, Sheriff 1956/57, Lord Mayor 1961/62, was one of many generations of that banking family to have been a Spectacle Maker, and our last Lord Mayor to date, 2019.

The mother Companies of the other eight varied greatly. Sir Francis Moon, Sheriff 1843/44, Lord Mayor 1854/55, was a Stationer and a Loriner, and became a Liveryman of this Company in October 1854, when he was already Lord Mayor Elect. His father was a gold and silver smith. He began as a print seller and developed into a large-scale print seller as has been previously reported. William Cubitt, Sheriff 1847/48, Lord Mayor 1860/62, was a Fishmonger. He was the younger brother of Thomas Cubitt, the builder of South Belgravia. He was re-elected to the Mayoralty at the close of his first year of office, probably as a consolation for his defeat in the contest for the parliamentary representation of the City, on the retirement of Lord John Russell.

Sir Alfred Newton, Sheriff 1888/89, Lord Mayor 1899/00 was a Fanmaker and a Liveryman of seven other Companies, of three of which he was also Master, so he probably had no time left to become Master of the Spectacle Makers! He founded the City Imperial Volunteers to serve in the Boer War and collected a large amount of money for their use, sufficient to provide pensions for the returning Volunteers, the last recipient dying in 1978.

Sir John Bell, Sheriff 1901/02, Lord Mayor 1907/08, was a Fanmaker and a Liveryman of three other Companies. He translated to the Haberdashers in 1907 in time for his election as Lord Mayor. Sir William Dunn, Sheriff 1906/07, Lord Mayor 1916/17, was a Wheelwright and a Liveryman of seven other Companies. James Roll, Sheriff 1909/10, Lord Mayor 1920/21 was a Horner and a Liveryman of four other Companies. From his arrival in London as "a small and friendless boy from the country", his own description, Roll served with the Pearl Assurance for 50 years and became Lord Mayor at the ripe old age of 73. Sir Alfred Bower, Sheriff 1912/13, Lord Mayor 1924/5, was a Vintner, one of whose claims to fame was that he was the founder of that well-known Fleet Street watering hole – El Vinos.

Coming up to modern times Sir Cullum Welch, Sheriff 1950/51 was translated to the Haberdashers before becoming Lord Mayor in 1956/57. When I joined the Company in 1965, there was still talk of the row which had ensued in the Court when this translation was requested!

The original purpose of a Livery Company was to defend and look after the standards of a specific trade for the benefit of the public. With, historically at least, most tradesmen having but a single trade, it seems odd, to say the least, that there were, are, and no doubt will be, individuals who seem to make a career out of joining as many Livery Companies as possible. This grandiloquent process of pot hunting seems a negation of the very idea of a Livery Company, though it does add considerably more votes come election time. Which is probably the reason for a number of our Lord Mayors becoming, eventually, spectacle makers. But I digress.

The Lord Mayor must already have served the office of Sheriff. Of the two Sheriffs each year, one is the Aldermanic Sheriff, and the other the Lay Sheriff. Sometimes when the Court of Aldermen gets it wrong, there would be years when there were two Aldermanic Sheriffs. The Spectacle Makers has had more than its share of Sheriffs. (See Appendix II). As already reported the Company obtained its Livery in 1809, and our first Sheriff was Lawrence Gwynne in 1818/19. There have been 35 Liverymen of the Spectacle Makers Company who have been Sheriff, in addition to those who eventually became Lord Mayor, though the Spectacle Makers may not have been their Mother Company. This makes double checking difficult, so there may be even more Sheriffs to come. (2018 saw the election of another Spectacle Maker Sheriff, Alderman Vincent Keaveny, whose Mother Company is the Solicitor's.)

This Spectacle Maker as Sheriff scenario, as with that of Lord Mayors, went in spells. Between 1847 and 1853 there were 6, between 1861 and 1866 there were 5 and between 1885 and 1898 there were 10. Of the 35 Spectacle Maker Sheriffs, 14 became Liverymen in the year they were elected Sheriff, and of these 9 had the Spectacle Makers as their Mother Company. This would appear to indicate that the Company had become a force to be reckoned with in the City of London civic affairs in the latter part of the 19th century. If one wanted to be Sheriff and had no livery allegiance, ours was the company to be with, and if you were already a Liveryman of another company being admitted to the Spectacle Makers would ensure many additional voters at the Wicket Gates.

With this record of Lord Mayors and Sheriffs, and, in the 19th century, a number of Common Councillors amongst our Liverymen and Freemen, at least 37 at one and the same time, the Company should be proud of the involvement its members have had in the Corporation of London, and the faith which those members had in the Spectacle Makers as a suitable launch pad for their City ambitions. (11), (12)

A complete list of Spectacle Maker Lord Mayors appears at Appendix I and of Sheriffs at Appendix II.

**

Having recently had occasion to send flowers for a funeral and used the services, as no doubt we all have, of Interflora, I realised that they had not always been around. When the Senior Past Master died in 1912, the Court Minutes relate that: *"the Acting Beadle had taken a funeral wreath to Torquay where Sir Horatio D. Davies had died."*

Admittedly people did not move around so much in the "old days" and so the funeral would very often have been local, but it wasn't everyone who had the services of an Acting Beadle. It was also quite a distance to Torquay. He presumably went by train, driving that sort of distance, now common-place, would not have been contemplated. That would mean a steam train which, though romantic, was highly inefficient, and think of his carbon footprint! (How nice it must have been not even to know what a carbon footprint was, even if such thoughts are not now PC. And they wouldn't have known what that meant either!!)

**

The occupations of our Freemen have been many and various

over the years, but there haven't been many firemen amongst them. In June 1897, William Cox, a member of the Metropolitan Fire Brigade, became a Freeman. At a Court meeting in June 1912 the following resolution was moved:

> *"That the hearty congratulations of this Court be unanimously and cordially accorded to Station Officer William Cox, M.F.B., a Freeman of this Company of 14 years standing for the conspicuous act of prompt bravery he displayed in rescuing two lives who must otherwise have perished at a fire which occurred at 196 Mile End Road, on 29th January, 1912, thereby earning the Victoria Cross of the Fire Brigade for Extraordinary gallant conduct signified by the award of a silver medal.*
> *The foregoing being seconded was put by the Master to the Vote and unanimously agreed to as well as that the said resolution be fairly written on vellum and presented to Station Master William Cox by Lord Aldenham the Master".*

**

Writing votes of thanks, and other congratulatory messages on vellum, was all the rage at the time. As previously mentioned before becoming Clerk, I had worked in the Town Clerk's Office at the Corporation of London. One of our tasks was to draft the various Committees' votes of thanks to their Chairmen, for somebody else to write them up on vellum. Quite a pleasant task for the first couple of years for the same Chairman but if, as they did, they lasted for a number of years, reference to Roget's *"Thesaurus"* became an absolute necessity. It was instructive to note the re-action of long-time committee members as they appreciated the lengths to which we had to go, each year, to say the same thing, a slightly different way. Usually the Chairman didn't notice.

**

In 1914, the Company paid £2-12-6 for a verbatim shorthand report of the speeches at the Livery Dinner. The best speeches on such occasions are ephemeral things, not necessarily worthy of transcription, but that's the Edwardians for you.

**

In February, 1915, a candidate for a Diploma claimed exemption from £2 of Stamp Duty, by reason of his having served as an apprentice to an optician. He produced:

"as evidence an Indenture which was so blotted and disfigured with red ink as also otherwise disfigured that it was thought desirable that the Acting Beadle should go to Peterborough to verify the documents".

The applicant's Master: *"certified in writing his belief as to the correctness of the Candidates statement"*. After that the Diploma was issued and the candidate wrote: *"a most ample expression of gratitude"*. So everyone was happy ever after – but for £2! Stamp Duty was avoided, a battle with officialdom won, but how much was the fare to Peterborough? £2 was probably a week's salary, but it seems an expensive way to prove a point for the Company?

**

Contemporary events, apart from the death of a Monarch, or a Coronation which affects the date of a Court meeting, are rarely referred to in the Court Minutes. The First World War, not unreasonably, proved an exception. Though there were few air raids, certainly compared to the Second World War, a vast number of men either volunteered or were conscripted, and women came more to the fore, taking on many of the jobs vacated by the men in the forces.

The first reference comes early on in November 1914, when Past Master, Sir Marcus Samuel, asked the question as to: *"whether Aliens could be and were admitted to the Freedom of the Company being answered in the affirmative by the Clerk it was Resolved Unanimously to postpone discussion on the matter until the next Court meeting"*. This Past Clerk would not have been able to answer that question in the affirmative, initially at least, unless they had been naturalised or came from the "old Commonwealth".

Be that as it may at its next meeting the Court, after due discussion, resolved:

"That it be a recommendation to the next Court viz. the propriety of not admitting to the Company during the present War any persons of German or Austrian nationality carrying on hostilities against Great Britain".

At the next Court the recommendation was agreed. A couple of years later the Court of Aldermen was to resolve that naturalised Germans should not be admitted to the Freedom of the City, and asked Livery Companies to ensure that a full Birth Certificate be produced, as a common practice had developed that potential Freemen only provided a Certificate of Registry of Birth.

But the War begins to appear more often and in June, 1915, Colonel Harry Lawson, a Past Master, was apologising for not attending a Court meeting: *"on account of his Military duties"*. Viscount Hill was another whose military duties were to prevent his attendance at Court meetings.

Despite the fact that, to Europe at any rate, this was the Great War, there were parts of the world which were not as yet aware of the implications. The request in June 1915, for: *"the loan of the Company's Plate and other articles of public interest"* for use in an Optical Exhibition in San Francisco, was, not surprisingly, declined.

Gallipoli in 1915, was notable in the Company records by the death of two Liverymen (and perhaps more, but not there mentioned). Major F.R.A.N. Knollys was serving with the 1st City of London Yeomanry (Rough Riders) and died of *"severe wounds"*. Though only some nine years a Liveryman, he had been active on the Company's behalf in that time. Amongst other things on his death, he established the Knollys Fund, with a legacy of £50 *"to be invested in any investments authorised by law for charitable Trust Funds with power to vary the investments therein from time to time and the income arising from such investments to be applied in the maintenance or the relief of any widow, son, daughter, brother or sister of a deceased Liveryman of the Company".*

The second Liveryman was Captain Robert Sebag-Montefiore, serving with the East Kent Yeomanry. He was also the junior Assistant of the Court having been sworn in 1912. He was the son-in-law of Sir Marcus Samuel, who, at that time had served as Master three times. Robert was the second generation of that family to have served on the Court of the Company.

Many men were being called to arms as the war continued and the Company's Diploma holders were no exception, and joining the forces could entail the closing of their establishments. In 1916, the Master, Sir John Rolleston, apparently off his own bat, though he subsequently asked the Court, offered:

"that in many of these cases the optician has an assistant, or relative, or close connection – of either sex – who, if more instructed in the conduct of an optical business, might be able to carry it on during the absence of the optician with the colours, so that, at least, complete closure could be avoided.
In this emergency, therefore, (the Company) offers to any such nominee of a diploma holder, free of charge, the services of the Official Instructor, Mr. Lionel Laurance, for a personal course of instruction in optics (in London) as full as may be possible within the limits of time at disposal, with the hope of thus rendering the assistance of such nominee more valuable for the object in view".

No such person could claim in any way the F.S.M.C., and the Company could refuse any application: *"without reason assigned"*. The Court agreed the proposal and instructed the Clerk, I imagine with all haste in view of the offer, to find out what fees Laurance was charging for each nominee, and also the fee per class. They were on good historical grounds for it had been the habit to allow the widow of a spectacle maker to take over his shop and continue in the trade, though admittedly the "trade" had become a good deal more technical and demanding in the ensuing 200 or so years.

The use of the phrase *"until the end of the war"* becomes more frequent and on the death of the Clerk, Col. Davies Sewell after 49 years service, no Clerk was to be appointed and an Acting Clerk, W. Sewell Singer, appointed *"until the end of the War"*. In the same way the fee to the Official Instructor, Lionel Laurance, increased to £100, *"until the end of the War"*.

Until the War, pensioners, some in their eighties, were expected to turn up to the Quarterly meetings to collect their pensions, but it then became the habit, and was continued, that their pension money was sent by post.

In 1916, the Lord Mayor and Sheriffs Committee asked whether, as the Company was associated with the Lord Mayor elect (Sir William Dunn) or the Sheriffs, whether they wished to take part in the Lord Mayor's Procession on the 9th November. If "yes" would they limit their carriages to two and provide a band. The Court simplified the issue by stating that: *"under the existing War conditions did not contemplate attending"*.

When an apprentice was taken on, the consent of the father was required. During the course of the War more and more often the consent of the mother is noted, with the father: "serving in H.M. Forces".

An approach was made in 1917, with other bodies, to the Board of Trade attempting to get the withdrawal of its prohibition to the import of articles containing gold so far as it affected the spectacle making industry.

Only partly affected by the War comes a proposal in 1917, from the B.O.A., to establish a combined examination with the Company, but under the control of the B.O.A. The Master and the Director of Examinations were asked to consider the proposal. They reported in April of that year. The main inducement from the B.O.A. side appears to be in the connection it had established during the War with the military authorities for testing the sight of recruits, and thus *"promoting an Official connection of much importance"*. The B.O.A. offered the use of a hall for examination purposes, and also seemed to consider that, with the limited resources of the Company, it would be a material gain for us to join such a scheme. Sir William Hart Dyke, in his report, shoots this last point down by pointing out that from the last accounts the B.O.A.'s income amounted to less than £900! Sir William continues:

"weighing the advantages suggested in Mr. Sutcliffe's proposals with the disadvantages, I cannot advise the Court to accept them. Our work on behalf of the optical industry has been fully recognised and considering our limited resources has proved most successful".

He continues by emphasising the valuable asset the Company Diploma was considered, and again mentioning that the examinations would be entirely controlled by the B.O.A. He ends:

"Were I certain that by accepting Mr. Sutcliffe's proposals we could attain some great results as regards training in Technical Optics I would make any reasonable sacrifices to secure the same. I can however see no guarantee for such a result in the scheme before

me". He ends on a prophesy which was a long time coming, some would say it still hasn't! *"In my judgement we should stand by the position we occupy until after the War when substantial efforts will be made by the L.C.C. and other educational bodies assisted by Parliament to secure the future of the Optical Trade. Other and better opportunities may then arise for our co-operation and support".* Not unsurprisingly, Sir William having read his report to the Court, *"it was discussed and afterwards Unanimously adopted"*.

Towards the end of 1917, the Court is advised of the death in action of Lieutenant Gerald George Samuel, the younger son of Sir Marcus Samuel, a Past Master.

The proportion of women taking the examinations increased in 1917, to 5 of the 11 passes in the May examination, though this was a trend which did not continue. Unexpectedly the first examinations after the War, those of May and November, 1919, out of a pass list of 39, 14 were "old Empire", and out of the pass list of the November exam of 48, 21 were old Empire. The Acting Clerk reported that: *"among whom were several Overseas men who having joined up for the War were about to return to their respective colonies"*.

At the end of 1917, the housekeeper of 19, Lincoln's Inn Fields, the Company's property at the time, was awarded a War Bonus of £1 a month on top of her generous £5 a month.

In early 1918, the Council of the London Chamber of Commerce make an approach to the Livery Companies: *"In these difficult times for the Trade, Commerce of Great Britain, and more especially of the City of London, it is quite evident that some special measures will have to be taken if the trade and commerce of London is not to suffer. In pursuance of its efforts to avert this misfortune, the Council of the London Chamber of Commerce, believe that the greatest help could be given by the closer co-operation with the*

Chamber of the Livery Companies of London." Briefly it was proposed to achieve this by encouraging the companies to reconnect with their trades. The Court were happy to pay the subscription of 3 guineas but wanted to know if there was any:

"likelihood of overlapping taking place in the objects of the City Livery Club and the London Chamber of Commerce". The City Livery Club had been founded in 1914 *"to bind together in one organisation liverymen of the various guilds... in service to the Ancient Corporation and in maintenance of the priceless City Churches"*.

Only partly attributable to the War, one of the tenants of 19, Lincoln's Inn Fields, asked, yet again, if the Company would contribute towards the cost of the installation of electric light in their premises. The Court declined on the basis that: *"it was an inopportune time to make such an installation owing to the increased costs of materials"*. The wiring of the building for electricity had first been raised in 1901, when the tenants had made the approach, and the Court heartily agreed, if paid for by the tenants. The Minutes remain silent on the point until the 1918 reference.

And so the War ends, though you wouldn't know this from the Minutes. The world had changed beyond recognition, but the Spectacle Makers continues on its same merry way. Perhaps this is the essence of the Livery Companies, to provide a solid, reassuring face to an ever-changing world. A stability to a world of chaos, carrying the standards, ethics and ethos of old to be tempered by slow change – let's hope so. It just seems a pity that in 1939 we all forgot that we had already had "the War to end all Wars".

**

The Court allowed the use in newspapers of a "Block Advertisement", which took the form of the Company arms (old style), Company name, names of various Company officials, together with the name of the individual and the note that they had passed *"the prescribed examination in optics and sight testing, has been granted the Diploma of efficiency and the right to use the affix F.S.M.C. He is therefore recommended as competent to prescribe glasses for correcting optical defects of the eye"*.

If a diplomate stuck to that form then no problem. However one such, either through error or deliberately, embellished his block by having printed on the left hand side *"COLE'S HONEY BALSAM will cure the Worst Coughs in the Least Time"* and adding *"1s. per Bottle, Post Free 1s. 2d."* To the right hand side *"SOLE AGENT for the Famous Cough Lozenges Nupines. 2d. per oz. 1s. for 8 ozs."*. This was considered gilding the lily a bit too much. The Diplomate replied to the Clerk's no doubt incensed letter:

"I must apologise for any breach of my agreement. I will see that the other part of the advert apart from the optical block is not published in future. I did not understand that this was not allowed or I Certainly would not have had it. The printer proposed printing that at the sides to fill up the space. Trusting this will be satisfactory". As no further action was proposed it presumably was.

The good opticians of Clacton-on-Sea, for this is where this heinous crime was committed, could now rest, grateful that their professional integrity had been upheld, and their colleague stealing a march snuffed out!

**

Sir Marcus Samuel had first raised the issue of the admission of ladies to the Livery in July, 1918. After a couple of Court meetings, it was unanimously agreed. Sir Horace Brooks Marshall was the Lord Mayor at the time, a Spectacle Maker, and as he was also the Master it was logical to invite the Lady Mayoress to join the Livery. So it was that Dame Laura Rebecca Marshall was admitted to the

Freedom at the Court meeting on the 25th September, 1919, the Court meeting being held in the Mansion House:

> *"the Livery Declaration was then read and signed whereupon the Lady Mayoress was clothed with a Livery Gown by the Acting Clerk and was afterwards the recipient of the hearty congratulations of the Master the Renter Warden and the Members of the Court upon being the first Lady to be admitted upon the Livery of the Company. Alderman Sir Marcus Samuel, Bart., the Senior Past Master present, in a felicitous speech presented the Lady Mayoress on behalf of the Company with a pair of Tortoiseshell Lorgnettes in a Lizard skin case to mark the interesting occasion of her admission this day to the Freedom and Livery. The Lady Mayoress gracefully thanked the Court for the useful Gift and the congratulations offered her, expressing pride at being the first Lady to be admitted on the Livery".*

Then all round the back for a brandy? Not quite - at the end of the Court meeting: *"the Lord Mayor and the Lady Mayoress kindly entertained the Members of the Court to Tea in the Drawing Room"* – oh how Edwardian, oh how Victorian!

It is unfair to put a modern spin on the words of our ancestors, or I would be wondering whether the use of the phrase *"interesting occasion"* by the Acting Clerk was a bit of male chauvinism. And whether the Lady Mayoress's thanks *"for the useful gift"* was a response in kind. Not that Lady Liverymen were as frequent as the leaves in Vallombrosa (according to Milton). The next lady admitted was Elizabeth Weston, an optician, in 1921, but after that a casual search does not reveal another lady admitted until 1939. But at least the gesture had been made, the cork coming out of the bottle, the glass ceiling broken or whatever phrase you prefer.

**

The Master in 1920, and indeed again in 1924-25, was, to give him his full title, Colonel and Alderman Sir Charles Cheers Wakefield Bt., C.B.E. (afterwards Viscount Wakefield of Hythe). Another highly successful industrialist to grace the Company with membership, Wakefield, born in 1859, introduced the Castrol brand, a name perhaps not as well remembered now as in previous years. He set up his own firm of C.C. Wakefield and Co. in 1899, which dealt in lubricating oil and equipment. Initially concentrating on lubricants for British and overseas railways, the rapid development of the motor car market created new opportunities for the firm. Wakefield introduced Wakefield Motor Oil, subtitled in 1912, the Castrol brand, as one ingredient was castor oil. The company was ahead of the rest of the industry, which had yet to realise the significance of the motor car, and they stayed ahead of the competition by two policies; massive and often topical advertising and advanced research.

The development of the aeroplane encouraged Wakefield to develop the Castrol R brand, an aircraft fluid which remained liquid at high-altitude temperatures, which received a unique testimonial *"when the Kaiser's chief of staff admitted to the Kaiser that the British had discovered the secret of non-freezing aircraft lubricant, which the Germans had been seeking for months"*. Developments in the mechanisation of farming were not overlooked with the introduction of Agricastrol in 1917. Between the wars many speed records were broken by cars, speedboats, motorcycles and aircraft, virtually all using the Castrol range of lubricants. The Company claimed that the Land Speed Record has been broken 21 times by cars using Castrol lubricants.

The money Wakefield earned through his company he devoted to philanthropic work, from which the Guildhall Library and Art Gallery, psychiatric treatment, research at Imperial Institute, British Academy lectures, setting up the Wakefield Trust to help All

Hallows by the Tower, Toc H and Tubby Clayton, and many other causes, greatly benefitted. *"His success could be attributed to a combination of foresight, courage and flair. For a business man, he had an unusually well-developed sense of obligation to the state as a guardian of society: he settled his tax bills without fuss or delay and strongly disapproved of covenants to avoid income tax on charitable donations. As Lord Mayor he floated the idea of calling a conference at the Mansion House to settle all religious differences and lay the foundations of a single great British church. This ingenious notion foundered on the indifference of the respective denominational leaders".* He died on the 15th January, 1941 and was buried at Hythe in Kent from which he had taken his title. *(13)*

**

There had been several attempts to set up a joint examination, usually from the B.O.A., who started from the precept that they would be in sole charge of any such examination, hardly a sound basis for negotiation, somewhat similar to the Conservative Party negotiating Brexit with the E.U. In 1920, the Court was approached by a Technical Optics Committee. This Committee was established by the Scientific and Industrial Research Department, Imperial College, the London County Council and the Northampton Institute and was an advisory body on "optical matters". It was currently considering "visual optics" and had established a Sub Committee which took evidence from amongst others, the B.O.A, the Pharmaceutical Society, ophthalmic surgeons and the Company's Official Instructor, Lionel Laurance.

The Committee proposed *"to consider the possibility of a combination of the S.M.C. and the B.O.A. with the Technical Optical Committee for the purpose of establishing a one portal system of examination, the setting up of a Register for qualified opticians, and the promotion of a Bill for the regulation of the industry"* the intention thereafter being that if the combination was agreed, the Diplomates would be members of the new body, as yet unnamed. In answer to a question as to what would likely to occur if the examining bodies did not agree to the proposal, the Chairman, Sir Alfred Keogh, *"thought that a Royal Commission would be formed to consider the matter"*. No pressure then!

The Court wisely referred the whole issue to representatives of the examining board as it:

"did not at the present time feel inclined to entertain the proposals put forward by Sir Alfred Keogh without further consideration".

Before the representatives reported to the Court, the Secretary to Imperial College of Science and Technology set out the circumstances for the proposals. *"The gradual decline from a position of pre-eminence of the Optical Industry of the United Kingdom has caused considerable anxiety in the scientific and manufacturing worlds for many years previous to the late War, but it was not until the full effects of that decline became manifest early in the war, by reason of the lack of optical instruments and high grade optical glass, that serious attempts were made by Government to remedy the defects.*

Fortunately, intensive research and energy of scientific men and manufacturers soon enabled the Navy and Army to possess the essential instruments and appliances which were essential for the successful carrying on of the war.

Among the grave defects which existed the dearth of scientific men for research was not the least, and even while the war was continuing the educational aspects of the problem was discussed by the Government, the London County Council and the Governors of Imperial College each eventually contributing funds to meet a scheme which was approved by all these parties." He went on to state that a special department for the highest education and research in technical optics, including optical engineering, was established in 1917, at Imperial College. This department was controlled by the Technical Optics Committee which itself consisted of *"representatives of the employers of the Optical Trades, a Glass manufacturer, with the representatives of the Navy, the Army, the Ministry of Munitions, the Royal Society, the National Physical Laboratory, and the Governors of Imperial College"*. It had special relations *"to the training of youths and workmen in Optical Science and manufacture"*.

Having emphasised the high level at which this Committee was operating, he went on to state that, with their concern in visual optics they had approached the various bodies as above related particularly as regards *"the education and standard of qualification needed for the practice of the detection and correction of errors of refraction. There can be no doubt that there is a great need for reform in much that relates to education and practice in the domain of Visual Optics. The existence of the present conditions of affairs cannot be contemplated with equanimity by those who appreciate the importance of vision as a factor in the maintenance of public health, whether in childhood, adolescence, or in those of mature or advanced age"*. The examiners, reporting that the Company should attend the proposed conference to hear more of the proposals, the Court agreed, and high power delegates were nominated, namely three Past masters and two examiners, Drs. Drysdale and Levy.

The representatives duly reporting to the Court agreed to:

"give the most sympathetic support to any Bill introduced into Parliament by the Technical Optics Committee of the Imperial College of Science and Technology having for its objects the regulation and control of sight-testing opticians and the protection and safe-guarding of the Public".

The caveats were: recognition had to be given to the Company for its past services, proper representation for the Company on any Governing Body to be constituted, and that holders of all Company Diplomas be entitled to be entered on the proposed Register, without further test or examination.

A further conference was convened to include, amongst others, 4 representatives of the S.M.C. and of the B.O.A. This conference set out the establishment of a single examination for the qualification of opticians in the United Kingdom. Candidates would have studied at recognised schools to an approved curriculum; previous experience and apprenticeship to be taken into account; candidates from the Dominions to be considered. A Council to be appointed which would establish a register, with power to add and remove; to organise the examinations and the approval of the schools and courses; to award Diplomas, and be able to award these diploma to current S.M.C. and B.O.A. Diploma holders. In other words a General Optical Council 40 years before its time.

So far so good! But in early 1921, problems arise. It was strongly argued in the Sub Committee, by J. Herbert Parsons and W.T. Holmes Spicer, that sight testing could not be thoroughly taught without medical training. In their view even medical practitioners at that time were not sufficiently educated in the subject, and a special qualification in ophthalmology was being introduced. The Sub Committee however accepted the original report, and the two dissidents put in a minority report. A subsequent letter from the Imperial College of Science and Technology indicated that, in view of what Sir Alfred Keogh was to report, no present action was to be taken beyond telling the London County Council of the current state of discussions. What Keogh had to report was that he was called to give evidence before a Ministry of Health Committee on the Causes and Prevention of Blindness, when he formed the opinion that the Committee would disagree with the proposals his committee would be making, and might ask Parliament to stop the examination of the eye by opticians. Imperial College's "no present action" can now be understood more clearly.

In the meantime, May 1922, Fellows of the Company teaching at the Northampton Polytechnic Institute were asking the Court to take some action on the activities of the London County Council who, in considering Section VI of the Third Burnham report (that's our Lord Burnham by the way!), were contemplating recommending that the Company's Diploma be not recognised as equivalent to a Degree. The Court referred this to the Board of Examiners on whose behalf Dr. Drysdale replied *"that the Diploma of the Spectacle Makers Company though giving evidence of a fairly high standard of general optical knowledge could hardly be advanced as constituting a University qualification of any kind, as it requires no evidence of general education or of any knowledge you have of a specialised subject. For this reason I cannot see how it could be accepted in lieu of any of the examinations of the University as at present constituted, and I do not think it would be politic for the Spectacle Makers Company to make application for such a recognition, unless there was a fairly good reason to suppose that any similar Diploma will be recognised by the University".*

The B.O.A. wrote in December, 1922, to tell the Court that the Ministry of Health Committee on the Causes and Prevention of Blindness, was strongly condemning the practice of sight-testing by opticians, and of any attempts for State Registration of opticians, and drawing attention to the uncomplimentary references to *"the certificates issued by your Company and those of other bodies"*. The Court, a little surprisingly, deferred consideration pending the actions of the Joint Committee of Qualified Opticians in applying for a licence from the Board of Trade. Surprisingly, in that a few months earlier when being asked for their co-operation in setting up the J.C.Q.O. and appointing representatives on the Council, the

Court had declined:

"whilst interested in the work this Council is undertaking and sympathetic with many of the objects it has in view, is of the opinion that no good purpose would be forwarded by appointing members of this Company to serve upon the Joint Council of Qualified Opticians and prefers to retain its independent position by not being officially connected with the same".

So ended the next attempt at a joint examination, that wasn't to come for another 40 odd years, and the impetus then came from within, rather than from without with some nasty strings attached.

P.S Despite the Court's reservations initially as regards the J.C.Q.O., various Clerks subsequently served as the Company's representative on that Committee. I did myself until such time as I, remembering as always that the Company served the public as well as the profession optically speaking, expressed a mild criticism of the way opticians viewed certain matters. I was taken aside by the Chairman to be told that *"if that was what I thought I needn't attend again".* For some reason criticism of the profession was not to be countenanced!

**

In 1921, the Grocers Company declined the Company request to hold a dinner in their Hall, whether on grounds of dates or something more subtle is not stated.

The Fishmongers' agreed to the use of their hall, at a date to be agreed in April, on the usual charges *"a fee of £10:10/- to cover cost of out of pocket expenses and an additional £5:5/- for gratuities for servants".* The letter stating these mundane facts is solemnly stuck in the Minute book. I suppose it is one way of keeping down the filing.

**

In October 1923, the Court were asked to consider an application for financial assistance from a Liveryman, H.E. Ellison, whose business was in Stamford Street, Blackfriars. Ellison was:

"formerly a Horse Cab proprietor in a good way of business but who, owing to the introduction of Mechanical traction, was now in needy circumstances by reason of the falling away of his business".

The Court was pleased to grant Mr. Ellison *"a special Donation of Five Pounds out of the Yarwell's Gift"*.

**

In March 1925, four Liverymen *"actually engaged in the work of sight testing and holding the Diploma of the Company"* wrote to the Court expressing their alarm at the limitations of the Company's examinations. Their concern was of the future status and success of the examinations, which twenty years before had set the standards: *"in the twenty years which have passed, optical knowledge and practice have naturally greatly increased. For instance, the old standard of 6/6 vision upon which the S.M.C. examination is based is now known to be inadequate and unsound".* The B.O.A., on the other hand, had recognised this and provided for it in its examinations. The increase in the number of examination candidates was because unqualified opticians were finding it increasingly difficult to obtain posts, as employers *"now usually insist upon their assistants having a qualification, in order to be eligible to undertake National Health Insurance Work".* They went on to say that, as the best firms throughout the country prefer their assistants to hold the B.O.A. diploma, it *"accentuates the inferiority of the present S.M.C. syllabus".*

As a consequence hundreds of S.M.C. diplomates have taken B.O.A. examinations and, *"paying much higher fees, both examinational and annual"*, there is great danger of the S.M.C. examination being regarded as a preparatory examination and therefore inferior. The B.O.A. examination demands *"a practical knowledge of objective methods, and skill in employing them, also requiring of its diplomates ability to recognise and to detect conditions other than refractive"*. The S.M.C. agreement requires this particular knowledge *"but so far has not called for definite instruction in, or provided in their examinations for, the testing of the skill necessary for the fulfilment of this obligation"*. For the above reasons, and in the interests of the Public, it was essential that the training should be further extended.

They went on to add: *"under the National Health Insurance Acts, optical benefit is now included and for nearly two years, about 70% of those receiving such benefit have passed through the hands of Opticians. A Royal Commission is now sitting and taking evidence regarding the administration and further extension of these and other benefits. One of the chief considerations urged by those who are opposing the continued entrusting of this work to the Qualified Optician is their alleged inability to detect conditions other than refractive"*. The Court referred the issue to the Board of Examiners. In due course the changes were made, but the Company tended to be a little behind in changes as regards practical matters, and was inclined not to upset the medical lobby, which at this time was not looking favourably on the optician.

**

When William Champness became Clerk of the Company in 1926, he naturally had a look at the past records and accounts of the Company. This set him a problem, as the books had not been kept, in any proper sense, for a number of years. As a result, the Acting Beadle had embezzled a considerable amount of the Company's money. It would prove impossible to quantify accurately the amount, but it ran into thousands rather than hundreds of pounds.

During the course of the investigation, an idea of the Company's financial system, at least as regards the examinations, came to light. The Acting Beadle received the entrance fees, sometimes amounting to more that £1,000 per examination, in cash or treasury notes and postal orders, either delivered personally to the office, or through the post. He then banked these in his own account, and used the money for gambling or the purchase of whisky, which he was drinking at the rate of a bottle a day. Some money he passed over to the Company, otherwise the "missing" amount would have been obvious.

"He has kept no account either of what he has received for the Company, or of what he has paid away. He states that he has not been in the habit of obtaining receipts for many of the sums he has paid, and for a large proportion of the alleged payments there are no vouchers."

I would suggest that even modern auditors, if they had the time after designing "tax avoidance schemes", might have spotted this one. The reason given by the Acting Beadle for his dishonesty was that:

"the late Mr. Singer (the Acting Clerk), *who was engaged at the Guildhall all day, had no time to attend to the business of the Company, and that everything was left to him; and he alleges that it was owing to the lack of supervision since the death of the late Col. Davies* (this is Col. Thomas Davies Sewell the previous Clerk who had died in 1916) *that he was tempted to be dishonest. I should also mention that the Acting Beadle says that from time to time he has handed to Mr. Singer various sums of cash, for payments Mr. Singer said he had to make, but of which no record has been kept. He says that Mr. Singer did not keep any petty cash book."*

Champness, in a subsequent report, his newly introduced Clerk's Report to the Court, states that *"I am of the opinion from what the Acting Beadle says that the temptation to misappropriation to which he confesses has largely been brought about by the absence of supervision and by a system of paying himself his salary, commission, head money etc., from the moneys he received without any check having been applied to prevent defalcations."*

When the cats away, or too busy elsewhere…

The Acting Beadle was, *"forthwith dismissed"*, though he had been allowed by Champness to stay on to supervise the shortly forthcoming examination but:

"in view of the impossibility of ascertaining the exact extent of the irregularities committed by the Acting Beadle no further investigation should be made, but that new accounts be started as from the present time".

As a side issue, but of some concern to the Company at the time, was the fact that the Acting Beadle had neglected to get 274 Freedom admissions stamped at all, which meant that some £800 Stamp Duty was in arrears. Should Somerset House extract the maximum penalty, the Company would owe some £3,540!

On a purely personal note it's quite "deja vue" to realise that the Court Minutes in 1926, are being written, no typed Minutes yet, in the unmistakable hand of Roland Champness, son of the new Clerk, and my immediate predecessor in office.

**

As usual topical references are rare in the Minutes, so it came as a surprise to find that in May 1926, the decision was taken not to postpone the May examinations *"on account of the Strike"*. The reason they were not postponed was that at least 150 of the candidates were in London, and I suppose, were expected to use their initiative to get to the examination centre. At the next Court the Pass List contained only 10 who had London addresses out of the 87 successful candidates. Either the number of Londoners had been badly miscalculated, or they were a particularly thick lot.

A slightly surprising consequence of the Strike was as regards applications for financial assistance. The May Minute states:

"Applications for grants and for relief and various other matters were in consequence of the difficulties arising owing to the Strike postponed for consideration at the next Court."

Five members of the Court attended at the May meeting, a bit below average, but at the next Court, only the Master and the Clerk managed to get there, thus not technically quorate, whether through the action, or reaction, of the Strike is not stated. At the July Court, referred to above, two candidates asked for their examination fees to be returned, which was declined, and, as this was an unusual request, may have been attributed to the Strike.

**

As to the General Strike, trouble had been rumbling around for some time in the mining industry, particularly as the machinery was out of date and the mines not sufficiently profitable. These were tough economic times after the War and there was a growing fear of communism. When the mine owners wanted to reduce wages by 13% and extend the hours from seven to eight a shift, this was the last straw. A million miners had been locked out of their mines and the T.U.C. decided on the 3rd of May to call a strike.

In solidarity huge numbers of other industries stayed off work, bus, rail, dock-workers, printing, gas, electricity, building, iron, steel and chemical works. On the 4th May it was estimated that up to 1.75 million people were on strike. Road and rail came to a standstill with no drivers, the roads choked with cars. Fighting broke out between the police and strikers. Food shortages loomed.

The Government, Conservative under Stanley Baldwin, acted quickly. The army was moved in to protect food lorries, thousands of special policemen recruited and a warship sent to Newcastle. The Government attempted to take control of the B.B.C., unsuccessfully, and produced a newspaper, *"The British Gazette"* to get their story out. They also arrested 374 Communists. But the strike did not have the support of the middle classes who volunteered to drive buses, lorries and trains. My father became a bus conductor for a time!

Secretly the T.U.C had been holding talks with the mine owners and called off the strike, having gained no concessions. The strikers were taken by surprise and slowly drifted back to work. The miners battled on until the November, when most returned to the pits with less pay and longer hours. Many remained unemployed for years. The General Strike had lasted from the 4th May until the 11th May. In 1927, Baldwin's government passed the *Trades Dispute Act*, which banned sympathy strikes and mass picketing. The T.U.C lost 2 million members by 1930, and the Labour Party won the election in 1929. Attlee's Labour Government repealed the *Trade Disputes Act* in 1946, to be reintroduced by Mrs. Thatcher's Conservative Government in the 1980s. So as usual who won what, why and was it worth it! (14)

**

Every now and again in the Court Minutes there is reference to the fact that the optician, and his professional/trade examination, has yet to be accepted by all and sundry, particularly in the medical world.

In January 1927, came the resignation of a doctor who, for reasons that will soon become apparent, must remain anonymous, was the Senior Examiner and the viva voce examiner. In January it appeared a simple resignation. Comes the 4th May meeting and the Court agrees to give evidence on the revised Optical Practitioners'

Bill. At a special meeting of the Court on 26th May, solely on the topic of the resignation of this examiner the Clerk reports: *"X has refused to give evidence before the Departmental Committee or to allow his name to be mentioned as an examiner, and that he had stated that when he was first appointed he undertook to do the work only as a temporary appointment with an express condition that his name should never be disclosed as an Examiner, and that his name had never appeared as such, and that Mr. Davidson* (a Past Master and currently Renter Warden) *confirmed that this had been the understanding; that Dr. X admitted that the work was profitable to him and that he received an unusually high fee for it, but he preferred that his brother practitioners should not know that he was doing the work and that as he now felt that he was in an anomalous position which was unsatisfactory both to himself and the Company the time had now arrived when the Court should consider whether they would not appoint another Examiner and allow him to resign."*

It was resolved that Dr. X *"be informed that the Company would not, in their written statement to the Departmental Committee, disclose his name, but that if the Master, when giving evidence, was asked to give the names of the Examiners it would be impossible to withhold them and also that the Court regretfully accepted the suggestion of Dr. X that he should retire"*.

Of course, all this took place 90 years ago. I am unable to comment on whether the optical profession is now fully accepted in all medical circles, but it would now all seem to be unnecessarily cloak and dagger and smacking of a possible plot for an Ian Fleming follow-up. The other oddity to modern ears is surely the fact that the Master felt duty bound to tell the truth to the Departmental Committee. No mention here of *"being economical with the facts"*, of telling only what he felt was expedient. A happy era or one of naivety? I leave the choice to you.

**

In July 1928, it was noted there were 2,398 F.S.M.C.s, of whom 908 were F.S.M.C only, whereas there were 1,856 F.B.O.A.s of whom 615 were F.B.O.A. only.

**

In the same year came the suggestion of an *"examination for those who only carry out prescriptions"* i.e. dispensing opticians, and though the examination was laid on there proved to be no takers. It was not until 1956, that the S.M.C.(Disp) was introduced, though candidates had been allowed, at one time, to take only the dispensing aspects of the optical examination.

**

A quick rise in status within the Company was not unique, happening even in my time, so far the record is held by Lionel Faudel-Phillips. Whilst he had obtained his Freedom by Apprenticeship in 1902, when his father, George Faudel-Phillips his Master, was Lord Mayor, he had to wait a bit for further promotion.

That came in April Court of 1929, when the 2nd Viscount Bearsted had declined to take office, and as a consequence it had been suggested to him, the Viscount, that he might like to resign, he had only attended two Court meetings, a hint which he duly took. It was then proposed that Sir Lionel Faudel-Phillips be made a Liveryman, and (purely by chance as he was lurking outside the Court room?) he was duly sworn. He had barely declared as a Liveryman, before it was agreed that he be made an Assistant, and he duly took that declaration. He had barely sat down than lo and behold, he is proposed seconded and agreed as the Upper Warden, and then took that oath. (And for the record, 6 months later he is elected Master).

Within the space of what, ten minutes, Sir Lionel had risen from a lowly Freeman to the office of Upper Warden - "Just like that". It isn't minuted that he made a speech of thanks for each elevation but, as at this time nothing seems to have been done without a speech, he probably did. This leads to the speculation, did he make three speeches of thanks, or did he telescope them all into one, and if so how did he know that all this was going to happen at the same time? I feel the hand of the Clerk at work, who had certainly, and not unreasonably, pressed Viscount Bearsted into taking action in the first place, and would have prompted members of the Court to make the right propositions at the right time. Probably wrote out the words they had to say into the bargain!

Sir James Gomer Berry, J.P. was also a quick riser. After an approach by Colonel Edward Lawson, following the death of Sir William Hart-Dyke, Berry was made a Freeman at the Court on the 18th February, 1932. At the same Court he took his declaration as a Liveryman closely followed by his election to the Court of Assistants. At the end of the year he was duly elected Renter Warden. Another of the newspaper clan had joined, for the Company at this time, as has been noted previously, was cornering the market in newspaper proprietors.

Berry may have been surprised that there were only three Court members present to greet him, albeit a Lord and a Bart. However, amongst the apologies were numbered two Lords, one Viscount and a Bart – quite a distinguished gathering, depending of course from where you look!

**

Whilst this brings to an end my trawl through three hundred years of the Minutes you may be pleased to know that this is not quite the end. There are some ruminations and appendices to come so, without more ado.

OBSERVATIONS

Whilst working on the archives a large number of lists of things and figures of all kinds have accumulated. The lists of Lord Mayors, Sheriffs and venues for Court meetings appear in the appendices. However rather than lumber the reader with a lot of figures it might be as well to summarise some of these figures, in particular the number of Freemen and Liverymen admitted each year, and the year Apprentices started and ended their terms of service. It might also be as well to own up to the fact that when the various databases, current and historical, were put together a few errors turned up which have yet to be sorted. I don't think they affect general trends as the variations are going to be small, but publishing rows of figures for each year which are later subject to minor revision will undermine faith in the accumulator of those figures, namely me.

As has already been noted the Company was very small at its inception and stayed that way for a number of years, most obviously because there was only a limited number of spectacle makers around at the time in London, or indeed in the country as a whole. From 1634 to 1759, the years up to 1666 are even more unreliable as the Quarterage books also went up in flames with the Minutes, the number of Freemen admitted was 323, an average of just under 3 a year. This was not a viable number and the Company, as with other Livery Companies, extended Freedom to non-spectacle makers. The increase in Freedom admissions was instant and over the next 49 years 844 Freemen were admitted, an average of just over 17 each year. The attaining of Livery Company status in 1809 saw a steady rise again, no doubt as the Company became better known, with 748 admissions to 1834, an average of just over 31 a year.

After 1834 with Gwynne, Harmer and Lainson becoming Sheriffs and Johnson, Carroll and Duke, Lord Mayors and with the Victorians ever increasing interest in the City and Livery membership, numbers took off. Between 1841 and 1853, 1,134 Freemen were admitted, these numbers were not to be equalled until the introduction of examinations at the end of the century. Whilst these 12 years were exceptional, between 1835 and 1897 a total of 2,422 Freemen were admitted, an average of 39 a year. With the introduction of examinations numbers steadily rose, though slowly at first, except for 1908 and 1909 when 251 were admitted. By the end of the period covered by this book, 1929, 300 admissions a year was not unusual. It may have been because students believed they had to become Freemen to obtain the F.S.M.C., a view not discouraged by the Company, or the very fact that they genuinely wanted membership of the oldest "optical" Company in the country, or even the desire to obtain as many affixes after their names as possible, or the simple truth that the passing of the examination gave them professional recognition, students joined in great numbers (as they did the B.O.A). Between 1898 and 1929, 3,336 were admitted to the Freedom, an average of just under 108 a year. Over the 295 years of which we have some sort of a record, 7,673 Freemen had been admitted.

Jumping on a few years, when I became Clerk the Company had in excess of 4,500 Freemen, all paying Quarterage albeit of a small amount, a figure which caused my fellow Clerks to go green with envy, offset somewhat when they were told that more than a third of these Freemen were in fact WOMEN (almost totally unheard of at the time as members of a Livery Company). "How did you manage" they asked aghast!

Admission to the Livery does not follow quite the same pattern. Not starting until 1809, admissions were in single figures until 1839,

161, an average of just over 5 a year. Then comes the same "bounce" as with the Freemen when admissions were in double figures up until 1882, namely 724, an average of nearly 17 a year. The difference comes in the years following, up to 1929, where apart from 1893 to 1899 and again from 1907 to 1911, admissions were in single figures. The vast increase in Freemen was for a professional purpose, to become recognised opticians, not because of an interest in the Livery and the City of London, together with their interest in anything medieval, which had driven the Victorians. Admissions between 1883 and 1929 were 375, an average of 8 a year. The total number of Liverymen to 1929 was therefore 1,260.

When it comes to apprentices I have to say that I was very surprised at the figures. In my ignorance I had assumed that the object of becoming an apprentice was to get "qualified" and to get a job. Some had paid a relatively high fee for the seven years training and, on paper at any rate, severe terms of service. The figures show that a surprising number did not finish their term in the sense that they did not take up their Freedom with the Company, though that is not to say that they failed to obtain employment elsewhere. Some lingered for a number of years after the basic seven required before taking up their Freedom, again to me surprising. After seven years I would have been counting the days to "demob" as it were and the chance of a job with more money.

As to the figures themselves, between 1666 and 1759 of the 323 who started their apprenticeship, an average of 4.5 a year, 170 took up their Freedom, just about 52%. Yet these are the years when apprentices of spectacle makers presumably intended to, or started out with the intention of, becoming spectacle makers. Between 1760 and 1809, when the apprentices would not necessarily have had spectacle maker Masters, 583 started their apprenticeship, a higher yearly average at nearly 12. However only 149 were admitted to the Freedom, some 25%. The period, 1810 to 1858, saw a vast increase in numbers, with 734 starting apprenticeships, an average of just over 15 a year, but of which only 167 became Freemen, just under 23%. As joining a Livery Company was "the thing" for young male Victorians many would presumably start apprenticeships as part of the experience, with no intention of completing. Perhaps the conditions of apprenticeship had not been pointed out to them in advance, after all sex was not a subject that was openly discussed in Victorian times, hence the necessity of the stork analogy. So when the farthing dropped (the modern equivalent being a penny) of what they couldn't get up to, even though Victorians didn't, they decided to opt out of apprenticeship rather than abstain from everything. Hence of the 23 who started in 1840, only 2 became Freemen, or of the 20 who started in 1848, only 1 took the Freedom.

After that and up to 1929 the number becoming apprentices was in single figures, 202, about 3 a year, but of these 80 became Freemen, 40%. This "conversion rate" is nearer that of the Company's early years, an indication that those starting an apprenticeship for the most part intended to finish it. When I was Clerk apprentices were still being admitted, though pretty infrequently. The reason was usually to keep alive the apprenticeship idea, mostly through an enthusiastic Liveryman parent, but probably without the restrictions historically imposed.

I have no way of knowing how the Spectacle Makers Company compares to other Livery Companies on this general issue of Freemen, Liverymen and Apprentices. It is fair to say that the Spectacle Makers has been able to stay closer to its "trade", eventually, than many other companies whose original "raison d'etre" no longer exists, either because the trade has become extinct or other modern professional bodies have taken over from trade training. The Society of Apothecaries has a similar basis in that the L.M.S.S.A. is still a recognised medical qualification, though looked down upon by the medical establishment. The

Spectacle Makers has had the advantage that, as one of the two earliest examining bodies in optics, it had been able to qualify the bulk of optical students, at least until 1980 and the establishment of the College of Optometrists. From that point of view the future looks less rosy but as this book is supposed to end in 1929 that is a speculation in which I need not indulge.

ENVOI

This archaic heading is intended to indicate that the three hundred years being up, I illogically intend to comment on the various centenary celebrations, encouraging the Company to out-do in 2029, the 400th, what has gone before. The first centenary, in 1729, appears to have gone by without any ceremony, but then as the Company was only recruiting about 3 new Freemen a year the drive probably wasn't there and I don't know whether, at that time, a 100 years was of any significance. For the Bicentenary things were looking up and a dinner was held on the 16th May, 1829. The Livery were invited and, according to the Minutes, 44 attended together with the Lord Mayor, 10 Aldermen and 8 Officers.

By 1929, the Company was in Tercentenary celebrating mood, if someone else organised it. There had been a discussion as to celebrating the event in the previous year and an Advisory Committee had been established. But it seems to have been a letter in *"The Optician"* in January, 1929, from a W.E. Hardy, later to become the first holder of the F.S.M.C. to become Master, which activated all minds. An Executive Committee, under the Chairmanship of Charles Hyatt-Woolf, Editor-in-Chief of *"The Optician"* was quickly assembled, with a Council of distinguished Vice-Presidents, under the Chairmanship of Sir Osborn Holmden, K.B.E., D.L, the Master of the Spectacle Makers Company. An S.M.C. Tercentenary Optical Congress was agreed upon to be held at the Northampton Polytechnic Institute together with a Trade Exhibition on the 10th September. There was to be a Commemoration Dinner at the Connaught Rooms on the 12th September.

A Memorial Volume was subsequently produced in which it was stated that *"The Congress, from an educational point of view, was of the utmost value, both scientifically and technically, and the opportunities given of exchanging knowledge and experience was of the greatest service"*. Over 40 manufacturers and organisations exhibited. There were some exaggerated statements: *"There was a feeling abroad that a new impulse for our profession and industry was desiderated – an impulse that would reveal to our own people and other nations the fresh young blood actuating this generation. Optics in Great Britain is arriving, and it is as well the world should learn of the fact"*. (Why do I believe the writer would have made a good Brexiteer?)

Amongst the organisations taking part were the British Optical Association, the Institute of Ophthalmic Opticians, the Joint Council of Qualified Opticians, the National Council for the Preservation of Sight, together with the Spectacle Makers Company. It was stated that nearly 2,000 people attended the Congress, at which twelve technical papers were delivered. The "group photograph", in two parts, certainly includes in excess of 150 people, plus a child in arms (perhaps that was the "fresh young blood" referred to). The President of the British Optical Association, proposing the toast to the Spectacle Makers Company, said *"the day, I hope, is not far distant, when there will be one examination, even if it is not a State one, and that in that one examination the S.M.C. and the B.O.A. would be working in close fraternity, not only of examinations, but in education, and that supervision and control which is so necessary to a well organised industry."* Hindsight I know, but if the B.O.A. had not consistently left the impression that of course in any such amalgamation they were to be the superior body it might well have happened sooner. Even as late as the 1960s their discussions with the S.A.O. left that body with the impression that they would become the B.O.A. branch in Scotland on any amalgamation. The result was a hastening of a joint S.M.C./S.A.O. examination!

Though not a "centenary" the Court eventually agreed to celebrate the 350th anniversary in 1979, after being encouraged by the Clerk, who in turn was being goaded by Joan James, the Assistant Clerk, to battle on after the first refusal. This time it was going to be organised by the Company and sponsors and contributors were sought from corporate bodies and individuals for a technical and social programme. There were two exhibitions, one historical in Apothecaries' Hall, the other a technological exhibition on the Anniversary Theme – *modern society's changing demands on the eye and vision* – at the London Press Centre. There were four days of lectures at the Press Centre, including reports on the six research projects sponsored by the Company. (The Freedom of the Company was given to all the lecturers regardless of their Nationality, a change in Company policy). There was a day's visit to Cambridge, both optical and non-optical in nature and three days of events organised by the Spectacle Makers' Society. This included three party visits to the Ceremony of the Keys at the Tower of London, following some behind the scenes arm twisting, after which the Clerk was told, by the Governor of the Tower no less, don't you dare apply for any more visits "in the foreseeable future".

The whole shebang had started with a banquet in Guildhall on the 14th May. Amongst the 704 diners, in no order of precedence were, the Lord Mayor and Sheriffs, H.R.H. the Duke of Gloucester, some half dozen Masters, the Master of St. John's College Cambridge, the Royal Society, Stockholm Institute of Optometry, the City Recorder, the Chief Commoner and the City University. There was still money left over after all the various celebrations and a 350th Anniversary Trust Fund was established.

It seems that each anniversary has been more lavishly acknowledged. What will 2029 have in store? How will they top what has gone before or will "austerity" still be the cry? Somehow

I don't think I will be around to have to make comparisons.

**

This really is the end of my trawl through things that caught my eye whilst working on the Court Minutes. I hope I have been able to cast some light on the by-ways of the Spectacle Makers Company as it developed over these years, from a small group of hard-up tradesmen, through its Freemen and Liverymen showing a growing interest in the workings of City Government, and its return to its trade roots with the examinations, from spectacle maker to optician. To come after 1929, was the official acceptance, obliquely, by Act of Parliament, of the trade as a profession, the Company growing its charitable foundation to a state where it would be able to take its rightful place amongst the City Livery Companies and remaining as an impartial and relevant part of the optical scene in the 21st century.

"May it flourish, root and branch, forever."

**

P.S. It only remains for me to clear up the mystery around the banners I alluded to earlier. In the 19th century "banners" were all the rage, as has already been noted. In simple terms these were an individual's or an organisation's coat of arms in flag, or banner, form. The armed forces seem to favour them as well, even to the present day.

There was also a passion to give these to your Livery Company, hence there are banners on display in Apothecaries' Hall and many other Livery Halls. There are lists of Banners given to the Company over the years in several of the Minute Books. These lists give me a twinge of conscience and at some stage the necessity to reveal a secret long lain hid – so why not now? So if you are sitting comfortably we will begin.

Many years ago, as the best fairy tales start, the then Clerk to the Society of Apothecaries came to me with a tale. They were busy doing renovation work about the Hall and under the Courtyard they had come across some very old and very musty "things" that looked rather reminiscent of Banners. Charles O'Leary, for it was he, said that the condition they were in was such that *"you wouldn't want to look at them and if handled would probably fall apart but you can if you want, but we have got the builders in who want to finish the wall"*. Taking the wink as a nod, and always relying on a fellow Clerk, especially when it suited my purpose, after all what the Hell do you do with mouldering Banners, I was happy to go along with the suggestion that we both left the sleeping dogs to lie, and agreed that the Apothecaries carried on building the wall which would effectively seal up these "things", including theirs, for eternity, or until the next rebuild. Should any Member of the Court feel a need to resurrect these Banners they know where they are – but they might disturb the ghost at the same time which, on all accounts, might be as well to avoid!

Well that is my version and my conscience now feels so very much better having bared my soul, as it were, rather than the Banners.

Where banners lie beneath – Apothecaries' Hall Courtyard – 2017. Modern Spectacle Makers' Office through the door immediately right of the steps.

References:

1. Based on an article by E.I. Carlyle in the *"Oxford Dictionary of National Biography"*.
2. Based on an article by H.C.G. Mattthew in the *"Oxford Dictionary of National Biography"*.
3. Based on an article by Huw Richards in the *"Oxford Dictionary of National Biography"*.
4. Based on an article by Huw Richards in the *"Oxford Dictionary of National Biography"*.
5. Based on an article by Edward Ullendorff in *"Oxford Dictionary of National Biography"*.
6. Based on an article by Adrian Smith in *"Oxford Dictionary of National Biography"*.
7. Based on a Wikepedia article.
8. Based on an article by David Brewerton in *"Oxford Dictionary of National Biography"*.
9. "London's Lost Department Stores" on the London History web site. "Hereford-heritage" web site.

10. Based on an article by J.R. Lowerson in the *"Oxford Dictionary of National Biography"*.

11. "The Alderman of the City of London" A.B. Beaven.

12. "My Lord Mayor" Valerie Hope, Weidenfeld and Nicolson.

13. Based on an article by T.A.B. Corley in the *"Oxford Dictionary of National Biography"*.

14. From the B.B.C. *"The General Strike of 1926"*.

APPENDIX I

SPECTACLE MAKER LORD MAYORS

John Johnson	1845	Spectaclemaker
Sir George Carroll	1846	Spectaclemaker
Sir James Duke	1848	Spectaclemaker
Francis Moon	1854	Stationer
William Cubitt	1860/61	Fishmonger
William Rose	1862	Spectaclemaker
Benjamin Phillips	1865	Spectaclemaker
Thomas Dakin	1870	Spectaclemaker
Andrew Lusk	1873	Spectaclemaker
David Stone	1874	Spectaclemaker
William McArthur	1880	Spectaclemaker
Sir Henry Knight	1882	Spectaclemaker
Robert Fowler	1883/85	Spectaclemaker
George Nottage	1884	Spectaclemaker
Sir Reginald Hanson	1886	Merchant Taylor
Polydore de Keyser	1887	Spectaclemaker
Sir Joseph Renals	1894	Spectaclemaker
George Faudel-Phillips	1896	Spectaclemaker
Lt. Col. Horatio Davies	1897	Spectaclemaker
Alfred Newton	1899	Fanmaker
Sir Marcus Samuels	1902	Spectaclemaker
Sir John Bell	1907	Haberdasher
Col. Sir Charles Wakefield	1915	Haberdasher
Sir William Dunn	1916	Wheelwright
Sir Horace Marshall	1918	Stationer
James Roll	1920	Horner
Sir Alfred Bower	1924	Vintner
Sir William Coxen	1939	Cordwainer
Sir Frank Newson-Smith	1943	Turner

Sir Bracewell Smith	1946	Spectaclemaker
Sir Cullum Welch	1956	Haberdasher
Sir Frederick Hoare	1961	Spectaclemaker

That comes to 32 who were Spectaclemakers at the time they became Lord Mayor. There is also the case of Sir William Lawrence (Carpenter) who was Lord Mayor in 1863 but did not join the Spectaclemakers' Company until 1880, so if you were loose with phraseology you could say that there have been 33 Spectaclemakers who have been Lord Mayor. That's at 2019, who knows more may come out of the woodwork.

In passing Lawrence was invited to become an Assistant in 1890, and at each succeeding Court it is reported that he was unable to attend to be sworn until in 1897, it was noted that he had died!

APPENDIX II

SPECTACLE MAKER SHERIFFS

(excluding Lord Mayors)

		Spectacle Maker unless stated
1818-19	Lawrence Gwynne	
1833-34	Alderman James Harmer*	
1835-36	Alderman John Lainson*	
1841-42	Alexander Rogers	
1847-48	Charles Hill	
1849-50	Donald Nicoll	
1850-51	George Edmund Hodgkinson	
1851-52	Richard Swift	
1852-53	Alexander Angus Croll	
1853-54	George Appleton Wallis	
1861-62	George Joseph Cockerell	
	William Holme Twentyman	
1862-63	Hugh Jones	
1863-64	Thomas Cave	
1866-67	Francis Lycett	
1871-72	John Bennett	
1885-86	Thomas Clarke	
1886-87	Alfred Kirby	Fanmaker
1890-91	William Farmer	Haberdasher
	Augustus Henry Glossop Harris	Loriner
1891-92	Harry Seymour Foster	Wheelwright
1894-95	George Hand	Loriner
1895-96	John Robert Cooper	Farrier
1896-97	Robert Hargreaves Rogers	Loriner
1897-98	Thomas Robert Dewar	Shipwright
1898-99	Clifford Probyn	Pattenmaker
1903-04	Alfred James Reynolds	
1909-10	Ralph Slazenger	
1912-13	Alfred Louis Bower	Vintner
1916-17	George Haysom	Basketmaker
1918-19	William Robert Smith	Apothecary

THE SPECTACLE MAKERS

1919-20	Curtis George Ashdown	Loriner
1927-28	Frederick Daniel Green	Farrier
1933-34	Alderman Isadore Nathan Jacobs*	
1937-38	William Henry Champness	
2018-19	Alderman Vincent Thomas Keaveny	Solicitor

* Did not attain the office of Lord Mayor

APPENDIX III

VENUES FOR COURT MEETINGS

17th century

Rayne Deare, Long Lane	1666-1673
White Hart, Old Bailey	1673-1678
Cage, Old Bailey	1678-1680
Coopers Armes, Muggwell Street	1687-1689
Citty Armes, Milk Street market	1680-1687/1689-1700
White Beare corner of Barbican	1694

Also used - Cork(?) Ale House behind the Royal Exchange, Sun Tavern behind the Exchange, the Kings Arms, Birchin Lane and Backside of the Exchange

18th century

Crown in George Yard, Lombard Street	1700-1701/1711-1712
Kings Head, Aldersgate Street	1702-1704
Kings Armes Tavern, Aldersgate Street	1703-1705
Fountain Tavern by Aldersgate	1705-1710/1714-1721
Blew Lyon, Aldersgate Street	1710-1713
Sun Tavern, St Paul's Churchyard	1721-1747
Queens Arms Tavern, St Paul's Churchyard	1747-1756/1758-1784
Sun Tavern, Ludgate Street	1756-1758
Pauls Head Tavern, Cateaton Street	1784-1802

Also used – Castle Tavern, Fleet Street, Chapter Coffee House, Paternoster Row and the Guildhall.

19th century

Baptist Head Coffee House, Aldermanbury	1800-1801
Kings Head Tavern, The Poultry	1803-1809
George and Vulture Tavern, Cornhill	1809-1822
London Coffee House. Ludgate Hill	1822-1853
The Albion, Aldersgate	1853-1902

Also used – Crown and Sceptre, Greenwich, Grocers' Hall, Stationers' Hall, Guildhall, Guildhall Tavern, Irish Chamber, Guildhall, L.C.C., Mansion House, the Old Bailey and the Master's office and that of the Clerk.

20th century

De Keysers Royal Hotel	1903-1914
Temple House, Temple Avenue	1906-1929

Also used – 15 and 22, Bishopsgate, Cannon Street Hotel, Carpenters' Hall, Daily Telegraph, Grocers' Hall, Guildhall, L.C.C., Shell House, and Vintners' Hall.

PICTURE ACKNOWLEDGEMENTS

I have made every effort to contact all copyright holders and thank them for permission to use the following pictures.

St. Botolph's Church: photo by Past Master Peter Mills.	Page 22
Map of London, 1572: Braun & Hogenburgh, (PD) via Wikimedia.	Page 32
Mrs. Salmon's Waxworks: *"Some account of the Parish of St. Clement Danes"*, [PD] via Wikimedia.	Page 35
The Globe Theatre: Wenceslaus Hollar. Old Moonraker. [PD] via Wikimedia.	Page 40
Cornhill in 1630: ©Lang Syne Publishing.	Page 41
London Stone, 1820: *"Old and New London"*, Thornberry [PD] via Wikimedia.	Page 44
Frost Fair, 1683: Thomas Wyke [PD] via Wikimedia.	Page 50
London in 1725: ©London Metropolitan Archives (City of London) (Ref.30395).	Page 63
Bow Church and Cheapside, 1750: ©Lang Syne Publishing.	Page 64
Hoare's Old Banking House, 1838: ©Lang Syne Publishing.	Page 66
Vauxhall Gardens, 1751: Samuel Wale [PD] via Wikimedia.	Page 68
Hyde Park on a Sunday, 1804: ©Lang Syne Publishing.	Page 73
Lords Ground in 1837: ©Lang Syne Publishing.	Page 75
Pasqua Rosee 1652 advertisement: [PD] via Wikimedia.	Page 79
From *"The Annals of Hampstead"* by Mr. Barratt as provided by M.J. Bassett.	Page 92
Photos of the Court Minutes by the Author.	Pages 97/99
The Norville Chest: Photo ©Jeff Smorley.	Page 106
Mr. Kittle's Handiwork: Photo ©Jeff Smorley.	Page 107
Temple Bar and the Devil Tavern: ©Lang Syne Publishing.	Page 111
Poultry Compter: *"Old and New London"*, Thornberry ©Brit. Mus. [PD] via Wikimedia.	Page 114
Map of London 1815: ©London Metropolitan Archives (City of London) (Ref:30600).	Page 130
Trial Trip on the underground, 1863: ©Lang Syne Publishing.	Page 131
The flushing lavatory: Joseph Bramah [PD] via Wikimedia.	Page 135
The London Coffee House: engraved by Rawle from a drawing by G. Shepherd [PD] via Wikimedia.	Page 167
The Spread Eagle: T.H. Shepherd ©London Metropolitan Archives (City of London) (Ref: 316232).	Page 172
James Harmer: Thomas Wright [PD] via Wikimedia.	Page 179
The Star and Garter: Postcard of 1890 [PD] via Wikimedia.	Page 195
Moon's Shop: *"Old London Taverns"* ©Brit. Mus. [PD]	

via Wikimedia.	Page 203
Claude Duval: William Powell Frith [PD] via Wikimedia.	Page 214
The Royal Exchange: Photo of 1895; ©London Metropolitan Archives (City of London) (Ref: 59465).	Page 221
Sir John Bennett: Leslie Ward [PD] via Wikimedia.	Page 228
Sir George Airey: Lock & Whitfield [CC by 4.0] via Wikimedia.	Page 234
19, Lincoln's Inn Fields: Photo, ©London Metropolitan Archives (City of London) (Ref: 73302).	Page 235
Exterior of the Great Exhibition, 1851: ©Lang Syne Publishing.	Page 237
Crystal Palace interior: J.McNeven [PD] via Wikimedia.	Page 241
Piccadilly Circus, 1952: ©London Metropolitan Archives (City of London) (Ref: 135528).	Page 245
Logo: from the Stephens Collection.	Page 249
Augustus Harris: Southwell Bros, 1862 ©National Portrait Gallery, London.	Page 253
An advertisement of 1890.	Page 255
Lord Mayor's Show: a print provided by John Salmon.	Page 260
Tommy Dewar in Egypt: ©John Dewar and Sons Ltd.	Page 274
The Onion Domes, Greenwich Observatory: a contemporary postcard.	Page 276
Bartholomew's Map of London c1900: Geographicus via Wikimedia.	Page 281
View from St. Paul's: H. Mason (PD) via Wikimedia.	Page 284
Lord Burnham: Leslie Ward [PD] via Wikimedia.	Page 286
Gamages late 19th century: Robert Cutts [CC by 2.0] via Wikimedia.	Page 297
Apothecaries' Hall: ©Andy Aldridge (https:flic.kr/p/piiVAZ).	Page 342

Printed in Great Britain
by Amazon